> "Build us straight, O worthy masters,
> Staunch and strong, a goodly vessel
> That will laugh at all disasters,
> And with ice and whirlwind wrestle."
> Longfellow.

Published
By
REARDON PUBLISHING
56, Upper Norwood Street, Leckhampton,
Cheltenham, GL53 0DU
England
www.reardon.co.uk

Researched and Edited
by
J.V. Skelton & D.M. Wilson

Text
by
D.M. Wilson

Layout and Design
by
N. Reardon

ISBN 1-873877-48-X

Centenary Edition

Cover Design
by
N. Reardon

Printed
through
World Print Ltd
Hong Kong

DISCOVERY ILLUSTRATED

PICTURES FROM CAPTAIN SCOTT'S FIRST ANTARCTIC EXPEDITION

1901- 2001

J.V. SKELTON
&
D.M. WILSON

BLUE ENSIGN

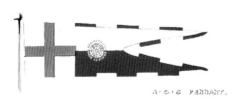

R.C.Y.S. PENNANT.

HARWICH YACHT CLUB BURGEE.

THE FLAGS OF THE SS DISCOVERY

All the Royalties from this book will be donated to the work of the
Scott Polar Research Institute, Cambridge.

Preface

The British National Antarctic Expedition of 1901-1904 fanned the flame of the Heroic Age of Antarctic Exploration. This numbers it amongst the most important expeditions of the period. Sailing aboard the purpose-built scientific research ship, *Discovery*, under Commander Robert Falcon Scott, the Expedition built on the achievements of its nineteenth century predecessors to become a crucible, from which current Antarctic scientific work and exploration emerged. Whilst continuing the British traditions of maritime exploration, the Expedition also occurred within a framework of international collaboration, being one of a series of European expeditions at this time that aimed to solve the mysteries of the unknown South. The British Expedition collected material that helped to answer some of the most pressing scientific questions of the day, principally geographic questions about the very existence of an Antarctic continent and the movements of the South Magnetic Pole. In answering these major scientific concerns, the first explorations into the interior of Antarctica were carried out and the gruelling hardships faced by Expedition personnel in doing so captured the public imagination. By merit of these explorations, the Expedition is often mis-represented as an attempt on the South Pole. It was not. It became, however, the foundation of such a quest and its significance is therefore often overshadowed by the events to which it gave birth: the subsequent Antarctic expeditions of Sir Ernest Shackleton, the last expedition of Captain Scott and the so called "Race to the Pole". Through these epic tales as well as its own pioneering work the Expedition has left a strong, if often unacknowledged, influence on our modern world.

Current opinion of the Expedition has been tarred with a post world war cynicism, which makes it considerably harder to think our way back to the exuberance of a pre-Great War world. Some of the Expedition's more recent critics have not shied away from substantial mis-representation, verging on blatant forgery of the archival record, in order to "show" the Expedition, or more particularly its leadership, to have "failed", or in order to suggest that science and exploration were not the principal aim of the Expedition but rather the handmaids of "British adventurism". Having no credible basis, except in the imaginations of their exponents, such accounts would not be worth mentioning, except that their influence has been widespread and pernicious.

It is against this background that we embarked upon a project to celebrate the centenary of this important Expedition. We desired to share something of the realities of our respective ancestor's experiences; something true to the history of the Expedition and the experiences and memories of the men who took part in it. Chief Engineer Reginald Skelton was the principal, but not the only, photographer for the Expedition. Dr Edward Wilson was the principal, but not the only, artist aboard. When the Expedition returned to England in 1904, these two men put together a large public exhibition in London's Bruton Gallery of the objects, photographs and paintings, which later toured in some of the provincial towns. It was a popular exhibition and started, amongst other things, a long public love affair with Emperor Penguins - the first images ever seen of Emperor Penguin chicks being secured by these two men. Skelton and Wilson also helped to illustrate books about the Expedition, principally Captain Scott's account, *The Voyage of the Discovery*. Such images were further used in the lantern slides for the public lectures given by Scott and others to immense popular acclaim. Our first inspiration for this project, therefore, was the Bruton Gallery exhibition and our own ancestors' illustrations for books and lectures that told the stories of the Expedition to the general public one hundred years ago. Our second inspiration came from the fact that in some sense we both "grew up" with the Expedition, with the stories and mementos collected by our ancestors in the form of scrapbooks, paintings and relics on the shelves and walls of our childhood homes. Most are now in Museums, considered too valuable to risk, being a part of our national heritage. Yet these private scrap books and mementos also formed an important part of our ancestors' memories of their achievements. It became our desire to share something of these with others on the occasion of the Expedition centenary.

Given these thoughts, we decided that it was appropriate for us to create a picture book, Skelton and Wilson edited by Skelton and Wilson - although, of course, we have included many images created by other Expedition members, as did our forebears. We had originally hoped to be able to identify all the pictures from the Bruton Gallery exhibition and to re-create it on the printed page. This has, for various reasons, not proved possible. Nevertheless, combining photographs, paintings, and some of the illustrations from the Expedition magazine, the *South Polar Times*, along with some advertisements from the Bruton Gallery Exhibition catalogue, has, we hope, enabled us to create something of a cross between the scrapbooks with which we grew up and an exhibition. In doing so we hope that it has re-created a flavour of the Expedition and its times and will allow interested members of the public to share in it.

This book is not, therefore, intended as a written history of the Expedition. Such a book already exists in David Yelverton's masterpiece *Antarctica Unveiled*. Nor is it a written history of the ship *Discovery*, which we have in Ann Savours' wonderful work, *The Voyages of the Discovery*. This book is intended to complement existing works. There is a basic text to act as an explanatory framework and we include extracts from our ancestors' diaries to act as a partial narrative. All but a few of the extracts from Reginald Skelton's diaries [RWS] are published here for the first time . Where necessary, we have corrected his spelling of names. For the diaries of Edward Wilson [EAW], we have kept to the format used by Ann Savours when she edited their publication. On occasion their viewpoints vary with their respective roles and experience and we have tried to maintain this within our limited framework. Edward Wilson, with the keen eye of a scientific artist, does not always see things in quite the same way as Reginald Skelton, with his bluntly practical naval problem-solving. In addition, Wilson wrote his diary for his family back home, whilst one function of Skelton's journal was to let off steam privately; the intended audience for such journals should always be born in mind by any reader when attempting to interpret such documents and the events that they relate.

It has been impossible, of course, to include every picture from the enormous number that are available from the Expedition. Skelton alone took over 500 photographs, although he didn't start to take photographs in any great number until half way through the outward journey; there are as many, or more, sketches and paintings by Wilson, before even considering the numerous contributions made by others. We hope, nevertheless, that we have gathered together a good selection to illustrate the key Expedition events. In some cases, however, such as the return journey of the ship from New Zealand to Portsmouth, few pictures seem to exist. Where possible the pictures are exhibited in a chronological format but since many events were occurring simultaneously, a few pictures are grouped thematically. Some images will be familiar, some rarely before published but we hope that on the occasion of the centenary of this great Expedition, the reader will be able to enjoy and savour them all. In so doing we hope that it will invigorate the memory of the extraordinary achievements of the officers and men of the British National Antarctic Expedition 1901-1904.

D.M. Wilson and J.V. Skelton. August 2001

SKELLY   BILLY

Acknowledgements

As is to be expected with a book of this size, a large number of people and organisations have been involved at various levels with the support and preparation for this project. What isn't necessarily to be expected is the extraordinary generosity of so many, through giving encouragement, spending their time assisting the project, granting permissions to reproduce pictures and/or offering financial support.

Firstly, this project would not have been possible without the generous support of our sponsors, John Dewar & Sons and Jaeger. We are very grateful to them for contributing towards the cost of publication, just as both firms contributed towards the support of the *Discovery* Expedition one hundred years ago. Their original advertisements from the Bruton Gallery Exhibition Catalogue are reproduced here, as is the advertisement for Greener Rifles, who have supported us in other ways. All the other advertisements that we have chosen to reproduce are for companies, which, so far as we are aware, have ceased trading.

Secondly, this project would not have been possible without the many years of work undertaken by David Yelverton FRGS on the identification of many of the British National Antarctic Expedition pictures. This work, and his kind generosity in sharing his expertise, have been invaluable.

Thirdly, this project would not have been possible without the support and assistance of the many institutions and individuals who now hold the pictures and documents from the Expedition. They all have our warmest thanks both for the assistance of their staff and/or their permission to reproduce some of their collections. Thanks in these regards are due to: the Scott Polar Research Institute, Cambridge (SPRI), in particular to the archivist, Robert Headland FRGS for his invaluable help and advice, to the Picture Library Managers Philippa Smith and Lucy Martin and to William Mills, the Keeper of Collections. All have spent a great deal of time assisting with this work. The majority of images in the book are from the SPRI collections: the paintings from their large holding of Wilson's works; the photographs principally reproduced from the Expedition lantern slides they hold and supplemented from photograph albums of members of the Expedition, particularly Wilson's and Skelton's own albums. SPRI also own the diaries of both Reginald Skelton and Edward Wilson from which we have quoted extensively. Warm thanks are also due to the Dundee Heritage Trust (DHT) who look after *Discovery* at her current home in Dundee, in particular to Gill Poulter, the Heritage and Exhibitions Manager, who also spent a large amount of time helping us; the extensive use of images from the *South Polar Times* has been made possible by the DHT, from a copy that originally belonged to Reginald Skelton. Thanks are also due to the Natural History Museum, London (NHM) in particular to the Zoology Librarian, Ann Datta, to the Archivist, Susan Snell, and to the Picture Library Manager, Gwyneth Campling; to Cheltenham Art Gallery & Museum (CAGM), and in particular to Dr Steven Blake, Keeper of Collections, and to the Bridgeman Art Library for the use of transparencies of Wilson watercolours in the CAGM; to the Master and Cheltonian Society of Cheltenham College, in particular to the College archivist Christine Leighton; to the Master of Dulwich College, London, in particular to the College archivist Dr Jan Piggot; to the Canterbury Museum, Christchurch, New Zealand, in particular to the picture librarian Kerry McCarthy; to the Abbot Hall Art Gallery and Museum, Kendall, Cumbria; to the Royal Geographical Society, London (RGS); to the Illustrated London News Picture Library (ILN); to Christie Manson and Woods Ltd (Christie's); to the National Aeronautics and Space Administration, USA (NASA); and last but not least to the many private individuals who have allowed us to reproduce from their collections, in particular to Neil Silverman.

Finally, we would like to thank the following for their support, advice and/or endless patience; Duncan Lawie FRSA; Dr Susan Solomon; Jacqueline Carpine-Lancre; and our publisher, Nick Reardon, who has put so much effort into the production of this centenary volume.

Needless to say the responsibility for any errors rests with us. In some cases it has been particularly difficult to decide which way round photographs should be printed as they were liberally reproduced using both orientations in period publications. Occasionally it has also proved difficult to date a picture precisely or identify the figures within it. If any errors still remain, we can but apologise and look forward to any corrections, so that they may be put on record for future researchers.

Authors' Notes

In keeping with the historical period, all units of measurement are given in imperial values. In the explanatory text we have included the metric conversion in brackets. Unless otherwise stated, distances are given in geographical (nautical) miles. One geographical mile is equivalent to 1.15 statute miles or 1.85 kilometres.

Readers should also note that the term "South Pole" was often used indiscriminately during this period as a synonym for the Antarctic region or for "Southern regions" in general and its use does not automatically imply the geographic Pole itself.

1: Introduction
July 1895 - July 1900

Sir Clements Markham,
President of the Royal Geographical Society.

In July 1895, amidst a gathering of the great and the good, the Sixth International Geographical Congress was hosted in London by the Royal Geographical Society. Its president, Sir Clements Markham, was in the chair for this prestigious meeting of leading experts in the geographical sciences. Amongst those present were Dr Georg von Neumayer (Director of the German Oceanographic Institute at Hamburg) and John Murray F.R.S. (later, President of the Scottish Geographical Society) who, like Sir Clements, had long struggled in their own respective spheres to encourage the exploration of the Antarctic regions. Finally, at this Congress, the combined efforts of these three men was to generate the will to achieve the expeditions that they had long desired. The hope was to fill in the last great blank space on the map of the world: Antarctica. To this end the Congress passed the following resolution:

"That this Congress record its opinion that the exploration of the Antarctic Regions is the greatest piece of geographical exploration still to be undertaken. That in view of the additions to knowledge in almost every branch of science which would result from such a scientific exploration the Congress recommends that the scientific societies through out the world should urge in whatever way seems to them most effective, that this work should be undertaken before the close of the century" [Report of the VIth International Geographical Congress, July 1895.]

Of course, there had been expeditions to the Antarctic regions before. Captain Cook had led a naval expedition in the ships HMS *Resolution* and HMS *Adventure* (1772-1775), becoming the first to circumnavigate the world in a high southern latitude and crossing the Antarctic Circle for the first time in 1773. It was his work that had disproved the myth of the Terra Australis Incognita, or Unknown Southern Land, as being a lost paradise. During this period there were also notable expeditions of the Russian navy under Admiral von Bellinghausen (1819-1821) aboard *Mirny* and *Vostok,* and less successful expeditions of the French navy. Further British naval expeditions followed up the commercial voyages in the Antarctic region south of South America, as the reporting of geographical discoveries by commercial ships was, with some notable exceptions, often unreliable. It was naval expeditions again, which led to the major Antarctic discoveries of the mid-nineteenth century, with the French navy aboard the ships *Astrolabe* and *Zélée* under Captain Dumont D'Urville (1837-1840) and the American navy, aboard some half dozen ships, under Captain Charles Wilkes (1838-1842), undertaking expeditions to unveil the hidden mystery of the Southern lands. It was the British Royal Navy aboard HMS *Erebus* and HMS *Terror* (1839-1843) under Captain James Clarke Ross which made the most extensive discoveries, however, with the penetration of what became the Ross Sea and the mapping of large parts of Victoria Land. By the time of the Geographical Congress these had been the last great exploring expeditions. For fifty years, European governments appeared to have decided that the pursuit of economic prosperity or prestige for their Empires was better served by the exploration of snow and ice in the Arctic, rather than the southern regions. It was not known, therefore, whether the scattered discoveries of land in the south were part of one continent or an archipelago of islands. Recent geological discoveries by the oceanographic expedition aboard HMS *Challenger* (1872-1876) had dredged up rocks of a continental origin in Southern latitudes but these had simply whetted the hypotheses of scientists rather than answering their speculations with any definitive proof. Nevertheless, the world at the end of the nineteenth century was changing. Britain had stronger maritime and trade interests in the Southern Hemisphere. Increasingly, too, the large whaling industry was looking to the South to compensate for the virtually exterminated stocks of the Northern Hemisphere. The questions that the scientists wanted to answer were of increasing commercial interest to European governments, particularly to Britain and its new rival, Germany. Unresolved navigational problems abounded in the Southern Ocean, principally because the magnetic pole had moved since Ross pinpointed it in the 1840's. Gauss's theories about the movements of the magnetic poles could not be verified because of lack of data from the South. There were serious problems in understanding Southern Hemisphere weather patterns or ocean currents because there was so little data from the Antarctic region, nor was there any great understanding of the Southern Ocean ecosystem, of such vital importance if whaling was to be a commercial success. Science was full of questions from geodesy and geology to biology and meteorology, which could not be answered without speculation about the nature of the Antarctic. Nevertheless, the issues could, it seemed, be refined to two primary questions considered to be of an importance high enough to be of national interest: where had the Southern Magnetic Pole moved to; and does an Antarctic continent exist? All the interested parties wanted the answers to those two questions above all others. To Sir Clements Markham this meant that what was required was a primarily geographical expedition and the scale upon which it would need to operate in order to answer these questions would necessitate a national enterprise.

So little was known of the Antarctic at this time, that Sir Clements joked that as much was known about Mars! It is sobering to realise, from our twenty-first century viewpoint, that if astronauts were launched for Mars tomorrow they would know more about where they were going than the men who were about to sail into the southern regions of our planet a century ago. What little was known had largely been acquired with the assistance of naval expeditions, and it was therefore a British naval expedition that Sir Clements, and others, expected would be necessary and hoped would be achieved. The immediate effect of the resolution of the Geographical Congress, however, was to help the Belgian explorer Adrien de Gerlache obtain the support of the Royal Belgian Geographical Society for his Belgian Antarctic Expedition which sailed in 1897 aboard *Belgica* and became the first expedition to over-winter in the southern ocean when it became trapped in the ice. He made extensive geographical discoveries in the region off South America but did not attain many of his objectives. The resolution of the Geographical Congress and the efforts of Sir Clements Markham also had the effect of enabling Carsten Borchgrevink to obtain the patronage of the media baron, Sir George Newnes, who was looking for exclusive stories of 'derring do' for his magazines. The result was a private British Expedition (although largely manned by Scandinavians) aboard *Southern Cross* (1898-1900) which wintered at Cape Adare on the edge of Victoria Land. Again, none of the key scientific or geographical questions were answered, although the expedition did achieve a 'Farthest South' by sledging a short distance over the Great Ice Barrier (Now the Ross Ice Shelf).

The fact that Sir George Newnes had seen fit to 'buy' his own expedition, achieving only moderate results, rather than assisting the national enterprise which Sir Clements hoped would achieve a good deal, upset Sir Clements, with some justification. Indirectly, however, it had the effect that he wanted. Sir Clements' initial efforts to interest the government in a national enterprise had largely failed; so much so that Sir Clements had enlisted the help of the Royal Society to found a joint enterprise, in the hope of raising the money. By November of 1898, however, Markham had only raised £14,000 mostly from Royal Geographical Society subscriptions, little having been contributed by the Royal Society. Ultimately the Royal Society's failure to raise significant funds was to cost it any say in the running of the National Expedition. In Germany, however, where Neumayer was similarly trying to mount a German national expedition, the British *Southern Cross* adventure had inspired sufficient interest to provide the necessary competitive impetus for central government to fund the entire German expedition. At about the same time, Markham had received a private donation from a London businessman, Llewellyn Longstaff, who offered £25,000 on hearing that the plans for the Expedition might have to be abandoned for lack of funds. Such a generous gesture meant that Edward, Prince of Wales, agreed to become Expedition patron and his son, Prince George (later George V), became vice-patron. These developments enabled a fresh approach to be made to the government in April 1899, which secured the promise of government backing of £45,000 spread over four years, providing the amount was matched from other sources. This was £15,000 less than had been asked for and a further £3,000 was needed to match it. With the Royal Society again failing to make any significant contribution, the Royal Geographical Society sold further investments which meant that its level of financial interest in the Expedition rose to nearly half of its assets. A further public appeal was also made. The resulting grand total of £92,000 in the Expedition Fund (equivalent to around £6 million today), was enough for the Expedition to become a reality.

Even though national rivalries had provided the impetus for government funding, the different expeditions nevertheless agreed to co-ordinate their scientific enterprises. At the suggestion of the Germans, simultaneous scientific observations were to be made, particularly in meteorology and magnetism, to obtain the best possible scientific data. The routes that the various expeditions were to take were also co-ordinated over polite dinners, to avoid duplication; the British Expedition being given the Ross Sea sector to explore in the wake of Ross. Other national expeditions were also now getting off the ground. Sir John Murray, who had been knighted in 1897 for his work on the *Challenger* reports, thought that the Expedition should, once again, be largely oceanographic, and decided to lend his weight to a Scottish National Expedition to achieve his ends; and a Swedish National Expedition too, eventually joined this international array of scientific enterprise heading South. The Heroic Age of Antarctic exploration was truly getting under way.

For Sir Clements Markham there remained two major obstacles to obtaining the departure of the British National Antarctic Expedition. The first was the committee of 33 members, with its numerous sub-committees, set up as a part of the joint venture to run the Expedition with the Royal Society, a structure which disastrously inhibited effective decision making. In part this was due to the Royal Society having substantially different ideas from Sir Clements and the Royal Geographical Society about the nature of the Expedition. The Royal Society's ideas were based on what they rather narrowly regarded as the pure sciences. They wanted a scientist, the geologist Professor Gregory, in charge of a scientific landing party whilst a naval officer took charge of the ship, which was hardly to be more than a taxi for their scientists. There was little room for major geographical exploration in their vision. Sir Clements wanted both scientific and geographical exploration, with geographical exploration having the priority, since he believed that it was the key to answering the most pressing scientific questions. Sir Clements also opposed a split command and wanted a naval officer to be in charge of the whole Expedition. This would also, in Sir Clement's view allow British naval officers the chance to prove themselves in peacetime, a romantic ideal close to his heart and central to his plans. Given that the Royal Geographical Society had obtained the Expedition funding the attitude of the Royal Society inevitably lead to board-room conflict which, together with the excessive bureaucracy, dominated the early months of preparation for the Expedition. Much to Sir Clements' credit, however, he never relinquished his wider vision of what could be achieved.

The second major difficulty was in obtaining a suitable ship for the Expedition. Because of the magnetic work that was to be undertaken the ship needed to be wooden, rather than metal, as any significant metalwork within 30 feet of the instruments would distort the readings. As no suitable traditional wooden whaling or sealing vessel was to be found, the job of building one was given to the shipbuilders of Dundee, who still possessed the skill of wooden shipbuilding, that elsewhere was a vanished art. Building a new ship meant that it could incorporate elements of design from the traditional Dundee whalers, from British naval vessels and from the famous Norwegian Arctic exploration ship, *Fram,* together with some innovative elements introduced by the Admiralty's chief constructor, William E. Smith. It was to become the first purpose built vessel ever constructed for work in Antarctic exploration.

The keel of the new ship was laid in March 1900. It was decided to name her *Discovery,* after a long line of illustrious exploration vessels bearing that name which had been commanded by some of Britain's greatest explorers; Hudson, Baffin, Cook, Vancouver and more recently Nares. It was a name deliberately chosen to 'continue the spirit of maritime enterprise' which Sir Clements felt had always been a distinguishing feature of the British nation and it was his earnest hope that the men who sailed in her would live up to those traditions. He would not be disappointed. In June 1900, with the official appointment of his favoured candidate, Lt. Robert Falcon Scott, as the commander of *Discovery*, the dreams of Sir Clements Markham, and others, were well on the way to being fulfilled.

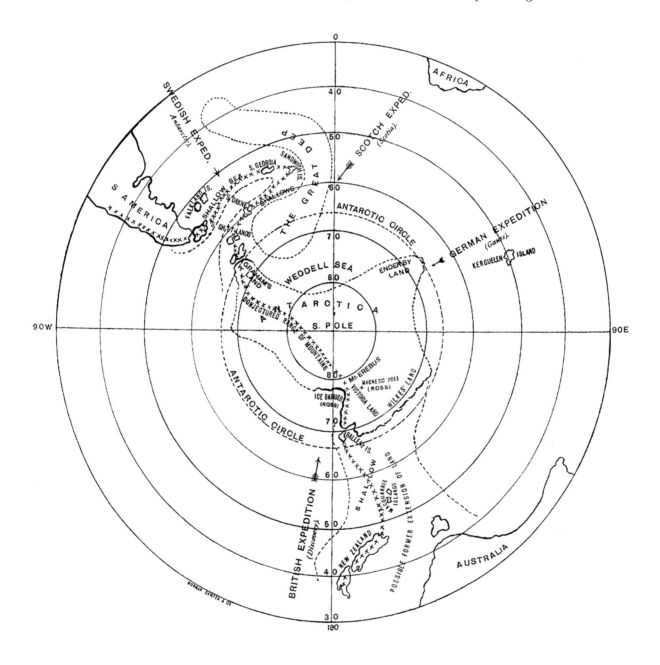

Map showing the spheres of operation of the European expeditions along with known coastline and scientists' projections for a continental coastline and mountain ranges. 1901

2: Expedition Preparations
August 1900 - 6 August 1901

At the age of 31, Scott had been serving as first Lieutenant of HMS *Majestic,* flagship of the Channel Squadron, when he was appointed to *Discovery.* He was a highly regarded young officer. Scott was promoted to the rank of Commander and released from his naval duties in order to take up his new role. The task that Scott and his future officers faced in preparing for their forthcoming Antarctic work was formidable. The political wrangling surrounding the Expedition had delayed their appointments until they had little time left to prepare and it continued to hamper preparations for some months after they started their work in August 1900. Training courses needed to be attended, books on Polar exploration read, officers and crew appointed and supplies secured. Much of the work fell to Scott himself.

Scott at once started work on selecting his team and soon had volunteers from amongst the officers of his old ship HMS *Majestic,* amongst others. From these he at once chose Lt. Michael Barne and the 29 year old senior engineer, Reginald Skelton, who would become the Chief Engineer of *Discovery* - once the appointments were approved by the naval hierarchy. Scott recorded that applying for Skelton's appointment was one of his first acts on behalf of the Expedition

"... and it was certainly a very fortunate one: from first to last of our voyage we never had serious difficulty with our machinery or with anything concerning it". [Scott p69]

Skelton was also to prove an invaluable assistant to the scientific programme, an indomitable sledger and a general favourite aboard. One of his most important roles, however, was taken up at Scott's suggestion:

"My Dear Skelton, just a line to advise you, if you have the time and opportunity, to work up the subject of photography. It will, I think, prove a matter of interest to you and of great service to the expedition..." [Letter from Scott, 12 Oct 1900].

Reginald W. Skelton R.N.

Whilst continuing his other Expedition preparations, Skelton duly did as suggested, and was to take his role as the chief photographer very seriously, producing by far the majority of photographs of the Expedition and also helping others to produce theirs. He organised the dark room as meticulously as he did the arduous work of the engine room and was undoubtedly one of those on the Expedition who lived up to the 'spirit of maritime enterprise' and initiative that Sir Clements was hoping for. Skelton's appointment to the Expedition came through in September 1900 and Scott immediately sent him to help supervise the building of *Discovery* at Dundee with Lt. Charles Royds, and in particular the fitting of the ship's machinery. He was also trained on other aspects of the Expedition work that might require an engineer, in particular the flying of the balloon which the Expedition was intending to use for aerial observation. In addition Skelton was involved in choosing the staff for the engine room:

"...the hands mostly from the Navy began to dribble in gradually, and I got one Quartley LS but I had to go to Portsmouth twice and Chatham once, to finish up my 4 leading stokers - and then I had to ask for another hand, which I got from the Merchant Service - a donkeyman RNR called Hubert...The four leading stokers are Lashly from 'The Dove', Whitfield from the 'Resolution', Quartley from Portsmouth, with me in the 'Majestic' and Page from Chatham."

Commander Scott, meanwhile, visited Norway with Sir Clements Markham in October 1900 for a series of meetings with experts in Arctic exploration, most importantly, perhaps, the famous Norwegian explorer, Nansen. Scott widely adhered to the advice that he received on matters ranging from dogs to equipment and the prevention of scurvy. Scott then travelled via Copenhagen to Berlin, for meetings with his German counterparts, before returning home for meetings with the Chief of the Scientific staff and his newly appointed deputy, Lt. A.B. Armitage of the Merchant Navy.

Up to May 1901, Scott shared the responsibility for preparing the Expedition with the appointed Chief of the Scientific staff, Professor Gregory. The latter, however, spent much of the time working at his post as the Geology professor in Melbourne, Australia, so most of the work fell to Scott in any case. Gregory did come to England in November 1900 to meet Scott and help to appoint some of the Expedition scientists. Amongst those interviewed was Dr Edward Wilson, a recently qualified 29 year old medical doctor who had come to the notice of Professor Sclater of the biological appointments committee whilst drawing at the London Zoo. It was with Sclater's encouragement, along with that of his uncle, who was an influential fellow of the Royal Geographical Society, that Wilson applied to join the Expedition. He duly arrived in London from his native Cheltenham for an interview on November 22. He had recently cut himself in the course of his medical duties and had developed blood poisoning and an abscess, so he had his arm in a sling. He was also not long convalesced from tuberculosis. He was nevertheless appointed as a second doctor to the Expedition, vertebrate zoologist and artist, provided that his health improved sufficiently. In fact, both Gregory and Scott were so impressed by him that when a medical decision was deferred to await improvement, they accepted his appointment in any case, provided that he came at his own risk; a position that was maintained even when he eventually failed the medical. At the time of Wilson's appointment he was expecting to be one of a landing party consisting of Gregory and six others who would be left by *Discovery* to over-winter on the edge of the Antarctic. He immediately set to work on specimens in the Natural History Museum, familiarising himself with the wildlife of the southern regions by helping Hodgson, the expedition biologist, to work up the specimens and reports for the recently returned expedition of the *Southern Cross*. He was later to regret these paintings, as he was required to depict seals that he had never seen alive. It is a matter of interest to compare the Weddell Seal Plate produced by Wilson for the *Southern Cross* Reports - nevertheless a reasonable example of Victorian wildlife art - with the plate of the Weddell Seal produced for the *Discovery* Expedition Reports, which is an intimate portrait of the animal and is as fresh today as the day it was painted. A better example of Wilson's development on the frontier of wildlife painting would be hard to find. Indeed, Wilson's Expedition drawings and paintings, along with his quietly spiritual and ascetic character, were to win him wide admiration. Amongst his Expedition preparations Wilson's appointment speeded up his own wedding plans and he was to be married to Oriana Souper just three weeks before the departure of the Expedition.

Dr Edward A. Wilson

The dispute over the precise nature of the Expedition eventually came to a head with the resignation of Professor Gregory in May 1901. Sir Clements and the Royal Geographical Society had finally achieved victory in the board room squabbles and Scott was at last given sole managerial control over the Expedition. Gregory left the Expedition several legacies, however. One was the hut that he had ordered for his shore party, which was based on an Australian outback shack - and became known to the entire Expedition as 'Professor Gregory's Villa'. The other was the appointment of Edward Wilson. Scott wrote:

"The original idea in appointing two doctors to the 'Discovery' was that one should be available for a detached landing party; but although this idea was practically abandoned, there were few things for which we had greater cause to be thankful than that it had originally existed, for the second doctor appointed to the expedition was Edward A. Wilson." [Scott p68]

Discovery was launched into the Tay at Dundee on 21 March 1901. This proved to be a very busy period for Skelton, who had much to do with the fitting out of the ship and the subsequent sea trials. It was also during this period that a leak was first located which meant *Discovery* going into and out of dry dock several times in the first year of her life. The source was never discovered and 'the Dundee Leak', as it became known, still plagues the ship to this day. A more serious incident, perhaps, occurred at the end of May:

"The ship did not leave Dundee on the 31st May owing to an accident to the propeller lifting gear, which was being tried, - the block of the purchase on the spanker boom broke when the propeller was at the top of the well, and let the whole thing drop, - it seemed at first as if the accident might be very serious, but the ship was immediately placed in dry dock, and it was found that there was practically no damage at all...the ship came out of dock at 10.0 on Monday morning 3rd June and left for London at 2.30 PM." 1901 RWS

In fact, the accident nearly killed Commander Scott, who had been watching the demonstration of the propeller lifting gear (a feature put into the ship for accessing the propeller in ice) and moments before had been standing on the very spot which the boom hit.

Discovery berthed at the East India Dock in London for stowing supplies. This was a period of very hard work for all members of the Expedition during a very hot English summer; the first of the reign of King Edward VII.

"Had a long day with Ory at the ship, as I had many things to finish up and unpack: the drugs, medical and surgical, and surgical appliances, also all the stationery and inks, taxidermic things, and what not; such a quantity of clothing too, all thick woollen things for the south which required a lot of stowing in the limited space at our disposal..." Mon 29 Jul EAW

In London, too, there was a seemingly endless round of social events and a stream of visitors to the ship, including meetings with many eminent polar scientists and explorers of the day, all keen to give advice and make suggestions.

To the relief of many aboard, they sailed out of London on 30 July, for Portsmouth where they had been summoned for an inspection by the new King, the Expedition patron. They swung the ship at Spithead in order to adjust their compasses and enjoyed a very successful royal inspection on 5 August. On the 6th they finally sailed out of the Solent and away from England's shores. The British National Antarctic Expedition was finally under way.

Expedition Preparations: Dundee March 1900 - July 1901

"In all these matters that refer to the machinery I want you to think out and decide every detail of improvement that may suggest itself to you only let me know what changes you arrange and especially should extra cost be incurred."

Letter of Instruction from Captain Scott to Chief Eng. Reginald Skelton in Dundee 28 Oct 1900

SS Discovery. View of Stern, Keel and After Frame being worked.
Panmure Shipyard, Dundee 1900

"On 25th Jul I went down to Aldershot to Colonel Templar R.E. to pick up something about Captive Balloons of which we are taking 2. - I went up in one a 1,000 feet." 1901 RWS

SS Discovery. View of Stern with part of the outer planking worked.
Panmure shipyard, Dundee 1900

SS Discovery. View of the Fore-end with the outer planking completed.
Panmure Shipyard, Dundee 1900

Expedition Preparations: Dundee 21 March 1901

"At 3.30 p.m. the dockyard and the neighbouring esplanade were crowded with people, a specially invited party occupying the platform in front of the bow of the vessel. Mr. Low, the chairman of the Dundee Shipbuilders' Company, presented Lady Markham with a pair of gold scissors, with which she cut the white ribbon holding back a bottle of Australian wine wreathed in flowers, and allowed it to swing against the steel sheathing of the stem. As the bottle broke, Lady Markham named the ship the *Discovery,* and a few moments later the vessel commenced to glide along the greased ways, and, gradually increasing in speed, shot out into the Tay with a magnificent splash. Two tugs were in waiting, and proceeded to tow the *Discovery* into the dock, where she was berthed beside the 90-ton crane where her boilers were lying ready to be put on board. The appearance of the vessel in the water was singularly graceful when the extraordinary strength of her construction was taken into consideration."

The Geographical Journal May 1901

The naming of the SS Discovery by Lady Markham, Dundee.
21 Mar 1901

Discovery glides towards the Tay, Dundee. 21 Mar 1901

Safely launched. Discovery,
on the Tay at Dundee.
21 Mar 1901

Expedition Preparations: Dundee March - June 1901

Discovery, not long after launching, at the Quayside in Dundee.
Mar 1901

Armitage at the compass during Discovery's trip from Dundee to London, 3 - 5 Jun. In the background Scott and Markham are talking with a third figure, (possibly John Murray)

The boilers being lowered into Discovery.
Mar 1901

"Ship should have left Dundee on May 31st although by contract she was to have been delivered on the 9th May, - but delays arose as to various items...as far as the hull of the ship goes, I believe the work and material to be very good, but any iron, steel or metalwork performed by the shipbuilder is perfectly disgraceful; and if it had not been for strict overseeing, the ship would not be fit to enter the Antarctic regions; - as it is I consider the ship in all main requirements to be well fitted, but this is by no means the fault of the shipbuilder." 1901 RWS

"On trial at full speed the ship had averaged 8.8 knots with 570 IHP. - on the way round to London we averaged about 7½ knots with 300 IHP, and did the whole distance to Gravesend on 14 tons of coal, 420 miles." 1901 RWS

Discovery's Trial Trip.

R.M.HEP 'SOUTHERN CROSS'.   PLATE II

Report on the Collections of Natural History made in the Antarctic Regions during the Voyage of the Southern Cross. Seal Plate II. Weddell Seal

E.A.W.pinx. H.Grønvold del.   LEPTONYCHOTES WEDDELLI   New Newman lith.

"In town, my work was mainly at the Natural History Museum, under Mr Murray. I had to learn bird skinning from the taxidermist, and also get to know all the southern birds and the seals. I set to work to draw them all roughly in coloured chalk, by way of practice in the use of them down south." London 1901 EAW

"We both worked, chiefly at the seal paper which I had to illustrate with 6 plates as well as write. And we finished it and them. Ory made a fair copy of the paper. I'm afraid it was very hurriedly done and will not do me much credit, but I trust I shall do better when I come home. It was hard to draw and colour seals one had never seen in the flesh." Sun 4 Aug EAW

***

"...and so with the church fully decorated with white flowers and lilies and with plenty of music and a general feeling of happiness all round, Ory and I were married on 16th July 1901, by Canon Escreet and Uncle Will Hopkins." Tue 16 Jul EAW

II.
NOTES ON ANTARCTIC SEALS.
COLLECTED DURING THE EXPEDITION OF
THE 'SOUTHERN CROSS.'

BY EDWARD A. WILSON, M.B., F.Z.S.[1]

(PLATES II.–VI.)

Owing to the death of Mr. Nicolai Hanson (the zoologist best qualified to have written an account of the Antarctic Seals), the task of describing his specimens has devolved upon one, who though at present unacquainted with these animals in a state of nature, has nevertheless a great interest in the work, from the fact that he shortly hopes to cover the same ground in search of the still (unfortunately) hidden treasures of knowledge concerning the Seals of the Antarctic

The start of Wilson's Southern Cross Seal Report

Dr and Mrs Edward Wilson on their wedding day

Edward Wilson trying on Officers' furs for the forthcoming Expedition in the garden at Westal, Cheltenham

Expedition Preparations: London June - July 1901

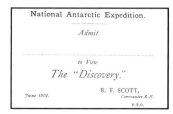

Visitor's viewing pass

Savage Club Farewell Dinner Menu for the Officers of Discovery

Ford, the Chief Steward, working below decks with two u/d men

Officers and Scientific Staff of the SS Discovery. 17 Jul 1901. L-R rear: Dr E.A. Wilson; W. Shackleton; Lt. Barne; Cyril Longhurst; Lt. Shackleton; Ch. Eng. Skelton; T.Hodgson; Dr R. Koettlitz. L-R front: George Murray; Cdr Scott; Lt. Armitage; Lt. Royds

"We had to attend several dinners in London notably, the Geographical Club at 'The Ship' Greenwich - The Royal Society at the Athenaeum, The Savage Club etc." 1901 RWS

"From this time onward we had but little peace. The summer was a very hot one, and the want of ventilation in the bowels of the ship, where we had to work, was very trying." Jun 1901 EAW

"On Arrival in London we were berthed alongside in the East India dock at Blackwall near No13 shed which had been laid apart for the Expedition, and where provisions had been accumulating for some time. - Coaling ship was the first job done, ... - it took altogether about 2½ days work, to get in 240 tons of coal." 1901 RWS

Worcester cheers Discovery as she passes

Discovery Leaving London

C.R.F.

"Cameras were going off in all directions, flags and hooters and sirens were making an immense noise and crowds were everywhere. We passed the *Worcester* who greeted us in grand style, but so did every craft we passed. It was a sensational affair, which would have been more enjoyable if one hadn't been so infernally hungry and hot and tired... But we all fully enjoyed it." Tue 30 Jul EAW

Expedition Preparations: Cowes 5 August - 6 August 1901

Left. Commander Scott is presented by Sir Clements Markham to King Edward VII, accompanied by Queen Alexandra and Princess Victoria.

Right. After the King's departure. L-R: Dr Wilson; Ch. Eng. Skelton; Lt. Shackleton; Dr Koettlitz; Cdr Scott (Wearing the Royal Victorian Order presented by the King); u/d lady; Sir Leopold McClintock; Admiral Markham (Behind); Mr Longstaff

"Proceeded to Cowes at 9.0 A.M. under steam and then the King and Queen, Princess Victoria and party came aboard to look round - Sir Clements Markham, Admiral Markham, Admiral Sir Leopold McClintock, - Mr Longstaff, who has given £30,000 to the Expedition, were with us - we were all introduced to the King in turn, and he then inspected the men, and afterwards the ship, over which they took a considerable time, and were evidently much interested, - Finally the men were fallen in, and the King made a speech to them short and to the point, - finishing up by presenting the MVO to Com'd Scott. - on the whole a rather good show. In the afternoon we all went to the 'Osborne' to write our names in his Majesty's book." Mon 5 Aug RWS

The Departure of Discovery from Cowes. 6 Aug 1901. The Royal Yacht, Osborne, is shown flying the Royal Standard to the port side of Discovery with the Royal Party on deck watching the departing ship. The Royal Yacht Victoria and Albert is shown astern. Many other prestigious yachts were also present for the "Cowes Week" Regatta of the Royal London Yacht Club

"I was very busy stowing goods down below when I heard that Ory was on board...Then we weighed anchor and began moving away to the west. They remained with us all the morning until we came opposite Yarmouth, when we began to meet some uneasy water, and then we had to say goodbye for several years. There were some tears, but not many, it was a gloriously sunny bright and breezy day and everything looked beautiful...Dear girl, it has remained fresh in my mind ever since, the happy sight of you in your grey dress and black hat waving your hanky to me till you were a mere dot in the tossing little launch altogether." Tue 6 Aug EAW

"Took ladies as far as Hurst Castle where they disembarked and went back in the steam boats, - All along we have been much troubled with numberless ladies, - who have if anything obstructed, rather than aided the work." Tue 6 Aug RWS

Alum Bay, the Isle Of Wight, from Discovery

" OH ALMIGHTY   GOD , WHO HAST APPOINTED ALL THINGS   IN HEAVEN
AND   EARTH IN A WONDERFUL ORDER,   BE PLEASED TO RECEIVE INTO
THY MOST GRACIOUS PROTECTION ALL WHO SAIL IN THIS SHIP.   GRANT THAT
OUR LABOURS MAY SHOW FORTH THY PRAISE AND INCREASE NATURAL KNOWLEDGE.
PRESERVE US IN ALL DANGERS OF BODY AND SOUL , NOURISH US IN ONE
SPIRIT OF GODLY UNITY AND HIGH DEVOTION AND BRING US HOME OH FATHER
IN LOVE AND SAFETY, THROUGH   JESUS CHRIST OUR LORD.   AMEN."

COPY OF INSCRIPTION IN PRAYER BOOK.

《 PRESENTED   TO THE "DISCOVERY" BEFORE LEAVING   ENGLAND FOR THE YET
UNKNOWN   SOUTH,   BY   THE BISHOP OF LONDON, WITH HIS PRAYERS AND BLESSING.

JULY . 15 1901.   A. F. LONDON. 》

3: The Voyage Out
7 August 1901- 24 December 1901

It took a week for *Discovery* to sail from England to Madeira, a chance for the officers and crew to get to know their new ship and forge themselves into a team. The scientists, too, were busy, testing out their oceanographic and other scientific equipment. All had to adjust to life at sea, including the ship-board pets. Scott's Aberdeen Terrier, Scamp, accompanied the Expedition as far as New Zealand, where he was left in the care of a family. The two cats, Blackwall and Poplar, accompanied the Expedition throughout, as did Armitage's Samoyed, Vinka. For the old naval hands the journey at this point was fairly routine, if very busy. For those from the Merchant Service or the civilian scientists, more demanding adjustments had to be made to life on a ship run to a naval routine. Chief Engineer Skelton, fully occupied in the engine room, was also suffering from severe toothache. Both these facts are reflected in the brevity of his diary entries and probably explain why he took no photographs during this period. Others, however, were eager to use their cameras, excited by the sense of adventure. Edward Wilson was busy with his paints, trying to catch the numerous moods of the ocean and the wonders of life that he was seeing around him. These differences were once again highlighted at Madeira, where Skelton was concerned with coaling the ship - the main reason for *Discovery's* visit - whilst Wilson had time to explore the island and was overwhelmed with the sensuousness of all that he saw around him.

Discovery sailed from Madeira on 16 August, leaving behind Dr H.R. Mill, a noted oceanographer and meteorologist, who had sailed part of the way to assist the Expedition scientists. *Discovery* only had the power to raise steam for short periods of time and was principally built with that capability for ice navigation. Her course, therefore, as with all sailing ships, was dictated by the need to follow the winds. From Madeira the course was set to follow the N.E. trade winds and they headed South East across the Atlantic. A few days out, Skelton's toothache became so bad that it was decided to operate. He had the tooth extracted under ether and caused "much amusement on deck over his loud and amusing songs and unparliamentary remarks as he was recovering from the effects..." Mon 19 Aug EAW

The ship was held up by a lack of wind in the doldrums around the Equator, so much so that they didn't 'cross the line' until 31 August. Here the ship was attended by the ritual visit of King Neptune and his court. Whilst Skelton notes it as a routine in his diary, Wilson was greatly astonished by the experience and recorded it in some detail. Falling in with the South East trade winds soon afterwards they started to make their way back across the Atlantic in a South Westerly direction. Here, they found the island of South Trinidad to be along their route, as had been hoped, and a landing was made. South Trinidad had been visited infrequently, and rarely by such a large team of scientists, so sizeable collections of the island's unique wildlife were made. One of the petrels was later deemed to be a new species and named for Edward Wilson, *Aestralata Wilsoni,* although many years later it was subsumed as a sub-species of the Herald or Trinidad Petrel. Here Skelton, having recovered from his operation, enthusiastically started to photograph in earnest but lost most of his pictures when his camera was broken in leaving the island. His diary entries nevertheless increasingly reflect his active assistance to, and interest in, the scientific programme - particularly the bagging and skinning of specimens. The skinning in particular had to be done quickly, but not until Wilson had first sketched the specimen, so that a record of the colours was set down before they started to fade.

Catching the Westerlies, they continued to sail towards South Africa, where they arrived on 3 October. Here, despite the continuing Boer War, they were met with warm hospitality, re-fitted and supplied. The principal reason for the visit, however, was to carry out magnetic work, so that their observations would have as many 'fixed points' as possible in order to work out the variations at sea and in the Antarctic. Skelton was quite caustic about scientists apparently having fun whilst he saw to the coaling of the ship. Nevertheless, before they sailed, he had time to visit the magnetic station and a prison camp holding Boers, along with attending the long list of social engagements arranged for *Discovery* officers.

Discovery sailed from South Africa on 14 October, leaving behind Mr George Murray, a noted oceanographer who had been temporarily assisting the expedition work. Owing to the fact that it had taken them much longer to reach Cape Town than had been expected, the next port of call, due to be Melbourne in Australia, was changed and the ship headed for Lyttelton in New Zealand. Much of the planned oceanographic programme was curtailed as they were falling behind schedule. Catching the Westerlies and entering the 'roaring forties' they started to experience rough weather and the diaries of both Skelton and Wilson reflect the efforts everyone made to continue the scientific programme despite the difficulties of time and motion. The enthusiasm of all aboard for recording everything that they saw meant that Skelton had particular difficulties in enforcing discipline in the dark room:

"The Dark Room is made too much of by almost everybody who wants to snap off any odd picture - the consequence being that it is impossible to keep things in order, one finds a developing dish has been used for washing out hypo or even for fixing, - I have put up rules in the Room specifying that everybody must clean up their own mess and replace water - but it is of course impossible to keep everything straight, especially as some of the photographers are exceedingly amateur." Thu 24 Oct RWS

When they had reached 47°S the ship's course was altered southward, being set for the centre of the Earth's maximum magnetic intensity, then in the region of 52°S 131°E, south of Australia. The plan was to head southward to the limit that the ice permitted and to record the changes in the Earth's magnetic force and dip. On 15 November, amidst considerable excitement, they sighted their first ice. They reached 62° 50´S 139°E, 200 miles north of the known Adélie Land coast, before turning north again, having completed their short scientific programme.

On 22 November they sighted Macquarie Island, and Scott was persuaded to stop for a few hours to collect specimens. Here Edward Wilson first became acquainted with penguins, on which he was to become an authority. Skelton was busy with his camera and helped to collect specimens. On 30 November *Discovery* berthed at Lyttelton, New Zealand.

In New Zealand the Expedition was, once again, offered warm and generous hospitality. Wilson spent a good deal of time working in the Canterbury Museum, Christchurch, on the biological specimens that had been collected to date which were now due to be shipped to the Museums back home. Skelton was busy seeing to the overhauling of the engines and the re-fitting of the ship which had once again been placed into dry dock to try to find the source of the famous leak. Barne, Armitage and the other magneticians were busy at the Christchurch Magnetic Observatory, setting up a land based station which would take part in the simultaneous readings that were to be taken on the 'term days' by the various expeditions and land stations. The arrival of Louis Bernacchi as physicist, the last officer to join the *Discovery*, helped with this. He had previously sailed with the *Southern Cross* Expedition. With the continuing scientific programme and the making of the final preparations to sail south, away from civilisation, the days in New Zealand were full of bustle. Added to this was an almost overwhelming round of social engagements, during which Skelton met a young lady, Sybil Meares, and fell in love. There were many thousands of visitors who came to see the ship, with special trains being laid on. When at last all was ready to depart, huge numbers of people lined the wharves or chartered tugs and other vessels to cheer *Discovery* out of Lyttelton Harbour. Bands played, hooters sounded and the crowds roared their good wishes. HMS *Ringarooma* and *Lizard* formed an honour guard and *Ringarooma* then escorted *Discovery* to Port Chalmers in Dunedin where she was to take on further coal. In the excitement of departure from Lyttelton several sailors climbed aloft to wave and cheer. AB Bonner, however, climbed atop the crow's nest and shortly afterwards, as *Discovery* reached the open sea and the last crowds of hoorahing well wishers turned back, he lost his balance and fell to his death on the deck below. He was buried in Dunedin, with full naval honours. Having buried their comrade and finished coaling the ship, *Discovery* was again cheered out of Port Chalmers by well wishers and her escorts until, finally, New Zealand and civilisation faded from view in the dwindling evening light. *Discovery* headed towards her unknown future in the south alone.

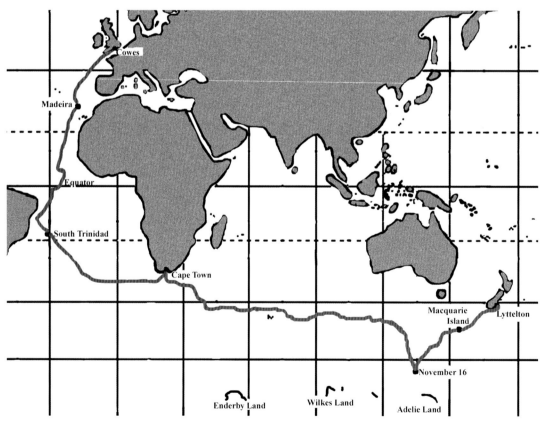

Map showing the approximate route of the outward voyage of SS Discovery to New Zealand. 1901

At Sea: Cowes to Madeira 7 August - 14 August 1901

Seascape

"I saw the sun rise this morning, a long streak of pink madder on the horizon, across which the sun passed hurriedly. All else was a dull dead grey, water and sky." Fri 9 Aug EAW

Bonito Fishing. Bay of Biscay

Group of Officers on the bridge. L-R: Skelton; Ferrar; Armitage; Barne (holding Scamp); Wilson

"Fine sunny, breezy day, Townet used very successfully in the evening. We "scientists" were busy all the afternoon till dinner time bringing up and re-stowing the emergency rations..." Mon 12 Aug EAW

"On the 14th stopped in the afternoon, to try the dredging and sounding arrangements" Wed 14 Aug RWS

Wilson's cabin

Scott

"Our Wine Caterer"; Wilson

Madeira 15 August - 16 August 1901

Discovery

"Took in 54 tons of Welsh coal the 1st day - I was ashore all day" Thu 15 Aug RWS

"Up the mountain road...The path was cobbled the whole way....with walls on either side or trellis work on which hung grapes, figs, Bougainvillaea, or honeysuckles, vaccinium, all sorts of beautiful creepers and fruits...the view looked down on the hot and sleepy town and the ships and the Atlantic Ocean, far far away into space...Well, it was a paradise!" Thu 15 Aug EAW

The Barracks Square

Bridge and street scene (detail)

"I then sat on the verandah and sketched the barracks square and the bullock sledges and sundry other very characteristic sights...I wandered about the narrow streets and the boulevard of Madeira all the morning, making pencil sketches of one or two of the multitudinous picturesque scenes that were to be seen there" Fri 16 Aug EAW

"We had ordered the wooden-shod wicker-work sleighs to meet us at the top, so in we got all three in one sleigh and a man hanging on with a rope on each side of the sleigh to save us from perdition. So down we went, sometimes at a break neck pace, very smoothly on these wooden runners on the cobble stones" Thu 15 Aug EAW

Bullock Cart

At Sea: Madeira to South Trinidad 17 August - 12 September 1901

Sunset. 28 Aug 1901

"Today we have had three or four really heavy tropical rains. And all round, but especially at sunset, when I went up the main mast, we have had the most splendid rainy sky." Fri 23 Aug EAW

School of small whales seen on 22 Aug 1901

"After lunch the King and Queen and their court arrived singing various chanties. After splitting two bottles of whisky, the show began. They addressed the Skipper, and introduced the court to him. It consisted of King Neptune in an elaborate crown, and black oilskins chalked all over with fishes, long tow hair and beard, and a trident on which was stuck a dried cod; his Queen in flowered silks, pink cheeks and a mass of thin rope twist all down her back, a Lulu hat turned up on one side with red paper roses and so on. She carried binoculars made of two wine bottles and a silver wand. Then came a ludicrous doctor with a stethoscope, and soap pills and screwdrivers for teeth. Then two constables for whom we had policemen's clothes in the acting department, and three men in yellow oilskins and tow wigs to catch and duck us in the sail bath. Then also the barber with an enormous wooden razor, a plasterer with a bucket of soot and flour and soap made into a fluid with tallow, and after him a man with a bucket of flour." Sat 31 Aug EAW

"On crossing the line the usual Father Neptune turned up and christened several people notably Hodgson, Wilson, Ferrar." Sat 31 Aug RWS

Crossing the line

Crossing the Line. Neptune's Court: Neptune (Allan); Queen (Mardon); and Tritons (Macfarlane, Pilbeam, Wild)

At Sea: Madeira to South Trinidad 17 August - 12 September 1901

"The heat is excessive. We are wearing our white suits. My cabin is the coolest of them all and early in the morning, breakfast time, it registers 84°F."
Wed 21 Aug EAW

"Cleaning department and adjusting bearings up to the 9th September, - completed intermediate and low pressure engines, - but were not able to get the high pressure done, consequence was when we started steaming at 2.15 P.M. on the 9th September, everything worked well and quietly except high pressure engine which made a shocking noise."
Sep 1901 RWS

Wilson, in tropical clothing

"Numberless flying fish. Saw also three splendid pink *Physalia*, or Portuguese men of war, which stood four inches out of the water at least and dragged long arms of a chocolate red colour." Mon 2 Sep EAW

"All the forenoon and afternoon I was sketching skies and doing a minute flying fish which was caught in the townet, an inch long." Mon 9 Sep EAW

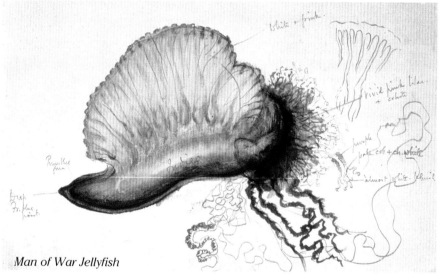

Man of War Jellyfish

Small flying fish caught in townet. 9 Sep 1901

Just after Sunset. Looking West. 9 Sep 1901

South Trinidad 13 September 1901

"Was called some time before sunrise to see South Trinidad, as I had asked. It was worth it. I made several sketches of the rugged broken outline. It was a most striking sight, this oceanic island, after so long seeing nought but clouds and sea and sky." Fri 13 Sep EAW

South Trinidad at Dawn

Within South-west Bay

Landing on South Trinidad. L-R: Koettlitz; Ferrar; Royds; George Murray; Cross; Wilson; Stoker Page; Gilbert Scott; u/d; Hodgson

"Two of the whalers were then lowered and manned. All of us scientists embarked with Royds as captain of my boat and the Skipper of the other...Our orders were to collect and bring on board everything of natural history interest that we could lay our hands on. We were all strung up like Christmas trees with bags and satchels and boxes and bottles. Most of us wore helmets or big hats, as the heat was intense."
Fri 13 Sep EAW

The Monument (Knight), Sugar Loaf and Noah's Ark, South Trinidad

South Trinidad September 13 1901

Fairy Tern, South Trinidad

Booby, South Trinidad

"Wilson...called my attention to some black breasted petrel flying about, - which I said I would try and capture...My total bag...amounted to

6 white breasted petrel with 3 eggs
1 black breasted petrel with 1 egg
4 gannet with 3 eggs
4 Tern with 3 eggs

On my way to the pier I found that I was cut off by the beach way, on account of high tide, - and going along the cliffs, I got into some very awkward places not able to move either way, and was also much troubled with cramp from carrying too much weight; - finally I had to drop my camera, birds, all except my gun on to the beach, - the camera getting badly smashed, - then walked round the cliff and then down to the beach by a safe path, - picked up my gear and arrived at the landing place, last and thoroughly fagged out, - on the passage off, - all my eggs got smashed, but the birds came off alright and turned out rather a good catch, - as of the black breasted petrel, there are no specimens and the white breasted only one specimen in the British Museum...Good hauls were made by other people on shore particularly Shackleton, - and a splendid lot of pictures were made by Wilson."
Fri 13 Sep RWS

Trinidad Petrel

Trinidad Petrel Eggs, Collected by Discovery

Dark morph Trinidad Petrel, sitting outside nest burrow

Skinning Birds on deck, after South Trinidad. L-R: Dellbridge; Skelton; Wilson and Hodgson

Cape Pigeon

"Up at 6 a.m. painting the heads and feet of all my birds. Same all the morning, and then! my word, skinned hard on till nearly 10.30 p.m. with intervals for eating. Skelton skinned some and Hodgson did a few, and Barne did one. I did the rest, about ten. We had to hurry on all we could, because they had already begun to stink by the evening." Sat 14 Sep EAW

Cape Pigeon

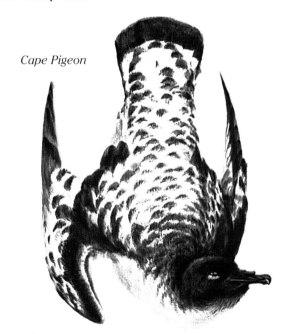

Cape Pigeon, hung up abaft the bridge

"Just before lunch we caught a Cape Pigeon with a tangle of thread lines let out from the stern. It was a very beautiful bird and I killed it with chloroform. It vomited a quantity of small red crustaceous matter. I spent the whole afternoon and evening sketching it in three positions." Sat 21 Sep EAW

"...caught one cape pigeon and Dellbridge caught another, - in the afternoon I caught a splendid albatross (Exulans) nearly 10 ft across the wings, and if his wings had been fully grown would have been more like 11 or 12 ft. Took photos of the bird. Big job skinning albatross, which Wilson and I myself did." Sun 22 Sep RWS

"Skelton hooked and landed an enormous albatross, 'Diomedea exulans', which weighed 15 lbs. and measured exactly 9 feet from wing tip to wing tip. He was freely photographed and then I sketched him. He was smothered with large lice." Sun 22 Sep EAW

Wandering Albatross

Dellbridge and u/d seaman holding a Wandering Albatross

South Africa 3 October - 14 October 1901

Table Mountain, Cape Town. 4 Oct 1901

"We came up to Cape Town from the S.W. rounding Table Mountain, along a magnificent rocky and precipitous coastline...the table cloth of cloud on the mountain kept rising and shifting to give us a view of shadow and sunlight among the mountain tops." Thu 3 Oct EAW

"In we went [to Capetown harbour]...and heard that all our letters were gone on to Simonstown, as they thought we were going straight there. But we got them the same evening, by telephoning, a few hours later. A few hours means a lot though, after two months of anticipation." Thu 3 Oct EAW

"Armitage and Barne started off to Simonstown with all their magnetic instruments, to set up a station, - All the scientists proceeded to the beach to have a good time." Fri 4 Oct RWS

Discovery at Simonstown

Between Cape Town and Simon's Bay, White Sands. 5 Oct 1901

South Africa 3 October - 14 October 1901

Magnetic Station near Simonstown

"We did very badly coaling during the forenoon getting in only about 80 tons, - but in the afternoon the gang was doubled and we also worked straight from a ship unloading at the same wharf, so that we got in all our coal 230 tons by 4 o'clock." Fri 4 Oct RWS

Barne (with two u/d men - prob. professors from the Cape University) at work with Unifilar Magnetometer

"Soon after leaving England, the Skipper had mentioned that provided the Admiral at Simonstown was a good sort we had every chance of getting a good refit, and a fair quantity of stores, such as only a good dockyard could supply, - but the actual case far exceeded everybody's ideas, we simply got everything we asked for and more." Sat 5 Oct RWS

"...we have received several invitations to various functions, - picnic on Tuesday afternoon, - dinner with the Governor on Tuesday, dinner with Philosophical Society on Wednesday, - observatory on Thursday, - dinner with Admiral on Thursday, - garden party at Admirals on Friday, - we expect to leave on Saturday." Sun 6 Oct RWS

"After lunch took the ½ plate camera ashore, and Scamp, and walked up the Hill to the Magnetic Station - deuce of a climb, - couldn't find the place for some time, and walked a good bit out of my way, but found it after a time; - Took 4 photos of tents etc." Fri 11 Oct RWS

"Hanging about the whole day swinging the ship, until at last it was done and we slowly steamed out amid the most energetic cheering from the battleships as we passed, with flagdipping and signalling and Naval band playing. We cheered and were cheered again and again." Mon 14 Oct EAW

False Bay, South Africa. 14 Oct 1901

Fish caught on a line, Oct.15.1901. in 35° 37½' S. 20° 34.'E. On the Agulhas Bank, South Africa. This fish was preserved in Spirit. Others of the same species proved excellent eating. "Discovery" Antarctic Expedition.

Fish caught on a line, 15 Oct 1901. 35° 37 ½´ S 20° 34´ E, on the Agulhas Bank, South Africa

"The morning was spent in preparing to fish over the Agulhas banks...Three large fish of one kind were caught and two bigger still, about 20 lbs. in all, were caught and I painted them before we eat them. They were very good indeed." Tue 15 Oct EAW

"In the dark room we suffer from the dishes being too shallow, they are all the ordinary photographic dishes, and I tried to get some specially deep ones, but they are not made. There is no doubt for photographic work in a small ship, - deep dishes should be specially made, - for developing not less than 2 to 3 inches deep - I have made a lead fixing dish myself about 2½ inches deep, which has the advantages of keeping the hypo-sulphite from splashing about and is unlikely to roll about when the ship heels over...It is impossible to do any work in the Dark Room with the ship moving." Thu 24 Oct RWS

In the Westerlies. The Monkey Poop.
u/d man at wheel

The Wheel

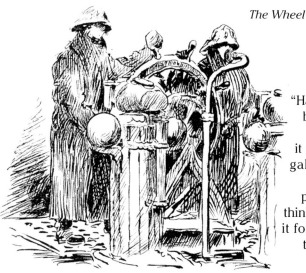

"Have made a bad weather sketching box which I hang round my neck and can sketch comfortably in it even when it rains and blows a gale and spray comes all over one. The paper keeps com- paratively dry - so: The Skipper thinks it's an excellent plan, and we use it for a barrel organ in our impromptu theatricals on the bridge."
Wed 30 Oct EAW

At Sea: South Africa to Macquarie Island 15 October - 21 November 1901

White headed Petrel

"Painting a bird which is swinging through 30° every few seconds is trying too. Things won't stay as you put them. Your water is hung on a hook, your paper pinned to a board and you hold your paint box. You yourself are wedged into the bunk cupboard and kept there by a boot on the chest of drawers opposite. You put your paint box down to settle a wing for the thirtieth time and down it rattles and the paints go all over the cabin. You jump to save the paint box and the corner of your board tilts the water tin off the hook and it empties into a drawer full of clean drawing paper; while a running drip takes the opportunity of coming from the skylight on to your painting of the bird you are doing. Everything is at such close quarters and everything trying to balance itself with the most indifferent success." Mon 4 Nov EAW

Grey Petrel. 2 Nov 1901

Albatross Lures

"The wind abated in the afternoon so much that I started fishing for Albatross, - had very hard lines, as I got no less than 5 in the triangle but the oncoming waves are so big that one cannot pull in all the slack, and the bird gets loose again,- one bird I hauled in a considerable distance before he got off, - he didn't like it much, - I was much disappointed, as two different species that got on are both very much wanted by Wilson."
Tue 29 Oct RWS

Grey Headed Albatross

"We each have to hand in to the Skipper a note book with our summary for the week, an excellent plan. These are all kept in his cabin, so that we can at any time see what is being done in the other departments. For example, I can get an idea of the food there is in the water, crustacean or animal food, by referring to Muggins' report, vegetable food by referring to Koettlitz's, ...all of which put together may explain now and again why a flock of petrels follows us for two days and then suddenly disappears en masse. In fact we hope to know all that can be found out about everything wherever we go." Sat 19 Oct EAW

"In the afternoon we stopped at 4.30 to sound and get specimens, crustacea, - diatons etc. the sounding wire carried away near bottom so we lost thermometer at depth about 2500 fathoms. Very satisfactory the way the winch hauls in the wire, faster than it goes out. - Took 2 photos of sounding." Fri 15 Nov RWS

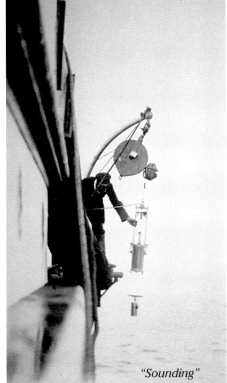

"Sounding"

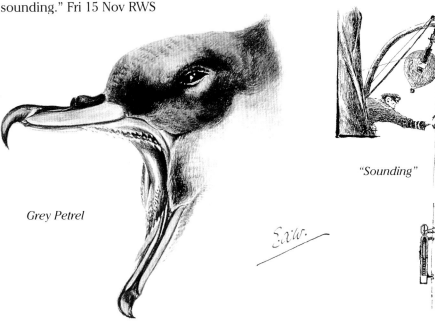

Grey Petrel

"Sounding"

Snow Petrel

"Suddenly however Michael went mad and rushed down the ladder and shouted 'Ice!' down the ward-room skylight. He slipped in his hurry and came a regular howler, but never stopped to pick up. All he had seen was piece of white ice the size of a soup plate, and yet in ten minutes there were bigger pieces all round us and everyone on the bridge to see it. Huge jokes and everyone in the most boisterous spirits and champagne at once ordered for dinner this evening." Sat 16 Nov EAW

Antarctic Petrel

First Ice

Blue Petrel

"This has been a most eventful day - We saw our first pieces of ice about 10 A.M. and it began to get thicker and thicker gradually until about noon we were constantly bumping pieces giving the ship rather a shock, - being under sail it was rather hard to avoid them... We proceeded again soon after 6.00 P.M. the ice began to get thicker and thicker, - a most marvellous sight, - quite the most wonderful I have ever seen, - about 9 we ran into solid pack and stopped dead, so we had to get up steam." Sat 16 Nov RWS

Wilson's Storm Petrel

"Skelton and I and Dellbridge the 2nd Engineer did the shooting" Sat 16 Nov EAW

Blue Petrel.
"This bird was shot to bits..."

"Looked over Wilson's sketches of the birds shot in the pack, they are splendid, - and should I think be of great use to the Naturalists at home as the descriptions of the birds, colouring, beaks, feet etc., in the British Museum catalogues are all wrong." Thu 21 Nov RWS

Wilson and Dellbridge Shooting

Macquarie Island 22 November 1901

"I told the Pilot that I would give him a bottle of liqueur if he could persuade the Skipper to allow us to land here for collecting. Off he went like a shot and soon after came up and told me he wanted the liqueur...we came opposite to a low lying shore at the foot of a valley which ran up into the island...Here on the flat we could see two or three red huts, wooden sheds, and soon after thousands of penguins all standing in crowds like an army of soldiers...I could see that there were colonies of the large handsome King Penguin and also of the smaller orange crested penguin." Fri 22 Nov EAW

Dropping the anchor at Macquarie Island

Chief Engineer Skelton photographing an Elephant Seal, Macquarie Island

"I went in the Captain's boat and steered her ashore to one of the huts...directly after landing the Captain spotted a seal basking just above the beach, - great excitement of course, and yells for a rifle, - no rifle forthcoming, so I got my camera out and took some photos quite close, - as I was taking a front view of the beast Heald, one of the seamen, was seized with a mania for murder and started belting the animal on the head, so my photo did not come off, and the camera was very nearly upset. Duncan and Heald then went on battering the animal in a most absurd way, until I got the stick from Duncan and finished it off with two good blows on the head and Barne put a shot from a mauser revolver into its head" Fri 22 Nov RWS

"...the poor beast woke up and gazed on us with its saucer-like eyes, and then being dissatisfied with the look of some 20 men and cameras, it opened its mouth to its widest, shewing a very old woman's set of teeth, poor thing, and gave a loud inspiratory sort of roar which startled us all. And then up went its tail end and it made a half dash at the camera, then it backed again into some long tussocky grass and a foul stinking stagnant pool of water, always keeping its mouth open most threateningly, till at last it couldn't stand things any longer and made another clumsy dash for the camera stand, which collapsed, and then the poor beast was sacrificed in the interest of science, as it was a seal we shall not see in the Antarctic."
Fri 22 Nov EAW

Macquarie Island 22 November 1901

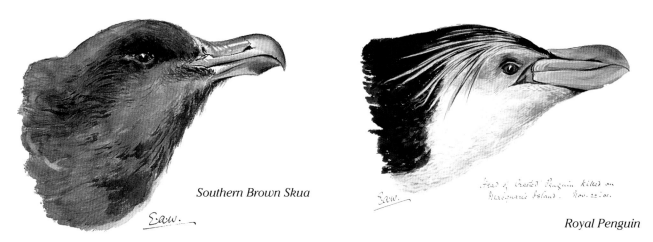

Southern Brown Skua

Royal Penguin

"Then we wandered off to inspect the penguin rookeries, and indeed they are the most strange sight I have ever seen. They were there in thousands and they lived on flats of rough loose stones, over which trickled water which had come down the valley, but all was stinking mud and in this wet filth the King Penguins were living and breeding." Fri 22 Nov EAW

Discovery anchored at Macquarie Island, from Penguin Colonies

"All this time, from 5.30 p.m. when we landed to about 8 p.m., the others had scattered with guns and cameras to try and find anything in the way of eggs or birds or what not, and the result was a really splendid collection for my department. We got the following:- King Penguins, Crested Penguins, Great Antarctic Skua gulls, Blue-eyed Cormorant, Black-backed Gull, Giant Petrel, Rothschild's Landrail. Eggs of King Penguin about a hundred, chiefly for food, excellent." Fri 22 Nov EAW

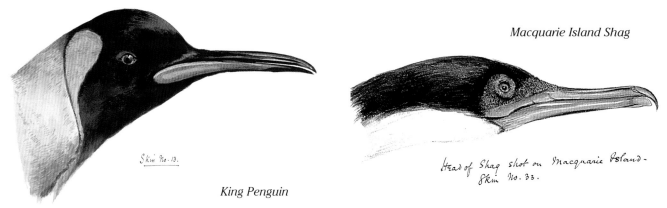

Macquarie Island Shag

King Penguin

At Sea: Macquarie Island to New Zealand 23 November - 28 November 1901

"Had Penguin Stew for dinner, - not bad."
Sun 24 Nov RWS

"Scrambled Penguin eggs for breakfast, practically colourless and tasteless."
Mon 25 Nov RWS

What a month, what a month what a month leg South

*Light-mantled
Sooty Albatross*

"The roast penguin turned out very fair - we also had the land rails we caught at Macquarie for dinner - I didn't care for them." Tue 26 Nov RWS

"Just before breakfast we had a roll to starboard of 56° which wrecked several cabins, and the amount of crockery broken was phenomenal." Tue 26 Nov EAW

Light-mantled Sooty Albatross

Some of the Crew at Lyttelton, New Zealand. 1901. On the Mizzen Boom L-R: ABs Vince; Peters; Wild; PO Evans; ABs Walker; Heald; Sailmaker Miller; PO Macfarlane; Carpenter Dailey; 2nd Eng. Dellbridge. On the Poop deck, L-R: Cpl. Blissett; AB Sinclair; Ldg Stoker Page; ABs Dell; Weller; Ldg Stoker Quartley; PO Smythe; AB Williamson; PO Allan; Ldg Seaman Pilbeam

Officers and scientists at Lyttelton, New Zealand. 1901. L-R: Dr E.A. Wilson; Lt. E.H. Shackleton; Lt. A.B. Armitage; Lt. M. Barne RN; Dr R. Koettlitz; Ch. Eng. R.W. Skelton RN; Cdr R.F. Scott RN; Lt. C.W. Royds RN; L.C. Bernacchi; H.T. Ferrar; T.V. Hodgson

New Zealand 29 November - 24 December 1901

"Miss Sybil Meares, prettiest girl in Christchurch" Tue 17 Dec RWS

"Started at 9 am with the Meares and drove out to the Maories Pah at Kaiapoi good show - dance in evening given by Ladies, - good show." Wed 11 Dec RWS

"Caulking of the ship proceeding... - A few of the ship's bolts and one or two other little places drip a little, but on the whole there does not appear to be any leakage from the outside to account for the amount of water that has been coming into the ship, - I should say this dryness in dock indicates that the leakage has been from the seams near the waterline, which have been sometimes exposed to sun and sometimes to water." Wed 4 Dec RWS

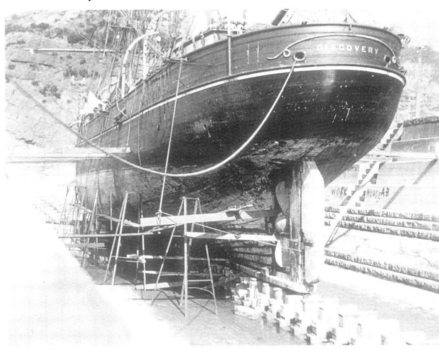

Discovery in dry dock, Lyttelton

"The old chief then addressed us in Maori and an interpreter told us all about it. Koettlitz and Hodgson replied, and Koettlitz was given a feather mat and a feather basket hat. Then they sang to us in Maori, then tea and cakes, then a visit to their very English church, and then after many photos were taken, we went off to an old Maori battlefield where we had an excellent picnic lunch, and a wander round the battle ground, where a monument has been erected." Wed 11 Dec EAW

Officers of Discovery visiting the Maori Pa at Kaiapoi. 11 Dec 1901. Visible, L-R with the Maori are; back: Barne; Hodgson; Scott; Ferrar; Wilson; front: Koettlitz, wearing the hat and cloak with which he had just been presented

The visit to the battleground Memorial near Kaiapoi

Discovery leaving Lyttelton, New Zealand. AB Bonner may be seen standing on top of the crows nest (inset), from where he was waving to the crowds of well wishers, shortly before falling to his death

"Well, we were all in the very best of spirits at getting off at last, the real work's beginning. No more looking back for sometime, no more fears lest something may crop up to prevent one from going after all. Now, neck or nothing, we are fairly started, thank God, and by His grace we shall do something worth the doing before we sight New Zealand and civilization again." Tue 24 Dec EAW

4: Something New Every Day
25 December 1901 - 8 February 1902

From New Zealand, the Expedition sailed across the windswept immensity of the Southern Ocean once again. Here the Albatross, and other seabirds of the true ocean, soar for days upon the rippling currents of the cold wind in their quest for food. For the team aboard *Discovery* it was time to re-adjust to ship-board life and to learn to work with new companions who had joined the ship in New Zealand. The scientific programme continued. Skelton was busy in the engine room, particularly when the ship was becalmed. He also relished applying his ingenuity to inventing gadgets to catch the seabirds that followed in their wake. Wilson set to work with his paints, recording any specimens that were successfully brought aboard, prior to their being skinned, dissected and prepared for museum drawers.

The frenetic activity of all aboard meant that the full celebration of Christmas day was postponed, at least until they reached the expected calm of the pack ice. New Year's Day 1902 was nevertheless seen in with plenty of raucous singing; over a bowl of whisky punch in the ward room and with grog on the lower decks. Many officers and seamen started the new year with a headache. By now they had sailed a good way south and sweepstakes were under way as to when the first ice would be seen. The first bergs appeared on 2 January and by the 3rd they were entering the pack ice. Here they started to collect specimens of the Antarctic seals and encountered their first Adélie and Emperor penguins. Bringing the seals aboard was hard work, as was dissecting and skinning them. Seal started to appear on the menu, and was considered by Skelton, amongst others, to be as good as beef. Dredging and sounding work was also started upon in earnest. Christmas Day was celebrated on 5 January, amidst the work of the scientific programme. By 8 January they were through the pack ice and into the open water of the Ross Sea.

They sighted the coast of Victoria Land on the evening of 8 January and landed at Cape Adare on the 9th. This was where the expedition of the *Southern Cross* had over-wintered, and the hut, surrounded by the messy remainder of Borchgrevink's supplies, was found and explored with interest. Bernacchi had spent a whole year living and working here as the physicist of that expedition and as a result he was very keen to take further magnetic readings for comparison. Wilson was most excited by the enormous Adélie Penguin rookery that surrounded the hut. He and Shackleton wandered the beach together collecting and photographing specimens. Skelton, too, was busy with his camera for much of the visit. Prior to departure they left a cylinder of letters for the relief ship to pick up when it came to find them the following year.

They sailed south along the coast of Victoria Land. Wilson was kept busy with his sketchbook and Skelton with his camera. Wilson had long since perfected a colour memorisation technique, in which he used a shorthand colour notation on pencil sketches, which allowed him to paint up the scene some time later. This proved the ideal technique for art work in the cold of the Antarctic. Skelton too, found the cold challenged his photographic skills:

"Hard at work developing photos, which are turning out well, but am troubled with sluggishness of developer owing to cold, frilling of negatives, and if one is not very careful, they get frost bitten in washing." Sat 11 Jan RWS

By 13 January they were in the lee of Coulman Island, sheltering from a gale; Skelton worked long hours keeping the engines going. However, they were able to land at Cape Wadworth on the 15th in order to set up another message post for the relief ship. From here they made their way round to Lady Newnes Bay where a large number of seals were slaughtered to start building up a supply of seal meat. A number of Emperor Penguins were also taken, two being kept alive as ship board pets for several days. Finding the way south blocked by ice, they worked their way back around the outside of Coulman Island and continued south. They were now in sight of the snow-clad peak of Mount Melbourne and hoped to enter Wood Bay - the closest known point to the expected location of the Magnetic Pole - but again the way was blocked by ice. The extraordinary quantity of new sights caused Wilson to note at this time:

"Another week come to an end. They go very quickly. There is so much to interest and so many new things to see and far too much to do." Sat 18 Jan EAW

Continuing to work their way southwards and charting parts of unknown coastline, they were in sight of the 12,000 foot (3,700 metre) volcano, Mount Erebus, by 19 January, when it was still 120 miles away. Mounts Erebus and Terror had been named by Ross for his ships and remained the most significant landmarks yet found in the South. The sight of them caused considerable excitement aboard. Now they were truly approaching the edge of the unknown. The ship continued grating, grinding and groaning its way southward through the loose ice floes. By now they were looking upon sheltered bays as potential winter quarters and they explored several on their way into McMurdo Bay. Here they once again found their way south blocked by ice and started to work eastwards along the coast of Mounts Erebus and Terror to Cape Crozier. From here they had their first sight of Ross's Great Ice Barrier. *Discovery* proceeded to sail along it, to see if the Expedition could unravel its mysterious nature. Dredging and sounding operations were carried out with some regularity and everyone marvelled at the extraordinary creatures that Hodgson was finding in the waters beneath them. As January came to a close the sounding operations suggested that they were coming towards the end of the Ice Barrier but fog meant that they did not get a good look at the new land that they had discovered until 1 February. They named it King Edward VII Land. It was the first significant geographical discovery of the Expedition. With the sea starting to freeze around them, and continuing fog making ice navigation dangerous, they wisely decided not to explore further, turning around and heading back towards McMurdo Bay. This was widely thought to be the most likely location to find a safe winter quarters, which Scott wanted to attain whilst the weather and ice conditions still permitted. At this point too, Scott outlined a general plan of campaign for the Expedition:

"We were today given an idea of the three years' programme of work. It is shortly as follows:- Make straight for McMurdo Bay; find good winter quarters and get settled into them as far south as possible. Spend the winter there. Give up next summer chiefly to sledging in three directions. One party to go due south from winter quarters. The ship to wait till its return. Other smaller parties and excursions to make out the immediate neighbourhood of McMurdo Bay and Erebus and Terror, and to come back to the ship. By this time the relief ship will have found our letters at Cape Crozier and will come to us in McMurdo Bay. The relief ship will now take Armitage and a party to Wood Bay to go inland for the Magnetic Pole, and wait for them till their return when they and the relief ship will return to Lyttelton. Meanwhile the 'Discovery' will have collected its sledge parties and will go up by Cape Adare and by Cape North and see if anything can be made out of Wilkes' Land, and when the season comes to an end, run straight up to Lyttelton, arriving there about the end of March 1903. Here we spend the winter months refitting, and then in December '03 we start south again to get further information about this east end of the Barrier where we found our new land. We go straight for this part and spend the whole summer working it out and then run up in March, out of the ice, and home round Cape Horn without going again to New Zealand at all." Sun 2 Feb EAW

Whilst returning westward along the Ice Barrier, *Discovery* anchored at a low point in the ice cliff and a landing was effected. Here, a magnetic party was sent sledging to the south across the Barrier, under Armitage and Bernacchi. They thought at the time that they had also achieved a 'Farthest South' but their later calculations indicated that they hadn't quite beaten the record which had been set in a similar manner by the *Southern Cross*. Here, too, a day was spent in launching the balloon which they had brought with them. Scott made the first ascent, the first flight in the Antarctic, and Shackleton made the second, during which he took the first Antarctic aerial photographs. Little could be seen from the balloon, certainly not any new land in the distance as they had hoped to discover. The Ice Barrier clearly reached over a considerable distance, or else there was no continent here after all. By 7 February the ship was once again at the westward end of the Barrier, passing Cape Crozier, and they re-entered McMurdo Bay on the 8th. This time there was little ice and they proceeded to explore the strange pinnacle ice formations that they found to the west and to look for suitable winter quarters in the icy bays through which they sailed. None was found suitable, however, and they followed the ice edge towards the eastern end of the bay.

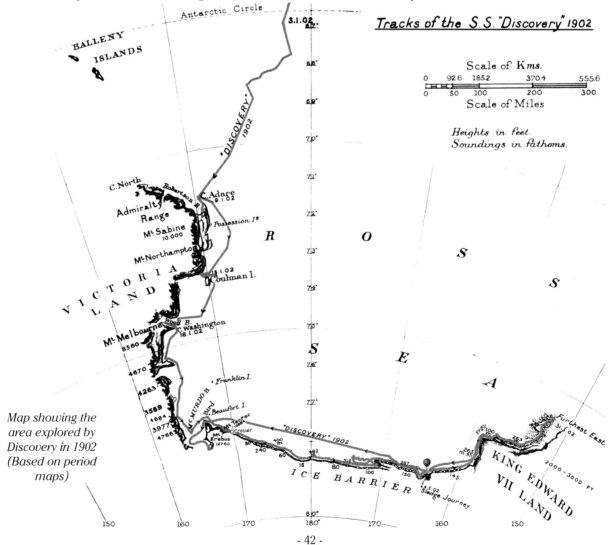

Map showing the area explored by Discovery in 1902 (Based on period maps)

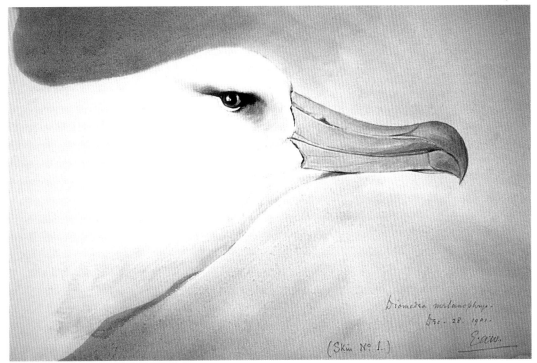

Black-browed Albatross. 28 Dec 1901 54° 54´S 171° 08´E

Black-browed and White-capped Albatross feeding astern

"Albatrosses very ravenous, tried all methods of catching them without success, until Dellbridge and myself tried bringing them up close with mutton fat and then throwing a grapnel." Fri 27 Dec RWS

Grey-headed Albatross. 29 Dec 1901 56° 54´S 170° 27´E

In the Pack Ice 3 January - 8 January 1902

First Ice sighted after leaving New Zealand

"Looked rather as if we were approaching ice about midday and Bernacchi felt so certain about it that he made bets on the subject with Koettlitz a bottle of fizz and Barne and myself a glass of port each, that we should see ice before dinner, - no ice appeared, so he lost his bets." Tue 31 Dec RWS

Discovery in pack ice

"After lunch we tied up to a large floe to practise skiing. Almost everybody went out and it was great sport. They seem fairly easy to get on with on level ice but it is difficult over rough and the skis seem to have a tendency to cross one another." Sun 5 Jan RWS

Officers on ski in the pack ice. L-R: Hodgson; Koettlitz; Wilson; Bernacchi; Scott; Barne (behind); Royds; Ferrar. 5 Jan 1902

In the Pack Ice 3 January - 8 January 1902

Crabeater Seal

"...it proved to be one of the crab-eating seals, a cow, very fair specimen, with its winter coat half shed." Fri 3 Jan RWS

"After lunch set to work with Walker our northern whaler and skinned this seal and made his skeleton. It was a winter coated...Crabeater - stomach full of shrimps...and remains of a fish." Fri 3 Jan EAW

Walker, with Crabeater seal on deck. 3 Jan 1902

L-R; Cross, Walker and Wilson, dissecting a seal on deck

Ross' Seal

"Royds sent down to say a seal was in sight, so Shackleton and myself took our rifles up, and putting 3 shots into him, finished him off, - he proved to be a good specimen of the Ross seal, Wilson was very pleased to get it, as there are only 5 specimens in all the museums of the world." Mon 6 Jan RWS

Ross' Seal on deck

In the Pack Ice 3 January - 8 January 1902

Sea leopard. ♀

Leopard Seal

"I was woken up about 2.15 A.M. by Wilson to shoot a seal which was close alongside, - I hurriedly put on trousers and coat, and with a rifle rushed up on deck - had to wait some time, before the ship was brought near enough, and then Shackleton and myself started firing, at the first shot the beast started off across the floe and it was only after 6 shots rapidly discharged that we brought him up just on the edge, - he proved to be a splendid specimen of a sea leopard - 10ft 10ins long and well over a ton weight - of course we could kill these animals easier if we shot them in the head, but that is not allowed as the skull is most particularly wanted intact." Tue 7 Jan RWS

"Skelton and Shackleton shot him, though he required 4 or 6 shots and very nearly reached the floe edge. He was near a ton in weight and took the whole watch to hoist him inboard, an enormous beast with a mouth full of teeth and a head bigger then a Polar Bear." Tue 7 Jan EAW

On deck at last. Leopard Seal, 7 Jan 1902

"This beast had an extremely fierce looking head, with large mouth and a most dangerous looking set of teeth, - I should not like to get very near one, on opening his stomach, an Emperor penguin was found, which must have been swallowed pretty nearly whole" Tue 7 Jan RWS

Leopard Seal chasing an Emperor Penguin

Exploring Victoria Land: Cape Adare 9 January 1902

"The magneticians were the first people to land with their instruments, - after that all the scientists went except Hodgson who had to go away in a whaler dredging, and half the ships company were also allowed to land." Thu 9 Jan RWS

L-R: Armitage, Barne and Bernacchi, taking magnetic readings

The Two Sisters, Cape Adare

"The place was the colour of anchovy paste from the excreta of the young penguins. It simply stunk like hell, and the noise was deafening...and bang in the centre of this horrid place was the camp with its two wooden huts, and a midden heap of refuse all round and a mountain of provision boxes, dead birds, seals, dogs, sledging gear, ski, snow shoes, flags, poles and heaven only knows what else." Thu 9 Jan EAW

Exploring Borchgrevink's Southern Cross Hut and abandoned supplies

"About 6 P.M. I went ashore with ½ plate camera and proceeded to take photos of shore, penguins etc...I took 12 photos on shore, and they have all turned out well, except one or two were frost bitten in washing." Thu 9 Jan RWS

"Want your dinner? Why you have only just had breakfast!" Adelie Penguins

"Our anemometer recorded the wind as blowing 70 miles an hour, and 90 during the squalls. - We tried to keep under the lea of the island of Coulman but were unable to do so, although we kept engines going slowly with one boiler, so as to keep ship's head right, we drifted some way north of the islands." Tue 14 Jan RWS

"The Captain and the geologist Ferrar went on shore with a party to fix a pole and a red cylinder of letters for the relief ship to pick up. I have put nothing into this cylinder, as I think in all probability it will remain where it is for many years." Wed 15 Jan EAW

Cape Anne, Coulman Island 13 Jan 1902

"C. Jones has been called C. Constance by Borchgrevink, but he had no right to name it, as it was named by Ross in 1841." Wed 15 Jan RWS

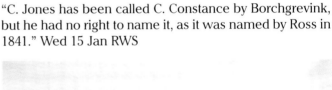

Cape Jones ("Cape Constance"), Coulman Island 15 Jan 1902

Cape Wadworth, Coulman Island   *Cape Wadworth, Coulman Island 15 Jan 1902*

Exploring Victoria Land: Lady Newnes Bay to Wood Bay
15 January - 19 January 1902

"The seals were dotted about broadcast on the ice. The penguins stood like little knots of men in the middle of their ice floes. The sky was deep blue overhead with large tracts covered with a filmy tracery of white clouds, brilliantly lit up in the sun." Wed 15 Jan EAW

"The captain...gave orders to kill 30 seals, which were to be skinned and taken on board for a winter stock of fresh meat." Wed 15 Jan RWS

"I suppose there were a couple of hundred seals in the inlet, all Weddells and we killed thirty of them, skinned them and shipped them as we wanted them for food...I had to superintend this beastly butcher's work, a duty much against the grain." Wed 15 Jan EAW

Sleeping Emperor Penguin, Lady Newnes Bay

Moulting Emperor Penguins, 15 Jan 1902, Lady Newnes Bay

"The seal meat is all hung up the mizzen rigging so with that and the sheep carcasses we look rather peculiar aft...I have been getting all the blubber put in a small tank with a steam coil which melts the blubber and I take off the oil from the bottom, - it works first rate, the oil seems to be very good, and I shall be able to use it for lamps or for lubricating the engines." Fri 17 Jan RWS

"Our two live Emperor Penguins seem very contented and comfortable in a small pen on deck. They are moulting and so it is quite natural for them to remain out of water and on a very low diet, as they do so in their wild state during the moult." Sun 19 Jan EAW

"Beautiful sight approaching Mt Melbourne and the entrance to Wood Bay." Fri 17 Jan RWS

Discovery at Lady Newnes Bay: sealing parties may be seen on the ice

Mount Melbourne, Wood Bay 19 Jan 1902

Exploring Victoria Land: McMurdo Bay, Mounts Erebus and Terror
20 January - 23 January 1902

Mount Erebus, 20 Jan 1902

"In the afternoon a Volcanic Peak appeared ahead which for some hours appeared to be Franklin Island, but afterwards turned out to be Mt Erebus, - with Mt Terror some way to the left of it. It was smoking very slightly and must have been over 120 miles off when sighted." Sun 19 Jan RWS

"We are getting down into McMurdo Bay, and at present there is no sign of land at the bottom of it; it must be very much (deeper) than the chart allows. (By deeper I mean it must go very much further back). On account of the weather we are able to keep very much closer to the land than any former expedition. - we consequently find many mistakes in the charted coast-line." Mon 20 Jan RWS

"This morning, we were under clouds for a few hours, but before midday the sky cleared and again we had the same beautiful sunshine and blue sky and were almost free of ice in open water under Mount Terror, and had passed Cape Bird and Beaufort Island...We gradually worked our way along towards Cape Crozier." Wed 22 Jan EAW

McMurdo Bay, 21 Jan 1902, the way south "blocked by ice"

Sailing past Mount Terror, 22 Jan 1902

The Great Ice Barrier 22 January - 7 February 1902

"Royds, the Captain and I went for a near mountain top...and had there a unique sight, and one that has never before been looked on. Out before us on the left was the open sea with a few bits of ice and streams of pack and new ice. Then came the cliff of the Ice Barrier stretching away like a coast line irregularly with one or two large bays and promontories, for near 60 miles as far as one could see with glasses. Then came the ice plain on which was setting a glorious sun, and miles and miles and miles of smooth ice plain." Wed 22 Jan EAW

The Great Ice Barrier

"We were steaming along the same kind of barrier all day again, the only difference being some water action on it in several big caves hollowed out of the ice cliff. We saw several big bergs, always interesting sights and delightful to look on, as their tints and tones change in every light." Sat 25 Jan EAW

Waterworn cave in the Barrier

A recently calved tabular berg from the Barrier, "The highest ice wall seen - 280 feet in height".

"Still steaming along quite close to the barrier, and continuing on soundings every 8 hours, - we have now got a continuous chain of soundings right along quite close to the barrier, which has never been obtained before, or anything like it, and I should think will be valuable." Wed 29 Jan RWS

Farthest East: King Edward VII Land, January 30 - January 31

King Edward VII Land

"Cleared up a little later on and about 6.30 real land was sighted, we were some time in making it out, but after dinner we got abreast a small mountain roughly I should say 3000 feet newly snow covered with 5 or 6 bare patches of rock sticking out of it; and ridge running from it to another mountain, and one in the distance, some way to the south; so that it seems to be a range of small mountains running pretty well south and north, - this is a most satisfactory discovery, as it gives so much more information towards the problem of the barrier, - besides, it has of course never been seen before."
Thu 30 Jan RWS

"...with the big telescope from the Crow's nest..."

"About lunch time we fastened the ship to a big heavy floe and the hands were occupied in taking in ice for water, which is at once melted by the steam hose from the main engines...on this floe we killed 3 splendid Emperor Penguins...Later on in the evening, with the big telescope from the crow's nest, I saw some thousands of Emperor Penguins...Obviously these were the Emperors' rookeries, which no one has found before, but...the whole big bay in which we were was quickly freezing and covered with new ice. Our only chance was to keep moving." Fri 31 Jan EAW

Emperor Penguin, Furthest East. 31 Jan 1902

Watering ship from a large ice floe. Farthest East

The Great Ice Barrier: Balloon Inlet, 3 February 1902

"The Captain was the first to go up...Shackleton next had a trip; and took some photos looking downwards, - he got an extreme elevation of 650 feet, - he spotted the sledge party in the distance returning, - but no signs of land...I am afraid as an assistance to Exploration down here it has not been a success, - still, it might have been." Tues 4 Feb RWS

"Yesterday the ship was in 78º 49´S. lat. and the magnetic party was in 79º 3´S. lat. Both of these are farther south than Borchgrevink and Ross." Wed 5 Feb EAW

Scott being lowered from the first Antarctic flight.

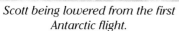

Balloon Bite: the first aerial photograph taken in Antarctica - Shackleton

The Barrier Sledge Party preparing to depart: Armitage, Bernacchi, Cross, Joyce, Crean, Handsley

Discovery at Balloon Inlet; the men are hauling seal meat to the ship

Return to McMurdo Bay: 8 February 1902

Iceberg off the Great Ice Barrier

"McMurdo Bay appears to be almost clear of ice, so we are to proceed, as far down as possible to find convenient winter quarters, - we have hopes of finding better and further south quarters than the granite harbour we looked into last month." Fri 7 Feb RWS

Looking seawards from fast ice near the Dailey Islands (Mt. Erebus in the distance), McMurdo Bay

5: Hut Point and Autumn Sledging
9 February 1902 - 22 April 1902

By the morning of 9 February *Discovery* was anchored in what became known as Arrival Bay. It became apparent, however, that a better anchorage existed to the south side of the small promontory by which they found themselves; it was to become known as Winter Quarters Bay. The ice had not yet completely left this area but since blasting it with explosives was not particularly effective there was nothing to be done but wait for nature to take its course. Nevertheless they were soon safely anchored, adjusting their position each time the ice moved away or the ice anchors were pulled in the wind. The task of erecting their huts ashore was started almost immediately and the dogs were also rapidly kennelled on the promontory, which was soon named Hut Point. With the ship remaining as living quarters for the winter, the huts were to be used for scientific work and storage, or in the event of an emergency. Whilst the construction work was undertaken local explorations were made and many of the features of their immediate surroundings were given names, including the newly sighted volcano to the south west - which was named Mount Discovery. One of the earliest revelations during these local walks was the fact that they were on an island, and that McMurdo Bay was properly a sound. The 'Parry Mountains' that Ross had thought to exist at the head of 'McMurdo Bay' simply weren't there. The features were rapidly re-named Ross Island and McMurdo Sound.

To the south of the anchorage, around the cape of the main peninsula which they named Cape Armitage, a further small island could be seen, later named White Island. Scott suggested that Wilson, Shackleton and Ferrar should undertake a journey to see what lay to the south of it and preparations were duly made for their first exploratory sledging trip. Due to uncertainties about the condition of the sea ice, they dragged a small boat called a 'pram' with them on their sledge when they departed on 19 February. This had to be hauled up through 'the Gap' - a low pass between the 750 foot (230 metre) Observation Hill and Crater Heights - a route that many southern sledge journeys would take in the future. Heading south towards the island, which they thought that they would quickly reach, they found that it was much further than they had anticipated. The three men had difficulty with their equipment and experienced minor cases of frost nip. Wilson rubbed the skin off Shackleton's ears as he had read that the treatment for frost bite was to rub it. Despite the sharp learning curve they kept their senses of humour. They attained the top of White Island and beyond it saw the vast snow-plain of the Great Ice Barrier stretching away to the south, rather than the hoped for Antarctic continent. To the west and south-west, however, was an extensive panorama of mountains with new ranges clearly visible. The men returned to the ship on 22 February having deposited their unneeded provisions and the pram for later collection. The spit upon which they left the supplies became known as Pram Point.

Whilst they were away, progress was made in completing the huts and in developing the scientific programme of the Expedition. Another matter was pressing on Scott's mind too, however, and this was the necessity of leaving further letters at the message post at Cape Crozier, in order to tell the relief ship where they were anchored. Such a trip also offered the possibility of exploring the newly found southern coastline of Ross Island. A string of minor accidents whilst making practice runs on the ski slopes, during which Ford had broken his leg and Scott had twisted his knee, meant that Scott couldn't lead the party himself. Royds, Koettlitz, Skelton and Barne were dispatched with Wild, Hare, Quartley, Vince, Weller, Evans, Plumley, Heald and eight dogs. Departing on 4 March, they made good progress for the first two days, but suffered from cold and frostbite, despite sleeping in their fur suits. By the time they were approximately half way to Cape Crozier, however, they had spent several days bogged down in deep snow. With such slow progress it was calculated that their rations would not see the entire party to the Cape and so Royds, Skelton, and Koettlitz continued whilst the main party returned to Hut Point with the dogs. Whilst exploring a new route back to the ship via Castle Rock, the wind suddenly got up and the returning party became lost in swirling drift. Disoriented, many of them fell down a steep ice slope in the confusion of snow and the party became separated. As stragglers started to arrive at the ship it became clear that a great accident had occurred and search parties were organised. The ship's hooter was sounded at intervals to aid the men's return. Over a dozen men formed search parties and Shackleton took a boat along the shore of what became known as 'Danger Slopes' to look for survivors. Eventually, all returned to the ship except for Able Seaman Vince, whom Wild had seen slide past him over a cliff, and Hare, the steward. After exhaustive efforts to find them, both of these men were presumed dead, not least because of serious cases of frostbite amongst some of the survivors. Much to everyone's disbelief, however, Hare walked back into camp two days later without so much as a scratch. Vince was never seen again. Meanwhile Royds, Skelton and Koettlitz had arrived at Cape Crozier and made several attempts to reach the message post at the penguin rookery. They were foiled on every occasion and turned for home without having posted the ship's mail, arriving back at the ship on 19 March.

Activity now centred on preparing the ship for winter and on one last autumn sledge journey: to lay a depot to the south for the next summer's sledging work. The lessons drawn from the previous sledging journeys took some days to put into practice and the Southern Depot party didn't finally leave until 31 March. Scott, Armitage, Wilson and Ferrar took the dogs and eight men, Macfarlane, Dellbridge, Walker, Blissett, Feather, Allan, Smythe and Williamson, to pull 2,000 lbs. (908 kgs) of supplies. The temperatures by now were excruciatingly cold, going down below minus 40 degrees (F and C). The dogs, which hadn't adjusted to the change of hemisphere and were going through their summer moult, suffered terribly and refused to pull. The men too found the cold unbearable - despite trying out new types of furs from those used by the Crozier party - and they got little sleep. After a few days, it was clear that they could not go on and so the supplies were deposited and the party turned for home, arriving back on 3 April.

The long Antarctic winter was rapidly drawing in. Wilson spent many of his days drawing illustrations for the newly founded ship-board magazine, the *South Polar Times,* of which Shackleton was editor. Additionally, no opportunity was lost to supplement the winter larder with passing seals; as well as providing specimens for scientific study, fresh seal meat was a regular item on the menu. The ship was settling into a winter routine of scientific work and leisure activities. On 8 April the scientific and dietary agendas met again, when a large party of Emperor Penguins was sighted a mile from the ship. These birds had not been seen in any numbers by previous expeditions and so were duly rounded up and slaughtered with more difficulty than their pursuers had envisaged. The Great Emperor Penguin Hunt, as it became known, was to enter the annals of the Expedition as an amusing story with which to regale dinner guests. Not that life was all made up of cosy fire-side chats or amusing stories. Life aboard ship, particularly at floor level, was cold and the damp caused by condensation a constant problem. Scott wrote his diary with his feet kept warm in a box of Saennegrass until the insulation in his cabin could be improved. With such temperatures and difficulties at this early stage of the season they could all only wonder what the true winter would bring: no-one had ever wintered this far south before.

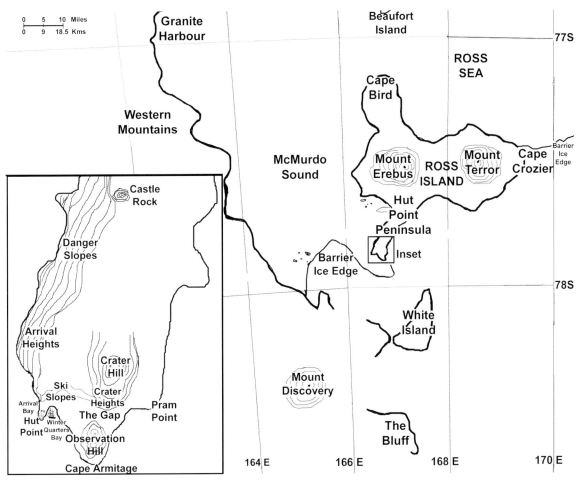

Map of the area of Ross Island showing Winter Quarters and autumn sledging locations 1902.
The scale is approximate (inset is not to scale)

Arrival at Winter Quarters: 8 February - 17 February 1902

"Going further south down the Bay we were stopped by fixed ice and forced to turn east and cross the Bay towards Mount Erebus, and here we found a small sheltered bay in which anchor was dropped, and the decision was come to that we should stay here and make the place our winter quarters." Sat 8 Feb EAW

"Several people went for walks round the bay, and in the afternoon later the Captain and myself went off right round the point, - when we got round, we could see right away to Terror on the southern side, - so there seems no doubt that Erebus and Terror are on an island and separated from South Victoria Land by a strait, - this is an entirely new discovery, - we have for the time named the peaked hill above the point at the end of the land Observation Hill, and a solitary volcano, very much like Erebus in shape but probably on the mainland to the SW, - Discovery Hill or Volcano." Sun 9 Feb RWS

Discovery, newly anchored in Winterquarters Bay. Hut Point behind

"The Captain tried exploding charges of gun-cotton in the ice ahead of the ship today, but the effect was practically nil except to blow a solitary hole; - there is no doubt that to do any good, a heavy charge is required, which should be exploded in the water under the ice." Tue 11 Feb RWS

*Breaking Winterquarters Bay ice
with gun cotton*

Discovery in Winterquarters Bay from N.E. head of the ski slopes. Arrival Bay is to the right over Hut Point. In the distance, Black Island (left) and Mount Discovery (right) may be seen

White Island and Pram Point: 19 February - 25 February 1902

"The Captain proposed today that Shackle and Ferrar and I should go for a sledging trip to the island and see what lay south of it." Mon 17 Feb EAW

"...we all began frost-bites...got the tent up, an awful business in such weather, as it flapped about in our hands like a handker-chief." Wed 19 Feb EAW

View beyond Observation Hill and Cape Armitage, to White Island

L-R: u/d; Wilson and Ferrar, before leaving for White Island, officers' sledging flags flying from the Pram

"We went on and on and on, with an occasional glimpse of the island in front of us, which never seemed even a little bit nearer than when we started." Wed 19 Feb EAW

Fractured mounds of blue ice, 4-5 feet high, NW of White Island

Wilson (left) and Ferrar astride a blue ice mound

"Bitterly cold it was, and our tea in our water bottles, though they hung inside all our clothes, was more or less frozen...It was a grand sight though. As far south as the eye could see was a level ice plain, the true Great Barrier surface, and no Antarctic continent at all." Thu 20 Feb EAW

"...we had to turn and make a long detour over a mile or two of tremen-dously uneven broken up pressure ridges to reach a spit of land where we could deposit our gear...and got in to luxurious comfort and a bath and a warm bunk at 10.30 P.M." Sat 22 Feb EAW

"Went out to the Pram Point to bring in our sledging gear...We saw an interesting sight in the bay. A school of very long Beaked Whales were sporting and playing and blowing, and breaching, a thing I had not seen before. One of them leaped quite clear of the water like a salmon, but as he was over 20 feet long it was rather a striking sight." Tue 25 Feb EAW

Settling in: February - March 1902

"The cook was put in irons today for insubordination. There was a lively scene on deck as he fought and was very obstreperous, but after sitting in the foc'sle till evening, with the prospect of sleeping there the night instead of in his bunk, he came to his senses and was liberated." Mon 10 Feb EAW

Discovery, not long frozen in, with Observation Hill and the Gap in the background

"There is to be one large living hut, and two observation huts, - the latter made of asbestos slates from the same company in Germany that made a hut for Count von Waldersee for his campaign in China - they were only ordered at my suggestion, and my specification, so of course I hope they will prove satisfactory. - I understand from Armitage that our latitude is 77° 50´, - should think people at home will be rather surprised when they hear we have wintered so far south." Wed 12 Feb RWS

"At 6.0 P.M. we played our football match officers v men, - which we won after very exciting play by 2 goals to 1. - Wilson and Ferrar were absent from our side, - Royds made a very good centre forward, and Mr Dailey was pretty good on the wing. - During the game an Adelie penguin came across the ice and stood on the touch line

Football match on the ice, looking towards Crater Heights

taking great interest in the game, - however, when any of the play came near it, it tried to join in - and going in for rather rough play, it had to be taken off the field." Thu 13 Feb RWS

"Ist fire in the Ward Room today - The mess keeps very warm, and I think we shall be a comfortable ship during the winter - there is of course a little dripping from the skylights and decklights, - and the cabins are very damp against the ship's side, - there is no doubt the side ought to have been lined throughout the living spaces." Mon 24 Feb RWS

"Landed 175 bags of coal for the hut, roughly about 15 tons... The magnetic hut...almost complete, and the roof and sides of the living hut, or 'Professor Gregory's Villa', are finished." Wed 26 Feb RWS

'Professor Gregory's Villa', Hut Point

Cape Crozier Sledging Party: 4 March - 19 March 1902

"...our orders were more or less to make for Cape Crozier and fix latest records to the mail cairn erected there in January, to let the relief ship know where we are wintering, - to take rough surveys of prominent landmarks, mountains, - try and find some distinguishing line between the Great Barrier and the Bay Ice, and if there is such a line - a tide crack that is, the 2nd party, Barne and self, to follow this up for as long as our time will permit." Tue 4 Mar RWS

Part of the Cape Crozier party (prob. Royds, Koettlitz, Wild, Quartley, Weller and Vince) in deep snow

"Good night...turned out about 7.0. On first seeing Royds he asked me if I would care to go on with Koettlitz and himself on ski with light sledge to fulfil rest of mission, the remainder [including the dogs] turning back - of course I snapped at the chance." Sat 8 Mar RWS

"We had finished dinner...when four of the sledge party returned to the ship empty handed - Wild, Weller, Heald and Plumley, all seamen. Barne, Evans, Quartley, Hare and Vince were all reported missing. Vince was said to have been seen to disappear over the edge of an ice slope and one of the dogs with him, and the sea was just below, so there seemed no doubt that he was lost." Tue 11 Mar EAW

Cape Crozier Party turned out in furs at Separation Camp. Showing Union Jack and four officers' pennants (Royds, Skelton, Koettlitz and Barne) with Royds, Koettlitz, Barne, Wild, Hare, Quartley, Vince, Weller, Evans, Plumley and Heald

"A terrible bad night, frightfully cold, - shivering all night. About 2.0 A.M. I went out and found the temperature -32°F, fairly low - we were having a most miserable time, - the furs quite inadequate to keep us warm; at 4.0 I went out again and found the temperature -38° and minimum showing -42° or 74° of frost - about as bad as I ever want to be in." Sun 16 Mar RWS

Danger Slopes near where Vince fell to his death in a blizzard.

"The first full page picture [in the *South Polar Times*], is a very good one of Royds, Koettlitz and myself dragging our sledge through a blizzard, - most realistic, though of course a very small proportion of it was like that." Wed 23 Apr RWS

Winter Preparations: March - April 1902

"The stoves on board are not quite satisfactory yet, they are inclined to smoke, - I must take them in hand, and make some alterations, - a long straight chimney seems to be the first necessity; - the ventilation of the living spaces also requires a little looking into." Mon 31 Mar RWS

March 30. Easter Sunday. The last Skua left us.

Winter Quarters from above the magnetic huts on Hut Point. Crater Hill and the Gap are visible beyond "Professor Gregory's Villa" and Discovery. Bernacchi is standing at left. An unknown figure to the right is walking dogs

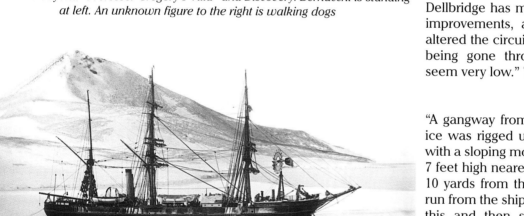

Discovery in Winter Quarters, showing the windmill in commission. Observation Hill is behind the ship, showing Cape Armitage; White Island in the distance

"We all get a bit aching all over when we come back to warmth after exposure to cold, but it passes off in a day or two. Some of Royds' party, after a fortnight out, found the ordinary ward-room temperature of 60°F. so hot that they couldn't sleep at all at night. Royds, after trying to sleep on the top of his bunk and bedclothes, at last had to go and cool in his pyjamas on deck at ten or fifteen degrees below zero." Fri 4 Apr EAW

"The windmill has been going along fairly well while I have been away, Dellbridge has made one or two little improvements, and the Skipper has altered the circuits, - the cells are also being gone through, their densities seem very low." Thu 20 Mar RWS

"A gangway from the ship to the Bay ice was rigged up today, - it is made with a sloping mound of ice about 6 or 7 feet high nearest the ship and about 10 yards from the side, - long planks run from the ship's rail on to the top of this and then steps are cut in the sloping snow, it makes a very good gangway, but shows signs of sinking the ice by its great weight." Sat 12 Apr RWS

"Windmill suddenly collapsed with a rattle in the blizzard, the iron plates clattering in the air." Sun 13 Apr EAW

"Expecting a storm from the Skipper about the windmill, but none occurred, - so I suppose he has thought it over reasonably. - He asked me for my verdict on the damages, and having inspected it, I told him that it was badly damaged, and that I did not consider it worth repairing but that it could be done; - as I expected, he wished it to be repaired." Mon 14 Apr RWS

April 13. Windmill collapsed.

Five unknown men standing on the new gangplank. Seal and mutton carcasses are clearly visible hanging in the rigging

Autumn Twilight: March - April 1902

"Spent the whole morning sketching the mountain range on the other side of our strait. Temperature just below zero Fahrenheit, and felt like it. One has to prepare oneself for this occupation, with jaeger hood, mufflers, great-coats, fur boots, wind clothes, felt gloves and fur mits etc. etc. and every now and then one has to do the cabman's swing to keep one's blood moving along the fingers. In a wind, sketching is quite impossible, but on a calm day with plenty of time one can manage, though it is not easy to draw quickly in fur mits." Wed 26 Mar EAW

Observation Hill from the foot of Crater Hill. Looking south west

Discovery in Winter Quarters looking towards the Western range, 28 Mar 1902

"Sunset very fine brilliant orange red horizon and water. Ice all gone out as far as Hut Point." Fri 11 Apr EAW

Sunset over the Western Mountains, McMurdo Strait, 11 Apr 1902

The Southern Depot Journey: 31 March - 4 April 1902

March 31. Depot sledge party left with 4000 lbs and 16 dogs.

"The journey is calculated to last three weeks and its object is to establish a depot of provisions on the farthest point of land due south from here, as a preparation for the big southern sledge journey next year." Fri 21 Mar EAW

"It was a most tiring day. The dogs had absolutely refused to pull at all. Our loads were consequently too heavy for us by about 1200 lbs., not to mention the fact that several of the dogs persistently refused to stand on their legs or walk and so had to be dragged along anyhow...we had only covered five miles in over five hours." Mon 31 Mar EAW

"In the morning, you put on frozen socks, frozen mits and frozen boots, stuffed with frozen damp grass and rime, and you suffer a good deal from painfully cold feet, until everything is packed up again and strapped on the sledges, and you are off to warm up to the work of a beast of burden. There's a fascination about it all, but it can't be considered comfort." Wed 2 Apr EAW

Three in a sleeping bag

"...a fine bright day, but the men are in three-men sleeping bags and complain bitterly of the cold at nights. So rather than risk a break-down we dumped the stores and four sledges and came home...Once their heads turned homewards, not a dog but pulled for all he was worth. True we had light weights now, and the dogs knew it. They never will pull when they feel a dead weight behind them, they give it up...Now we had only two lightly loaded sledges, which the dogs managed without any help at all and we got home by 6. We kept our flags flying all the time partly, I at least, because I liked to see it flying and partly to show them at the ship that we hadn't turned back because anything was wrong." Thu 3 Apr EAW

Wilson, ready to depart on Southern Depot Journey

A SLEEPING BAG FOR THREE

SLEDGING PANNIKIN AND SPOON.

"They had had such extremely low temperatures, -40° to -50°, perhaps more, and a whole day in which the temperature didn't rise above -35° that the Skipper didn't think it wise to be out - quite right too I think...Their minimum thermometers were out of order, so they were unable to record the minimum, but they actually observed -47° before turning in. - with that temperature there was every possibility of losing the dogs, which would be unlucky this year." Thu 3 Apr RWS

Sledging in April.
Camping after dark.

FINNESKOES

April 3. The sledge party returned.

April 3rd.

- 64 -

The Great Emperor Penguin Hunt: 8 April 1902

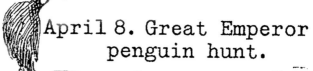 

April 8. Great Emperor penguin hunt.

"Just as I sat down to dinner, news was brought that some 30 Emperors were in sight...we drove them gradually in a body up to the ship from about a mile away...and were trying to pen them all into a circle of wire netting. Skelton had come out in a hurry with no mits and a thin balaclava. Both his ears went and his hands were going, burnt by the wire netting, so he went back for clothes and had an uneasy time when his ears began to come to life again." Tue 8 Apr EAW

"I felt alright in about ¼ hour, and putting on a helmet and mits went out for the finish; I found Wilson and Cross, with the assistance of the others had started to kill them, by putting in a lancet or a thin spike like a bradawl at the back of the head severing the spinal cord, and then going into the brain; if done neatly the animal is practically dead at once, and no blood comes out to spoil the feathers, - I had a very good bradawl with me and killed mine very neatly." Tue 8 Apr RWS

"It was not a pleasant job, in any way, but an opportunity not to be missed, for no one has ever seen this bird in any numbers before and it is our duty to bring back as good a collection as we can." Tue 8 Apr EAW

"After breakfast I took several photos of the penguins, dead, alive, being weighed." Wed 9 Apr RWS

Weighing the dead Emperor Penguins - men unidentified. The photograph also shows Discovery's boats on the ice and a live penguin chained to them

6: The First Winter
23 April 1902 - 23 August 1902

On 22 April the sun sank below the horizon for the last time in four months. This marked the start of the true winter and offered an excuse for a party. As a result 23 April was seen in with appropriate style on the decks of *Discovery*: both Skelton and Wilson thought it a "merry dinner". It was also the day chosen to publish the first volume of the *South Polar Times,* which was presented to Scott during the evening's festivities. Its contents caused considerable amusement and the single volume rapidly made the rounds of the ship. In order not to offend those whose submissions had not made the cut for the *Times,* a smaller volume was also produced and named *The Blizzard* but it was widely accepted that the contents of this were considerably inferior to those chosen for the *Times.* Preparing submissions for future issues occupied aspiring contributors for many hours throughout the winter darkness.

Life aboard continued as a steady routine. A winter awning was raised on 25 April which helped to protect the deck from snow and also had a beneficial effect on the insulation of the ship. The scientific programme continued to occupy a considerable amount of time. The long, cold hours of darkness posed a constant challenge to those who braved the freezing conditions in order to tend to the exterior scientific instruments; meteorological and physics equipment at the various shore stations needed regular attendance. Wilson walked most days to the top of Crater Hill with Shackleton in order to read the thermometer at the outlying weather station here. Royds, or his substitute, read the thermometers at the starboard meteorological screen every two hours. On calm days, when the temperatures plummeted, even the slightest slip in concentration resulted in frostbite. The silence on such days was deep and penetrating. Wilson often stopped to sketch on his walks: the astonishing colours of the Antarctic twilight, or the shimmering aurora etched against a jet sky glistening with stars. These pictures were often acquired with a considerable amount of pain as cold fingers were warmed back to life after two or three minutes of rapid drawing; the process being repeated until the field sketch was completed. Many of the drawings were used in issues of the *South Polar Times,* which were produced once a month, and some worked up to full watercolours. During the winter months Wilson also worked up many of his rough sketches from the previous season into presentable form.

Some days, however, the weather was so severe that it was impossible to venture outside. Guide ropes had been erected from the ship to Hut Point for such eventualities but in a very severe blizzard even the short distance to the huts or the starboard meteorological screen couldn't be attempted. During such periods the men were trapped in the ship listening to the screaming fury of the storm outside, whilst the relatively warm temperatures of such blizzards increased the damp misery of condensation. The hurricane force wind of just such a blizzard on 2 May destroyed the experimental windmill for a second time. Skelton and his team had spent many hours trying to keep it working. Scott finally accepted that the windmill itself was not physically up to Antarctic winds and the rest of the winter had to be spent with candles and paraffin lamps rather than electric light.

In addition to the work of the scientific programme and the amusements of the *South Polar Times,* preparations also needed to be made for next season's sledging journeys. Skelton worked hard on the development of a Plane Table for surveying and automatic sledgeometers to record distances sledged accurately. Such work was in addition to the challenges provided by the stoves, which often smoked, and to the recurring problem of condensation. The routine maintenance work of the ship and its programmes also generally fell to Skelton and his team:

"My people have their hands full almost every day, repairing, pots and pans, buckets, - lamps etc. making candlesticks, - the crew seem very careless with the gear, and never think of the trouble of repairs." Wed 30 Apr RWS

Discovery also had a well stocked library, so no-one was short of relevant reading material. Skelton could be found reading books such as Nansen's *First Crossing of Greenland,* Greeley's *Handbook of Arctic Discoveries* or Payer's *Voyage of the Tegelhoff* (about the discovery of Franz Joseph Land). Such books circulated around the ship and issues found in them often sparked intense debates over subjects connected to their future explorations. Skelton and Armitage had several rounds over the use of ski, which Skelton favoured. Debating was a particular winter sport aboard and was formally organised on one day of the week: issues from whether an Antarctic Continent existed to compulsory school sports were aired. Several theatrical evenings were also organised: Royds arranging musical evenings, including a "Minstrel Show", and Barne producing a full blown play entitled "Ticket of Leave". Rehearsals and the production of scenery and costumes was a further occupation. Model making and craft work were popular pastimes as generally was the exercise that Scott insisted everyone should take when possible. Perhaps the most enthusiastic and often heated attentions, however, were given to the numerous games played, from Shove H'a'penny and quoits to cards and chess. Wilson thought that Ward room chess, in particular, deserved comment:

"Every evening we are treated to a chess quack. The Skipper and Koettlitz invariably disagree, the former always in a facetious manner if winning, but if losing, always in a cantanker which K. soon picks up. Armitage and Bernacchi also quack over chess most evenings, but one always knows in this case what is coming - invariably the same remark: 'Come along Bunnie, do! How slow you are!'." Tue 29 Apr EAW

The half-way point of this winter routine was marked in grand style. Mid-winter's day was celebrated on 23 June with the messes decorated from top to bottom for an "Antarctic Christmas". Elaborate carvings of ice were made for table pieces and quantities of special food and drink consumed. Skelton recorded the event with some difficulty as flash photography was still a clumsy and unpredictable process. Everyone enjoyed themselves, however, and proceeded to undertake their work with renewed vigour over the next few days. The return of the sun was approaching - and with it an ambitious programme of sledging. Both Skelton and Wilson felt that they hadn't achieved half as much as they had hoped through the winter and yet no-one had been idle. The routine of the winter months continued so that by the time the sun returned on 22 August most people were ready for another small party, which was duly thrown. It was with some relief that everyone realised that the long months of winter confinement were nearly over. With so many men of diverse backgrounds more or less confined to a small area of bare comfort, there had been surprisingly few open rows aboard but, perhaps, an inevitable degree of tension. Bernacchi, who had over-wintered before, put this success down to the continuance of naval routine and discipline, however artificial. *Discovery* had come through her first winter more successfully than either of the other expeditions that had previously wintered and better than many that were to follow. Nevertheless, everyone was itching to leave the ship, to feel the sun on their faces and to get out to work in the fresh air.

Red glow on the smoke of Mount Erebus. Winter 1902

METEOROLOGY.

Kew Observatory.

Wilson, reading the thermometer at the meteorological station on Crater Hill

"...with Shackle went up to top of Crater Hill, taking a spirit minimum thermometer, aneroid and compass to found a little observatory of our own there, which we can visit two or three times a week on clear days in the winter and so have an object for our daily walk. The hill is 950 ft. high...It takes us about two hours to go there and back, snow all the way, up hill and down and a splendid view of Mount Erebus and all the sea and country north and south." Wed 16 Apr EAW

Barograph

"Everyone has volunteered to take turns at the meteorological nightly observations, - they have to be recorded every 2 hours, and it means one staying up all night to go out at 12.0, 2.0, 4.0, 6.0 and 8.0 A.M. to the screen about 200 yards astern of the ship. Royds takes all the daily observations, and we each get a night out every 11 days, - my first night tomorrow night." Fri 25 Apr RWS

Marine Barometer

Fixed Screen.

The starboard meteorological screen, with Observation Hill and the Gap

The starboard meteorological screen with figure (probably Royds) looking towards the Western Mountains

"There are five recording instruments out of doors and they are worked by weekly clocks. Two are hygrographs for recording the relative saturation of the air by moisture, the other three are thermographs for recording the temperatures. There are also two barographs inboard. All the instruments out of the ship get full of drift snow every time there is any wind, and every Monday morning is spent by Royds in cleaning them, winding them, and putting new paper charts on the drums, a miserable job. They have to be overhauled every day to see that they are going and to see that the glycerine ink isn't used up or frozen." Sat 9 Aug EAW

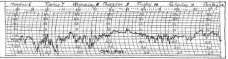

Thermograph Record.

Early Winter: May 1902

"The weather is simply terrible, no-one could face it. - It was rather lucky for me that about 6 P.M. I went in to the Skipper and told him that I doubted whether the windmill would stand it, if the weather got much worse. - Well it is all finished now." Fri 2 May RWS

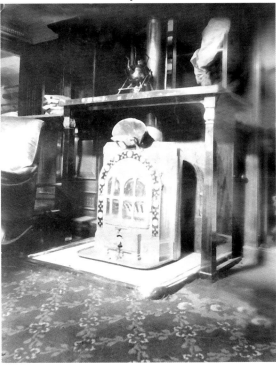

The Ward room stove

"Most of the chimneys of the stoves have been blown away, and the stoves smoke badly, - the awning is also getting a severe shaking. - I believe the greatest velocity recorded by the Robinson anemometer was 120 miles in 2 hrs." Fri 2 May RWS

Discovery in Winter Quarters, after the second major blizzard. The remains of the windmill are on the forward deck

"The Skipper is everlastingly planning out new theories and new methods of observation and temperature and formation of ice and freezing of sea water, an endless and difficult job, which keeps various people everlastingly hacking holes in the floe down which they drop saws and thermometers and other things, and up which come seals to breathe and investigate. He has always got some new idea for obtaining new facts, an excellent man for this job, full of theories and ingenuity - and always thinking." Fri 23 May EAW

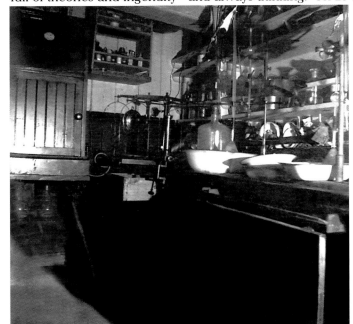

Laboratory aboard Discovery

Winter 1902: The *South Polar Times*

May 1902

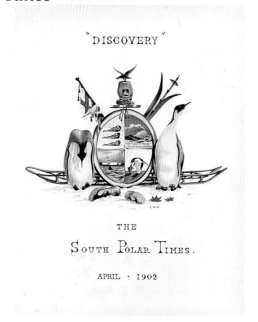

"DISCOVERY"

THE
SOUTH POLAR TIMES.
APRIL · 1902

"The 'South Polar Times', first number, was presented to the Captain after dinner, and I think was thoroughly appreciated by every one, even those who appeared in the caricatures. Only one copy has been produced and this has been made as complete and perfect as possible under our circumstances, in the hope that the whole thing may be thoroughly well reproduced with all the illustrations when we get home." Wed 23 Apr EAW

"In the afternoon I went down to the Editor's office, of The South Polar Times, and helped [Shackleton] to finish printing 'The Blizzard', - a sort of supplement to the S.P.T. - the articles are all by the men, except Editorial, and as their ideas mostly run to Poetry, the result is very amusing, though perhaps it would not be exactly admired by the Laureate." Thu 1 May RWS

Shackleton

"I spent the evening getting silhouettes of some of our mess, and succeeded in getting decent ones of Royds, Shackleton and Barne." Mon 19 May EAW

Royds

"Shackleton's typewriter broke down this afternoon, and he was in great despair that he wouldn't be able to use it, but I managed to patch it up for him so that it is quite as good as before, - it is a Remington, and is full of the most cunning little mechanical contrivances." Wed 21 May RWS

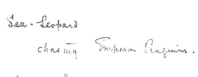

Sea-Leopard
chasing Emperor Penguins.
S. P. Times - May. 1902.

Barne

Winter 1902: Debates and Theatricals

EN ROUTE FOR TERROR THEATRE.

"Theatrical News

I⠀⠀⠀⠀a singsong will take place on Thursday next (May 1st) at Professor Gregory's Villa residence. Performance commences at 7.0 P.M.

II⠀⠀⠀⠀a discussion will take place in the Ward Room on Friday next May 2nd at 7.0 P.M. Lieut. Armitage in the Chair. Subject - 'Woman's Rights'." Thu 1 May RWS

"Ticket of Leave: a screaming comedy in one act", The Antarctic Theatrical Company at the Royal Terror Theatre, Professor Gregory's Villa, 25 June 1902. L-R: standing: Pilbeam (Joe); Weller; Cross; Feather (Thos. Muggetts); Allan; seated: Buckridge (Mrs Quiver) ;Wild; Gilbert Scott (Mary Ann)

"The Dishcover Minstrel Troupe", the Royal Terror Theatre at Professor Gregory's Villa. 6 Aug 1902

"Clarke the cook's mate brought down the house with his Gaelic chorus 'McPhairshn swore a feud'. He was excellent. It was a funny show altogether, as we were all very cold (or rather the place was). We were all in our hoods, blouses and overcoats and felt boots, and the place was darkened by the light of a few oil lamps, yet we all enjoyed ourselves and the choruses were full and hearty." Thu 1 May EAW

" 'Ticket of Leave' - very funny, - [Gilbert] Scott made a very good female slavey! I took flash light photos of the audience and the performers." Wed 25 Jun RWS

"In the evening we had a debate on sledge travelling. Of course every one speaks, and sometimes we have great fun. Bernacchi is nearly always amusing. Lays himself out to be absurd and succeeds. They are not bad sport and have been very successful on the whole, though I think signs are not wanting that we have had almost enough. Everyone has so much work to do and feels that the winter is slipping away without getting the work intended done. All the same, this feeling seems to come particularly on Tuesday nights when a debate is on, and isn't anything like so strong on every other night of the week when cards are on. Every single day cards begin after dinner and go on till midnight, often later I believe. Poker had a long reign, whist followed, now bridge. Chess had an innings, also dominoes. Wall quoits is played off and on. It has become a fixture over Queen Alexandra's portrait." Tue 8 Jul EAW

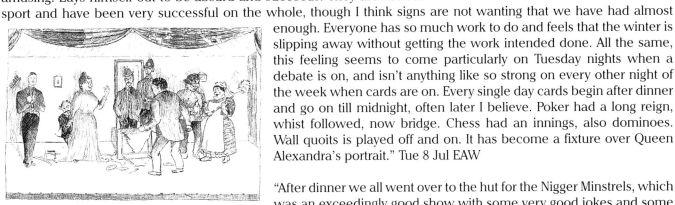

June 25th⠀⠀Concert and Theatricals.

"After dinner we all went over to the hut for the Nigger Minstrels, which was an exceedingly good show with some very good jokes and some very bad ones...Some of the men are born clowns and the singing was very fair indeed." Wed 6 Aug EAW

Midwinter: 1902

Moon over the Western Mountains, McMurdo Strait

"At 10 P.M. it fell dead calm and cleared to a brilliant moonlight, so we all went out for a walk. It was a wonderful night...Sounds carried an immense distance. The stillness was almost uncanny...I could easily imagine we were standing not on the Earth but on the Moon's surface. Everything was so still and dead and cold and unearthly." Thu 22 May EAW

"Almost 10 P.M. it was so absolutely calm, that a splendid echo could be heard all round the hills, when the dogs barked. - the silence here simply can't be understood unless one has actually 'heard' it." Sat 14 Jun RWS

Midwinter Dinner: 23 June 1902

"The mess deck was most gorgeously and elaborately decorated with wreaths and garlands of coloured paper, after the manner of a German Christmas tree. This is an old Naval custom it appears and the men all put their pet photographs out on the mess deck tables. Everything is clean and bright and on the stokers' table was a large block of ice carved into the head of a frost king with a crown, with a hot poker. Also a dish with ices made of condensed milk and chocolate vanilla etc. of which we each had to partake." Mon 23 Jun EAW

The Ward Room (clockwise): Bernacchi; Hodgson; Wilson; Armitage (hidden); Barne (standing); Royds; (standing); Shackleton; Skelton; Ferrar; Koettlitz and Scott (Obscured by the flash)

"I got my half plate camera, and the flash light apparatus ready and while the men were at their Christmas dinner took a photo of each side. - Bernacchi gave me a hand." Mon 23 Jun RWS

We had also a very prettily decorated table, with bunches of holly (artificial) and berries, and a lot of little union jacks and printed menus and each of us a small thumb top with our initials on it for racing against each other." Mon 23 Jun EAW

The Starboard Mess (left to right and front to back, by bench): Pilbeam, Walker; Cross, Allan, Macfarlane; Kennar, Duncan

"At the beginning of our dinner I took 2 more of our mess, but Ford worked the flashlight, and didn't bring it off very well, so they may not come out. A jolly good evening, - Songs, games, etc, - old Koettlitz was very amusing, - Everybody went very strong." Mon 23 Jun RWS

The Port Mess (left to right and front to back, by bench): Crean, Wild, Weller; Heald, Croucher, Peters; Plumley, Page, Hubert; Whitfield, Quartley

Our Midwinter Day 22nd June.

June 23rd Christmas Day
        Festivities.
     No signs of
     depression in
     the Colony.

"BEATS ALL COMERS".

OVER FIFTY
MEDALS AWARDED.

DEWAR'S
"WHITE
LABEL"
WHISKY

. . Awarded the . .

Grand Prize

Highest possible award
over all Competitors,

St. Louis Exposition, 1904.

Winter Scenes: July 1902

Aurora and Moon over the Western Mountains, McMurdo Strait

The moon shining through the Gap

"I then went out and saw a fine aurora display, curtains and beams, running up from horizon to zenith." Sat 5 Jul EAW

"We could see right away to the northern horizon. Ice floe and open water leads all the way up the strait. And the most fiery carmine red that I have ever seen, burning in the sky and reflected from the ice floe, and over this a canopy of ponderous black water clouds." Sun 20 Jul EAW

Discovery in Winter Quarters, looking north towards Hut Point, Carmine sky.

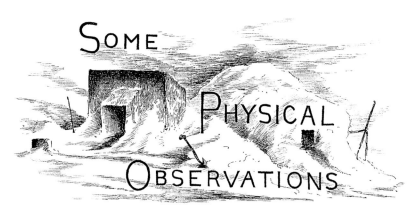

Some Physical Observations

"Bernacchi got his Eschenhagen magnetic instruments fixed up in one of the Asbestos Observation Huts today and started it working, - it shows every sign of being most successful, I believe, - the records, which will be continuous, show most remarkable magnetic storms to be the normal state down here." Sat 1 Mar RWS

Bernacchi emerging from the Magnetic variation studies hut

"An earthquake was shown today on the seismograph to have happened somewhere on the earth, between 8.0 and 10.0 P.M., - it will be interesting to hear where it was when we get back." Mon 26 May RWS

"This was the first night that no observations were possible at the screen on the floe. Everything was choked with snow and no one was allowed to leave the ship. One couldn't see a yard, indeed it was hard to open one's eyes at all for the drift. Royds was reading the anemometer on the screen in the afternoon and was simply blown off the ladder. Bernacchi had to go to his magnetic hut and did most of the journey on hands and knees. These things sound funny, but it is no exaggeration to say that ten yards from the ship you may be as completely lost as ten miles. You can see nothing but white drift and the roar of the wind is utterly bewildering. You cannot consult with anyone because you can't hear him, even if he shouts in your ear. I know nothing so terrifying as these blizzards." Fri 18 Jul EAW

"We finished the pendulum observations at about 8.30 and started off to the ship - The Blizzard was much worse so thick I couldn't see Bernacchi at all 3 yards off, - he knew the way very well so I followed him;...- reached the ship after having been out 1½ hours - Bernacchi had face and wrists pretty well frostbitten. I got a slight one on the right cheek, and my trousers full of drift. - Altogether a very narrow escape. - we were never more than ¼ mile from the ship and generally under 200 yards." Thu 31 Jul RWS

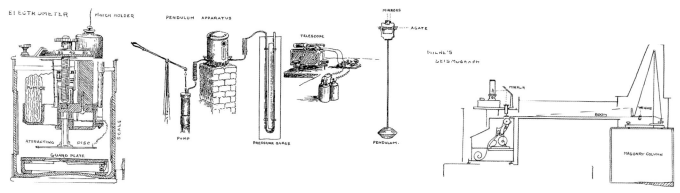

The Return of the Sun: August 1902

Mount Erebus and Castle Rock, 16 Aug 1902, midday

"Shackle and I went up harbour slope and across the snow plateau to Castle Rock. We went round the foot of it, under a sheer cliff of 400 feet, to the other side and got a splendid view of Mounts Erebus and Terror and the little rocky islets in Erebus Bay. It was a very beautiful sight and the Castle Rock itself is immense and very grand. I made some sketch notes and we got back to tea at 2.30, the longest walk we have had, this spring." Sat 16 Aug EAW

"At 12 went up harbour hill with Shackleton where we saw the sun, the whole sun, and nothing but the sun for a bit, for it was a great joy to see it again quite clear of the horizon and quite free of clouds." Fri 22 Aug EAW

```
Aug 19th   The ice broke out up to Erebus Islets.

Aug 22nd   The sun returned.

Aug 23rd   Commemoration Dinner for Sun's return.
```

7: Spring Sledging
24 August 1902 - 24 October 1902

Late August 1902 found the officers and crew of *Discovery* making the final preparations for the forthcoming sledging season. Skelton, Dellbridge and Lashly were hard at work building sledgeometers and the Plane Table. The increasing hours of daylight were improving the mood of everyone aboard as the Antarctic world emerged from winter darkness. The daily tasks of the scientific programme were carried out as usual, if with a little more ease than under the rigours of winter. The dark winter months had also seen the birth of several litters of husky puppies. With the return of the sun, many of these were now at the age of sweet incorrigibility. As they played in the sun-lit snow they proved an irresistible lure for spring-time photographers.

The sledgeometers were soon tested during a dog trial trip from 2-5 September. Scott, Wilson, Shackleton, Skelton, Ferrar and Feather, the Boatswain, took 14 dogs spread between four sledges. They explored the coastline up to what would become known as the Erebus Glacier Tongue and the Dellbridge Islands and turned back when they approached open water. Scott charted the unknown coastline, Ferrar undertook geological investigations and the dogs were tested in a newly developed harness. This was found to work well, but chaffed so much that it was re-worked using hemp instead of steel rope. Skelton tested the new sledgeometers which pleasantly surprised everyone with their accuracy, having an error rate of less than one percent. Despite the freezing temperatures and wind causing considerable discomfort, the trial trip was deemed a success.

Further exploratory parties were soon on their way out into the field. Royds led Koettlitz, Lashly, Evans, Wild and Quartley from 10-19 September, on an exploration south-west, towards the area of Mount Discovery where they succeeded in starting to survey the area around Brown and Black Islands (Brown Island was later re-named Brown Peninsula). Armitage led a reconnaissance party from 11-26 September towards the Western mountains, consisting of Ferrar, Gilbert Scott, Cross, Heald and Walker. Scott himself was soon out again with Shackleton, Barne and two teams of dogs. They made a reconnaissance trip to the south, in an attempt to reach the Bluff. This trip was cut short by a blizzard and they were only out for two days. Blizzards and low temperatures, down to -53°F (-47°C), were experienced by all the parties. Attempting to sleep in three man sleeping bags, lying in various states of dampness with freezing temperatures or bad weather, tested the men to the limits of their endurance. The trip to the Bluff, with supplies for the depot, was finally accomplished between 23 September and 4 October when Scott, Shackleton and Feather completed the trip. Koettlitz, Bernacchi and Dailey were also out from 23 September to 2 October exploring ice formations to the west of McMurdo Bay near what were to be named as the Dailey Islands. Therefore, neither Koettlitz, the senior doctor, nor Scott, as commander, were present when a serious threat to the Expedition emerged on 26 September.

Armitage's party returned safely to the ship having explored the area around New Harbour where they had tried to ascend some way into the mountains - but were trapped in their tents for some days by a blizzard. The routine medical examination of the men upon their return, however, revealed the presence of scurvy amongst the sledging party. This was a considerable shock as strenuous efforts had been taken to avoid an outbreak. The true cause of scurvy was as yet unknown. The most popular theory of the time suggested that scurvy was caused by 'tainted' food (i.e. food poisoning), particularly if it had been tinned; a theory which Koettlitz devoutly upheld. For this reason Wilson and Koettlitz had tasted most of the tins of supplies as they were opened throughout the winter, in order to avoid any 'taint' infecting the ship with the dreaded mariner's disease. Its sudden presence was thought to place the entire Expedition in a serious predicament and there was concern for those parties who were out in the field. The sledging parties nevertheless returned safely, with Scott now believing that they had sighted the southern coast of Victoria Land heading to the south and west of the Bluff. The entire summer's sledging plan would be based on this assumption. Once all were aboard a full medical examination was carried out of the whole ship's company, but no definitive signs of the disease having spread were found. As a result, Royds, Skelton, Lashly, Evans, Wild and Quartley were permitted to leave for Cape Crozier, to complete the job of putting a letter at the message post for the relief ship, a task that had been attempted the previous autumn. Those who remained started to spring-clean the ship, to remove any possible germs, particularly in the galley. It was also decided to increase the amount of fresh seal meat that was being eaten, to two meals per day, to avoid any tainted food. Wilson, Barne, Cross, Walker, Dell and Weller therefore went out on a sealing expedition that lasted for four days. The outbreak of scurvy greatly perplexed the doctors. The spring-cleaning had found nothing particularly unhygienic aboard and all of the tins of food had been tasted to avoid any taint. Wilson was beginning to suspect that the answer lay in fresh meat alone. One result was the inclusion of fresh seal meat in the provisions for the forthcoming Southern Journey.

The Crozier Party returned on 24 October. They had experienced extremes of weather, with temperatures down to -58°F (-50°C). They had, nevertheless, carried out the delivery of the letters to the message post. In the event, Skelton lead the party from camp, since Royds had twisted his ankle. So it was Skelton who made one of the most important biological discoveries of the entire Expedition: an Emperor Penguin breeding rookery, below the cliffs of the Great Ice Barrier, where it met Ross Island. The birds had never been seen breeding before and - with the exception of one dubious possible specimen - their eggs never collected. Wilson was astonished to hear that rather than finding eggs, the party had found chicks that were already some weeks old. Three were brought back alive to the ship which he then proceeded to sketch, creating the first ever paintings of Emperor chicks, to complement Skelton's first photographs. With notes and cross-questioning Wilson started to work on unravelling the extraordinary breeding cycle of these birds - with increasing astonishment. Wilson wanted to leave and study the penguins immediately but with the scurvy outbreak apparently brought under control by an increase in the seal meat ration, he was due to head off in a matter of days on the great Southern sledging trip. Scott had chosen Wilson and Shackleton as his companions for the great adventure: to sledge south across the Great Ice Barrier and into the unknown. The penguins would have to wait.

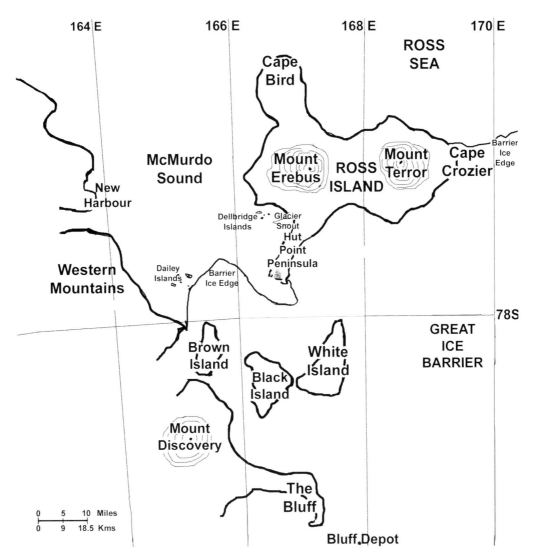

Map showing the general area covered by Spring sledging trips: 1902 (scale is approximate)

Antarctic Spring: September 1902

"...in taking the midnight observations I had a nasty fall in the dark, for in stepping from one screen to another, at a height of six feet from the floe, the wind swung me round and I stepped into mid air and came a cropper into the screen, bruising myself under the armpit and wrenching my shoulder. Happily no real damage was done either to the screen or to myself." Mon 1 Sep EAW

"A fine clear day. - Mt Discovery and the Western Mountains look lovely in the sunlight now. - we are getting the sun well on the ship now. - The after part of the awning taken off today." Sat 13 Sep RWS

"A beautiful morning, so I went out with Hodgson to a fish trap hole off C Armitage with my camera, and took 3 photos of the ice crystals which come up on his trap line." Fri 19 Sep RWS

Hodgson with Ice Crystals on the fish trap line off Cape Armitage

Royds by the starboard meteorological screen, with puppies playing by the ship

Discovery, showing the wind scoop around the ship after the first winter

Dogs: Spring 1902

"After we got well away from the ship yesterday, the Skipper handed over the leading team of dogs to me so I am now carrying on with them - it consists of Nigger, - The Kid, and Brownie, - 'Nigger' is a splendid puller, - the strongest dog and King of the pack. - The other two are small but keen, especially The Kid. Brownie is always looking out for seals, and he pulls with that one idea of coming across some...[on pitching camp] Nigger and Brownie of my team started to eat 'The Kid', and I had some trouble to get them off. Had to sing out for assistance." Wed 3 Sep RWS

"These [photographs] I have [developed] today have been mostly individual dogs a very difficult subject." Sat 20 Sep RWS

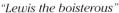

"Lewis the boisterous"

Nell with pups

"Most extraordinary thing, - 3 men went out on ski down to Turtle Island, and found the two dogs which have been missing for nearly 3 weeks; - they had killed a seal, which in dying had rolled over on to the chain of one of the dogs, 'Birdie', and had pinned the latter's head to the ice so that it could only move about 6 inches; - the other dog had remained by it ('Snatcher'), - and kept it warm, and they had subsisted on what they could get from the seal. The skipper will be glad to get them back, as they had both been given up for lost." Sun 28 Sep RWS

Buckridge with Vinka's puppies

Sledge pups

The Southern Journey: 30 October 1902 - 3 February 1903

Christmas Day Camp. L-R: Shackleton, Scott & Wilson

"As a result of today's medical examination I told the Captain that both he and Shackleton had suspicious looking gums, though hardly enough to swear to scurvy in them." Wed 24 Dec EAW

Farthest South Camp: Mount Markham, Shackleton Inlet and Cape Wilson

"The Captain and I went for a ski run this afternoon to the south, but saw nothing and were compelled to return when we had gone a mile or two, as we were afraid of losing our camp, the weather was so thick. Tomorrow, whatever happens, we must turn north again, our furthest southern point being 82° 17´ S.lat." Tue 30 Dec EAW

The short exploration from the Farthest South camp. Wilson stands in front of the Cape named for him. Scott is lower down, towards Shackleton inlet. Shackleton remained in camp and took the photo

"We started off on ski to try and reach bare rock and bring some specimens for the geologist...but after covering a mile or more of it we came to impassable crevasses, and then saw that the land snow slope ended in a sheer ice cliff...which decided us to retrace our steps as, even if we reached it, this ice foot would prevent our reaching rock." Wed 31 Dec EAW

Mount Longstaff - farthest south land seen

Sledging past Mount Markham, Shackleton inlet and Cape Wilson

Impassable crevasses. The large tide crack (with Scott) which prevented land being attained

The Southern Journey: 30 October 1902 - 3 February 1903

"We threw off 25 lbs. of dog food this evening, and I killed the remaining two dogs, as we didn't see our way to getting them home alive."
Wed 14 Jan EAW

"Since the last blizzard Shackleton has been anything but up to the mark, and today he is decidedly worse, very short winded, and coughing constantly, with more serious symptoms...which are of no small consequence a hundred and sixty miles from the ship, and full loads to pull all the way." Wed 14 Jan EAW

"Mount Discovery and the Bluff are in sight again now, so we feel we are nearing home." Wed 21 Jan EAW

"...we saw the black flag that marked our Depot A...Here at the depot were the remains of many camps and here too were letters from the ship for us all...Excellent news of all the other sledge journeys, no mishaps." Wed 28 Jan EAW

The Bluff depot (Depot A)

Camp on the Ice Barrier with fog-bow

Camp with a view north to the Bluff. 25 Jan 1902

The Southern Journey: 30 October 1902 - 3 February 1903

"We met them abreast the depôt 7 miles out, no dogs with them, Wilson and the Skipper pulling two sledges on foot, Shackleton walking alongside on ski. They looked as if they had had a pretty rough time. - The Skipper and Wilson looked fit, but Shackleton looked very weak and seedy and his hair very much bleached. The Skipper's first question was about the ship and if everybody was alright." Tue 3 Feb RWS

"...as we turned Cape Armitage we saw the ship decorated from top to toe with flags and all the ship's company up the rigging round the gangway ready to cheer us, which they did most lustily as we came on board...Then came the time for a bath, and clothes came off that had been on since November the second of the year before, and then a huge dinner." Tue 3 Feb EAW

Wilson, on return from farthest south

Plasmon

Is Fresh Milk reduced into an enduring dry and soluble Powder. 100 pints of Milk make about 3lb. of Plasmon. It adds enormously to the nutritive value of any food with which it is mixed.

Lieut. E. H. Shackleton, R.N., late of the " Discovery," on the Antarctic Expedition, recently made the following spontaneous announcement:

SIRS,

I have much pleasure in testifying from actual experience as to the excellence of Plasmon preparations. We used them continually during the National Antarctic Expedition, and the Plasmon Powder was one of the principal items of food on the Southern Sledge journey in which Captain Scott, Dr. Wilson, and myself made the world's record for further South. Another sledging party practically lived on Plasmon during one journey they made. I have had occasion to fit out Polar Expeditions for other people since my return to England, and have always included a quantity of Plasmon preparations among the provisions.

I am, SIRS,

Yours faithfully,

(Signed)   E. H. SHACKLETON.

Plasmon Cocoa.

Is Best Pure Cocoa combined with Plasmon.

Plasmon Oats.

Best Scotch Oats scientifically mixed with Plasmon.

Plasmon Powder, in pkts., 9d., 1/4 & 2/6.   Plasmon Cocoa, in tins, 9d., 1/4, 2/6
Plasmon Oats, in packets. 6d.   Plasmon Chocolate, in croquettes and bars.
Plasmon Arrowroot. in tins.   Plasmon Biscuits, in several varieties.
Beef Plasmon, in tins.

INTERNATIONAL PLASMON, Ltd.,

66a, FARRINGDON STREET, LONDON, E.C.

West End Depot: 56, Duke St., Grosvenor Square, W.

At the Ship: Summer 1902 - 1903

"Armitage has been busy... making arrangements for the celebration of the King's birthday - Sports and a concert to be held on the 8th, Saturday, a whole holiday, and a special feed on the 9th Sunday." Thu 6 Nov RWS

"The prizes [were] presented by the Princess Lobodon Carcinophagus - Scott dressed up as a female - an uncommonly pretty one too, - and Allan as an attendant. - caused great amusement." Sat 8 Nov RWS

"During the forenoon, Koettlitz cut his crop of mustard and cress, which has grown very well in the Ward Room skylight, and served a fresh crop, - also some lettuces and radishes...I helped Koettlitz to make mustard and cress sandwiches for all hands - they were tremendously appreciated." Sat 8 Nov RWS

"The silk Union Jack presented by the 'Discovery' and 'Alert' was hoisted at Hut Point at 8 o'clock and the ship 'dressed' in honour of His Majesty's birthday." Sat 8 Nov RWS

"We had tea a bit early; and went up [the] ski-slope to watch the toboggan contest. - The first heat started was Cross and Scott V Quartley and Hubert - The latter pair had made a Canadian bob-sleigh and Quartley evidently knew something about it as he worked it very fairly well, - it was made of the roughest materials, - a plank, - the runners of old barrel staves, and the bogie in front of a cross plank and barrel staves with a central bolt, - it was the slowest sledge of the lot, but they won all their heats and the final through good steering and having no capsizes. Cross and Scott capsized or they would have won this heat...Tremendous interest was taken in the whole thing, - it was great fun to watch, and certainly the best managed sleigh won" Sat 8 Nov RWS

At Cape Crozier: 3 November - 20 November 1902

"In the afternoon about 5 pm - Royds sledge party from Mt Terror arrived. They have had a very enjoyable time, no low temperatures, - and successful results; - bringing back the one thing everybody wished for, - an Emperor Penguin's egg - They found it in the little line of hummocks where the Emperors roost, - almost entirely buried, and Blissett spotted it just as they were leaving. They had to dig all round it with ice axes as it was frozen in. I should like to have found it myself." Mon 17 Nov RWS

"On their visit to the Adelie rookery, - they found the birds there in full force and laying eggs...they started away with 200 eggs, - but some got broken on the way back. - They managed to have enough for 2 a day each and brought back enough for 1 all round the ship's company and 2 for each officer." Mon 17 Nov RWS

*Royds,
with Adelie Penguin*

Blissett and Plumley with Adelie Penguin eggs

"At breakfast we had our penguin eggs, - Koettlitz blew one of his and one for Ferrar and Hodgson blew his - though he put his thumb through one and broke the other. Koettlitz didn't make much of a job with his; - both mine blew very well, - I strapped them together well; and made first rate specimens. Afterward I scrambled the eggs and had them on toast. Every egg was cracked through being frozen." Tue 18 Nov RWS

Emperor Penguins at Cape Crozier

Adelie Penguin

*Biological specimens: L-R: Emperor, King and Adelie
Penguin eggs. The Emperor's egg was the first scientific
specimen collected of this species*

At the Ship: Summer 1902 - 1903

McCormick's or South Polar Skua

Onlookers encourage Lt. Barne and the sledge party
(Smythe, Plumley, Williamson, Crean & Weller) as he leads off to explore to the south-west; 12 Dec 1903

Decr. 25 Christmas Day. Gloriously warm fine weather. A good
        basket of fish caught with hook and line.
        Those who had sufficient energy and love
        of fishing were now able to indulge in
        an epicurean dish nearly every day.

The Western Journey: 29 November 1902 - 18 January 1903

"Ship gave us 3 cheers at leaving and several photos were taken, - we looked a fine party leaving 21 strong. - Sail up and a good stiff fair breeze." Sat 29 Nov RWS

The departure of the Western Parties. 29 Nov 1902

"The Western Mountains have been obscured by clouds all the time, probably I shall not get a photo of them at all if it goes on. - about 6.0 we had to turn off again towards the moraine to get a camping ground. - arrived there and camped at 7.0 in a regular little gully, - broke off icicles to fill the cooker with." Sun 30 Nov RWS

"we are opening out the scenery well, - have now arrived at a big open valley between the foothills and the high Western Mountains, entirely filled up with ice and snow, - Took a photo at lunch of Western Peaks..." Fri 5 Dec RWS

One of the sledges, heading west

Camping on morainic ice, near the Eskers. 1 Dec 1902

View of the Western Mountains from half way up the Blue Glacier. The highest peak is Mount Lister. 4 Dec 1902

The Western Journey: 29 November 1902 - 18 January 1903

View up Glacier Valley. 12 Dec 1902

"...we camped at 6.15 as there was a strong breeze, - weather didn't look favourable and we had come to a moraine, - a convenient place being found in a hollow to leeward of some granite boulders, - for all 4 tents, - the boulders are grey granite and each must be over 200 tons - 1 over 250. - To our South is an enormous Talus heap, - towering up some 3000 ft above us, and forming a slope to the Knob Head Mountains." Wed 24 Dec RWS

"Erebus and Terror showed up plainly during the afternoon, down another glacier to the north of the one we have come up, - they must be 100 miles off. - we have now also a splendid view of the back of the Western Mountains, - they are almost as steep on the inland side, as on the sea side. - they look incomparably finer on this side. We camped for the night at the foot of what looks like the last rise to the inland ice, with a sharp turn to the West. I took 4 photos for the day." Sat 27 Dec RWS

Christmas Camp in the glacier moraine, spur of Terra Cotta Mountain

"After going about 2 miles Allan reported to Armitage that Macfarlane had collapsed and could go no further - he complained of shortness of breath and a pain under the heart, and Armitage said he looked very bad, - others of that party also had the same complaint - though not so badly, - particularly Wild, Duncan and Walker. So Armitage told them to camp and remain there while our party goes on to complete the journey - leaving Allan in charge. - I was very glad he did not tell me off, - I fully expected to be, and of course I am keen to get on and get to the highest possible height. The complaint is I suppose due to the exceptional altitude. - our party all seem very fit." Fri 2 Jan RWS

Looking down the glacier towards the Western Mountains

Allan's rest camp. Depot Nunatak is visible in the distance (Armitage, Gilbert Scott, Evans, Quartley, Buckridge, Allan, Macfarlane, Handsley, Duncan, Wild & Walker)

The Western Journey: 29 November 1902 - 18 January 1903

"...found him hung up by his harness, over 20ft down,...Evans made a bowline and lowered the rope. Armitage put it round him and we hauled him up - it took 5 to do it. The Rope of his harness was only 1 inch, - and if that had gone nothing could have saved him, the crevasse opened out and went on beyond sight. - It was about as nasty a show as I've seen, and I don't wish to see any narrower escape." Tue 6 Jan RWS

Depot Nunatak, taken on the return journey

The cliffs of Finger Mountain. Wild (left) and Armitage pose in the wind-scoop. 9 Jan 1903

"After breakfast Armitage and myself went off towards the cliffs to get specimen of rock etc...and then we found a very big Bergschrund, - 100 feet deep, and almost vertical sides but in one place we found a slope where we could get right down amongst the stones that have dropped from the cliffs. - It looked such a fine place that we thought it worth a photo and Armitage went up again and yelled to the camp for the camera. The Rocks echoed the sound so much that at the camp it shouted like 'Help' - and we saw all the men immediately start running as hard as they could towards us, - some grasping Alpine Rope, ice axes, and others the Brandy bottle, - when they came close enough Armitage shouted again and then they heard. - It was all very amusing and caused a good deal of laughter...Wild finally arrived with the camera, and I took the photo - we had a search amongst the boulders and took specimens. The cliffs are formed...of dark and light strata - the dark being granite seems to stand back a good deal and the quartzite forward, forming rubble shelves." Fri 9 Jan RWS

"Crossed a medial moraine, of which I took a photo - this was unfortunate as it turned out to be my last plate, and it would have been decidedly useful later on." Sat 10 Jan RWS

At the Ship: Summer 1902 - 1903

Digging out the boats

"Great progress made with one of the boats, nearly free." Wed 12 Nov RWS

"Royds has got a lot of work done, - succeeded in getting out the boats but with a lot of trouble and they are mostly damaged. - They all had to be sawn out." Mon 19 Jan RWS

"Dellbridge has had steam up in the Donkey boiler since the 2nd week this month, and has got both main boilers filled with fresh water ready for steaming, and both Feed Tanks. The ship's tanks have also been filled with 20 tons fresh water, all from ice melted in the Engine Room Tanks. Several burst pipes have occurred, but they seem to have been only the small ones under 1½ inches diameter, and Dellbridge has repaired them all." Mon 19 Jan RWS

Watering ship
Evans, Cross and Heald

Morning Brings Relief: 24 January - 2 March 1903

"A great Day: - Just after midnight Kennar came running aboard from Hut Point, and reported the relief ship 'Morning' in sight 10 miles away; - almost everybody went out to have a look, - very excited, especially Bernacchi, - I didn't turn out, but sleep for some time was out of the question." Sat 24 Jan RWS

"The crew gave us 3 cheers when we were close and we replied. - Scrambled aboard and shook hands with everybody and then went down to the Ward Room...we had dinner soon after we arrived and then got into our mails." Sat 24 Jan RWS

Officers aboard the relief ship Morning at Lyttelton, New Zealand. L-R: (back) Midshipmen Somerville, Pepper; (front) Lt. Doorly, Lt. Evans, Ch. Eng Morrison, Lt. England, Capt Colbeck, Lt. Mulock, Dr Davidson

"...we got news that Barne was coming back from the relief ship with about 11 others. They arrived shortly afterward, and we found them to consist of Capt Colbeck, - Doorly, Morrison - and young Somerville. We had a very merry dinner, - 16 sitting down to the table, lengthened as much as possible; - we had Champagne unlimited and Bernacchi's liqueurs, Egyptian cigarettes and cigars, all luxuries brought out by the relief ship, not to mention fresh mutton and potatoes. I was president and gave the toasts, after the King. - The return of the South Sledge Party, - Capt Colbeck and the officers of the Morning, - and a silent toast to those who died in the cause of science 'our dogs'." Tue 3 Feb RWS

Armitage and the Discovery party greet Captain Colbeck and the Morning upon arrival in McMurdo Bay

Hauling fresh supplies from Morning to Discovery, Mount Erebus in the distance

The departure of Morning

"Far away in that cold white land
In the home of the Great Ice King
Braving his fury, daring his wrath
When honour and glory are showing the path
God will keep them from harm and scathe -
Till the 'Morning' comes with the Spring."

Songs of the Morning. Morrison and Doorly

9: The Second Winter
3 March 1903 - 6 September 1903

The late autumn of 1903 saw earnest preparations being made aboard ship towards the second winter. Large stocks of seals and skuas were built up to supplement the mutton brought from New Zealand by *Morning*. Skelton thought their total bag of skuas to be in the region of 700 birds. It was a chance too, for the new boy to settle into the steady routine of life aboard *Discovery*. Lt. George Mulock, a Royal Navy surveyor, replaced Shackleton in the Ward Room. The six men of the lower deck who had returned home weren't replaced:

"Mulock came with us in Shackleton's place, so we are now 11 in the Ward Room, 4 Warrant Officers, 5 Petty Officers, 4 Leading Stokers, 2 Domestics, 1 Cook, 10 Able Seamen - all Royal Navy except 3, Armitage, Weller and Clarke, - so I hope we shan't have any more trouble with the men now - personally I'm very glad my two bad characters have gone, Page and Hubert." Mon 2 Mar RWS

One of the most pressing problems faced by Skelton was the difficulty of lighting the ship. Apart from candles and oil lamps Skelton also experimented with acetylene gas lighting, which took some considerable effort to perfect. Despite the fact that it did not reach all parts of the ship by the time the winter awning went up on 21 April it was a general success, providing more light than oil lamps or candles. Nevertheless, Skelton's greatest problem over the second winter was the same as everybody else's, with the exception of Mulock: the novelty had gone. By now the ship's company were experienced Antarcticans; the Antarctic winter had lost its power to astonish. The long hours of frigid darkness, punctuated by the furore of blizzards, became dull and oppressive, little relieved by the routines of ship-board life. The scientific work and its associated winter hazards had attained the hallmark of other lengthy scientific studies, becoming a chore, if highlighted with moments of interest when something out of the ordinary occurred. By now, however, the ordinary prevailed. Even the *South Polar Times* had become something of a routine. Bernacchi had taken over the editor's role after Shackleton's departure and provided the normal run of ascerbic wit within its pages. Yet that was the rub; it had become a part of 'normal' life. Nor was there any distraction to be had in undercurrents of tension as, with the troublemakers gone, there was less friction during the second season; which isn't to say that there was none at all. In the absence of general excitement there was a corresponding increase in practical joking. Barne famously dressed in his officers' furs and hid in a tide crack, growling and crawling on all fours in an effort to trick Koettlitz into thinking that he was a bear; he only succeeded in making him rather cross. Such pranks didn't always hit their mark, particularly where Koettlitz, often the butt of them, was concerned. In between such highlights, the second winter was spent reading, debating and playing games:

"On the mess deck there is work for all hands up till midday, the rest of the day they have to themselves. All hands go out everyday for exercise and fresh air if their work is not out of doors. Some of the men sleep the afternoon away, but the majority do odd jobs, many making models of sledges, matchboxes, etc. or washing clothes, and in the evening most of them play cards or read, many of the seamen being able to give their opinion on the books of any recent novel writer you like to mention. Just now there are sudden uproars of shouting every now and again as a game of bezique is won by somebody. They are coming to the end of a tournament and the prize is an enormous medal with the King's head, made out of a chocolate box cover." Mon 25 May EAW

Mid-winter was seen in with the ritual feasting and jollity. It provided a welcome break from the every-day and an indication that the sun was slowly making its way back - a day all of them longed for with every passing hour of darkness.

For Scott, the long winter hours were spent in planning a second sledging campaign, which he organised to try to answer the riddles posed by the first. Although they had broadly defined 326 miles (607 km) of new coastline on the journeys to the south and south-west, they still needed to ascertain whether this was continuous or not. Therefore a journey was again needed to the south-west. Wilson wanted to go and study the Emperor Penguins at Cape Crozier; and Scott also wanted the answer to riddles posed by Armitage's journey to the west; was there a western coast to Victoria Land or was his newly discovered ice sheet continuous to the magnetic pole, in which case, could they reach it? Scott discussed various plans over the winter, and particularly sought Skelton's advice on plans for the Western Journey. The entire second season's work would be aimed at answering these riddles with the reduced manpower and equipment now available.

The long, dreary days of darkness came to an end with the sun's return on 22 August, although the sun seekers aboard had to wait until the 25th to see it because of overcast weather. The brightly coloured phenomena of the spring twilight excited more interest than the previous year. They heralded the arrival of the new sledging season and its promise of escape from the confines of the winter and its ordinary routine. With light returning to the world, the men of *Discovery* could once again let out a sigh of relief. They had achieved another Antarctic 'first' and survived a second winter.

Polar Biology

"The fish trap was hauled this morning and 54 small fish taken, weighing in all about 8 lbs. They weighed this cleaned. They are a species of 'Notothenia', looking like a Toad fish or Miller's thumb. Hundreds of thousands of amphipods come up swarming on the seal scraps like a mass of shrimpy maggots. You can hear them moving, a disgusting mass." Wed 29 Apr EAW

"Went out for a walk to the fish-trap, - only 18 fish in it, though it has been down 2 days...we had fish for breakfast this morning and very good they were; - it will be a pity if the supply gives out." Sun 3 May RWS

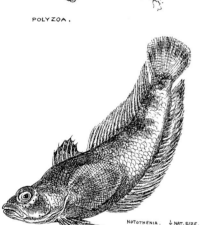

POLYZOA.

NOTOTHENIA. ½ NAT. SIZE.

Hodgson on his round of the fish traps

NYMPHON, A SEA SPIDER

SEA-FIR

THE HYPERIDS OR AMPHIPODS "ARE FREEZING IN THE MASS".

"THE ISOPODS ARE VERY SMALL."

NAT. SIZE.

"AND WITH WORMS."

OF PTEROPODS
HE SAVES A WRECK AT LEAST.

DIATOM

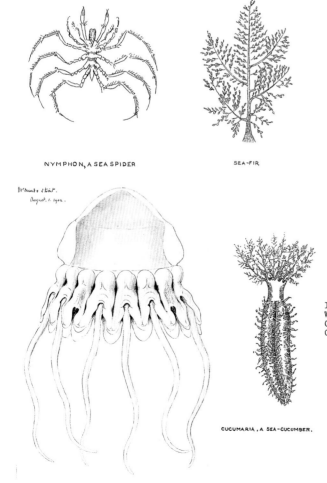

McMurdo Strait.
August 1. 1902.

CUCUMARIA, A SEA-CUCUMBER.

PERIDINIAN

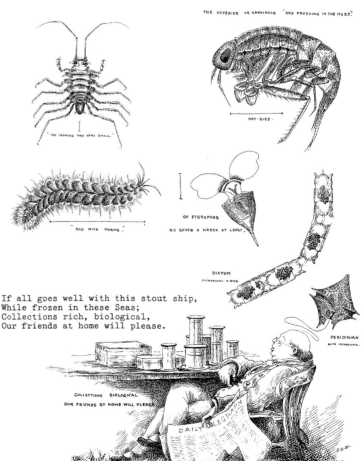

If all goes well with this stout ship,
While frozen in these Seas;
Collections rich, biological,
Our friends at home will please.

COLLECTIONS BIOLOGICAL
OUR FRIENDS AT HOME WILL PLEASE

Autumn Colours: 1903

"After dinner I often spend the evenings painting odd sketches made round our winter quarters and my attempts at the splendid afterglows and sunsets and twilight colouring which we get so much of now, all being done at the ward-room table under the public eye, afford a good deal of amusement." Mon 4 May EAW

Mount Erebus. 26 Apr 1903

"Went up the hills. Seven dogs came with me, otherwise my walks nowadays are always alone, so that I can sketch and potter as often and as much as I think fit." Mon 4 May EAW

"Walked out to C Armitage to see Michael dressed up as a bear, for the benefit of old Koettlitz walking out to his thermometer, - Koettlitz discovered Bernacchi lying down near, which rather gave the show away, and although he didn't mistake Michael for a bear, - he walked straight on, and came back to the ship very angry; - he can't understand a joke." Sat 6 Jun RWS

Crater Hill from Harbour Heights. Noon, looking south-east. 8 May 1903

Midday in May

The Aurora Australis: Winter 1903

Auroral corona

Discovery in Winter Quarters with Aurora

"Lay down from 10 to 12 and then was constantly out to watch a splendid aurora. From 12 to 5 a.m. there was a constant play of arches, bands, streamers and banners in the sky. Twice a corona was formed in the zenith, the streamers all rising from the horizon till they met in a large star overhead. Once a long waving banner crossed the zenith. It was altogether the most lively aurora I have seen as yet. Though there was no pink, the light was all between lemon yellow and a pale green." Tue 7 Apr EAW

"...saw a very good aurora, which this time formed a corona almost overhead. Very extensive arches of diffused light which rose from the south and east forming waving curtains as they approached the zenith. This period of the moon's absence has given us a good deal of aurora on most afternoons." Sun 31 May EAW

"At 4.00 P.M. we had a most lovely auroral display; quite the best I have seen, - a complete and much folded curtain extending from the South West behind Black Island to the East and above Observation Hill, - its movements were very quick horizontally and there were some very bright spots in it with an occasional little green colouring." Sun 19 Jul RWS

Discovery in Winter Quarters with Auroral streamers and curtains stretching from Crater Hill, past Crater Heights, the Gap and Observation Hill beyond Cape Armitage towards Black and White Islands

Midwinter: Winter 1903

```
WE  WISH  ALL  OUR  READERS
           A
         MERRY
       MIDWINTER.
```

"Sir Clements has written a song about us called 'Intrepid Souls', rather a dirge." Sat 24 Jan RWS

Turtle Soup

Halibut Cutlets

Roast Beef

Plum Pudding
Jellies

Devilled Skua

Pineapple
Muscatels & Almonds

Coffee

Vegetables   Potatoes
              Fonds d'Artichokes

Winter Quarters,   June22nd. 1903

"...at 7 we sat down to our own Christmas dinner to which the four Warrant Officers had been invited, namely the Bo'sun, the Second Engineer, the Chief Carpenter and the Steward. They were great fun and enjoyed themselves well. I had the Carpenter next me at dinner, the nicest of the four. We had the remains of the champagne that was sent on board specially for the King at Cowes. It was by no means bad stuff. The Carpenter asked me what it was about three parts through dinner. He said it wasn't like any champagne he had ever drunk, because it 'didn't seem to do you any good'. He had done his best and been unable to get any forrarder on it. We had a most lavish display of dessert thanks to the boxes I opened yesterday, and it was very much appreciated, not only today, but as long as it lasted afterwards." Mon 22 Jun EAW

WOULD I MIND OBLIGING YOU WITH A SONG ?

"Antarctic Christmas Day special meals, fresh beef etc. - Christmas cakes. We had the Warrant Officers in to dine with us making a party of 15 altogether; a very good dinner. Turtle soup, fresh beef etc. and King's champagne. Armitage proposed the toast of the Skipper, - I don't think the latter cares very much about such things, and personally I don't quite see the force of doing it; - that sort of thing goes a long way with certain types; - but I should say the Skipper is quite commonsense enough to be above it." Mon 22 Jun RWS

"After dinner we had some cockfighting, - a set of Lancers and various songs, - Armitage made a brew of hot punch, - altogether we had a fairly merry evening, - turned in at 12.45." Mon 22 Jun RWS

"After dinner on midwinter night, I forgot to mention, that the second number of our 'South Polar Times' was published, a very fat number of over 70 pages." Wed 24 Jun EAW

Winter 1903

"The 1st number of the 2nd volume of South Polar Times came out and we had a special dinner to celebrate the going of the sun. The illustrations of the SPT are very good, - there is a truly fearful caricature of the Pilot." Thu 23 Apr RWS

"Altogether the work is precisely what it was last year, and carried out even more keenly and profitably, because more is known now by experience and everyone has his job cut and dried. Work inboard is only hampered by the fact that having no light in our cabins, everything has to be shifted off the ward-room table for every meal and the meals are rather straggling, so that one's hours for work are curtailed." Mon 25 May EAW

YE LONG ANTARTIC (K)NIGHT

"Have started writing letters, so as to be up to date for the next mail despatch in 1904." Thu 11 Jun RWS

"Evening, tin candlestick making in the galley. Cross is there also, making model of pram in German silver, Blissett making model of the crow's nest in wood and German silver, Lashly making something too, Clarke and Williamson working at arithmetic. So that the galley becomes a sort of workshop between 7 and 10 p.m., the galley fire coming in handy for the soldering irons." Wed 8 Jul EAW

THE PILOT

"Nothing of importance has happened since I last wrote this up. Day follows day with more or less the same routine and events." Wed 8 Jul RWS

"This evening we had a temperature of -53.4°F at the screen, the record up to date, and so far this month averages below -30°F, so that the monthly mean also bids fair to be a record." Fri 10 Jul RWS

"Yesterday evening I gave a magic lantern show to the Ward-Room and Warrant Officers, - of the slides I have made from 50 or 60 negatives of varied subjects, - they show better on the screen than I expected." Sat 25 Jul RWS

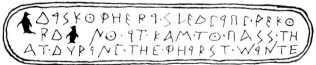

The Return of the Sun: Winter 1903

Opalescent alto stratus and snow drift; looking north. 17 Aug 1903

"One takes much more interest perhaps in the sky changes in these regions, than one would elsewhere. Even the most phlegmatic individuals are woken up by one of the rose pink glows or afterglows. The fact is, one has few distractions and when one is out, the only thing that moves or changes perceptibly is the sky, with its clouds and light and shadow, and one swallows every bit to satisfy the craving that results from the monotonous life we lead during the winter months." Sun 19 Jul EAW

"If a dozen vivid rainbows were broken up by a heavy wind and scattered in wavy ribbands and flecks of curl and fleecy cloudlike forms to float against a background of dull grey, one would have something like the beautiful appearance of this cloud colouring." Sun 16 Aug EAW

"Most beautiful prismatic colouring of the sky and clouds to the North. From 10.0 A.M. until 1.30 P.M. we had most lovely prismatically coloured clouds and mother of pearl clouds." Sun 16 Aug RWS

Castle Rock below Mount Erebus, looking north-west 2 p.m. 3 Aug 1903

10: The Second Sledging Season
7 September - 25 December 1903

Monday 7 September saw a six man party (Royds, Wilson, Cross, Williamson, Blissett and Whitfield) leave the ship for Cape Crozier. It was clear from visits the previous year that the Emperor Penguins laid their eggs early and Wilson wanted to be there. Upon arrival at the rookery they were astonished to discover chicks that were of comparable age to those obtained by Skelton in October 1902. It slowly led Wilson to the extraordinary realisation that these birds laid their eggs during the Antarctic Winter. The large number of frozen eggs and chicks that they found nevertheless provided Wilson with valuable specimens, although eggs with live embryos had eluded him. The early start to the sledging season meant that the party was experiencing very cold temperatures, however, and with no fresh eggs to study they decided to go back to the ship. It was to be a cold return, recording -62°F (-52°C). With them they also carried two live chicks that were lovingly cared for by Cross and Wilson, who chewed seal meat for them on demand. Nevertheless, one died soon after reaching the ship and the other in early November.

Scott's wish to have all the sledging parties back by Christmas, in the hope of releasing the ship, meant that other parties were also out early. Leaving instructions with those who were to remain behind to prepare and re-supply the ship for sea, Scott led a six man party (Scott, Skelton, Dailey, Lashly, Evans and Handsley) to the Western Mountains on 9 September to lay a depot for the forthcoming exploration to the west. He managed to pioneer a new route onto the Western (Ferrar) Glacier from the sea ice, therefore removing the need to travel via the Blue and Descent Glaciers as Armitage had done the previous year. This boded well for a rapid ascent to the plateau on the main journey with plenty of time left for exploring the inland ice. Barne, too, was out early, leading a six man party (Barne, Mulock, Quartley, Smythe, Crean and Joyce) to lay a depot for the forthcoming exploration to the south-west. His party also experienced bitterly low temperatures, down to -67°F (-55°C) and possibly below -70°F (-57°C), as one morning they rose to find that the spirit had frozen, shattering the thermometer column. They were not unhappy to have laid the depot and be safely returned to the ship by 20 September. Joyce had been the only casualty, freezing his foot, which Barne and Mulock had saved by slowly warming it upon their own bare chests. He was nevertheless fit in time to leave on 6 October with the main South-west Party.

The brief interludes between journeys provided time for recuperation, for rest and relaxation; time to watch the returning spring wildlife or to catch up on writing journals. The return of the wildlife also meant that there was once again plenty of fresh meat to eat. One particularly welcome change to the ship's diet was a large fish caught by Weller on 1 October, an incident which also caused considerable amusement. Weller had announced its capture to the assembled ship's company who came to help him to land his large catch. On the end of his harpoon, however, was found a seal and not a fish. Weller was mercilessly teased for his 'big fish' story until Skelton, cleaning out the seal hole at which the alleged catch had taken place, found the fish, minus its head which had been bitten off by the seal, floating amidst the surface debris. Weller had the last laugh and amidst great good cheer, everyone had a large fish dinner that night.

It took two weeks for Barne's South-west Party to reach the Bluff depot, which to their surprise had moved some distance from its original bearings of the year before. This provided the first definitive proof that the Great Ice Barrier wasn't a stationary mass of ice but was an Ice Shelf moving inexorably towards the sea. Their progress was hampered by headwinds, poor visibility and blizzards. The support party (Dellbridge, Pilbeam, Wild, Allan, Croucher and Heald) had to turn back from a position further north than had been hoped for. Nevertheless, Barne led his party into the inlet discovered the previous year and later named for him. Here they found a large glacier and not a frozen sea channel, so showing that the coast line was continuous. Perhaps the most important discovery, however, was achieved when Barne managed to work his way ashore in order to obtain geological specimens, which proved to be continental in nature. Barne so understated the achievements of the party when they arrived safely at the ship on 13 December that its true accomplishments were not recognised for some time.

The Western parties, too, were away promptly, leaving on 12 October and making rapid progress under sail. Quickly progressing up the Western (Ferrar) Glacier they had travelled as far up as the Knobhead Mountain when disaster struck:

"After lunch we examined the sledges and it was a tremendous shock to find all but one gone so badly that they wouldn't last out the journey, - nothing could be done so it was decided to depôt almost everything except a week's supplies and come back to the ship for necessary repairs starting again without the supporting parties." Sun 18 Oct RWS

The necessary return was immensely frustrating. Arriving back at the ship on 21 October the main parties were on their way westward again by the 26th. They once again made rapid progress, Scott being determined to make up for lost time and achieve the objectives of the second season's programme. They scaled the glacier at an astonishing pace, despite difficulties with the weather and the loss of the handbook that helped Scott to work out their precise latitude and longitude. Always resourceful, Scott improvised a way to make the calculations and pressed on.

Arriving at the Depot Nunatak on 4 November they struggled to climb the next ice-fall towards the summit in rapidly deteriorating weather. They camped with great difficulty and remained trapped in their tents by a blizzard for the next six days. This further delay meant that Western Geological Party (Ferrar, Kennar and Weller) went its own way on 11 November, rather than pressing further westward. As this party slowly worked its circuitous route back towards the ship, Ferrar would discover plant fossils near Finger Mountain, so proving that Antarctica had once had a warm climate. Fossils had, of course, previously been found in the northern area of what we now know as the Antarctic Peninsula but had not been widely publicised, nor was it clear if the lands were connected. The finding of these fossils so far south would cause a small sensation in scientific circles upon the Expedition's return. Meanwhile, Scott pushed the Western Summit Party on at a punishing pace. By now they had achieved an altitude of 8,000 feet (2438 metres) and the combination was too much for Handsley, who collapsed. Handsley and Feather were therefore returned to the ship under the command of Skelton and Scott pushed on with the two fittest men, Lashly and Evans. Having given up any idea of the magnetic pole, although still taking readings to help establish its precise location, Scott's aim was simply to travel as far as possible, in the hope of finding the west Victoria Land coast. The small summit party achieved an astonishing sledging journey, which would have equalled the crossing of Greenland, but no coast came into view. They safely returned to the ship on Christmas Eve, having also discovered a new valley which became one of the great geographical finds of the Expedition: the dry valleys of Victoria Land, extraordinary snowless deserts which have intrigued scientists ever since. The discovery of any western coast had, however, eluded them, which in itself was significant. The distances covered suggested that such a coast did not exist, the inland ice in all probability continuing for hundreds of miles: a scale that could only mean that the land was continental.

The third major sledging journey of the season was led by Royds south-eastwards across the Great Ice Barrier. The South East Barrier Party (Royds, Bernacchi, G.Scott, Cross, Plumley and Clarke) was sent to see if the Barrier's eastern shore could be determined; the fact that no land could be seen after sledging 155 miles helped to define the true scale of the Barrier. The party also took a series of controlled magnetic readings away from any residual magnetism present in the coastal mountains in order to help locate the magnetic pole. Further observations made by Royds' party, such as the variation of temperature in Barrier crevasses, provided evidence that the Barrier was afloat, a significant discovery.

Other important results were yielded by some of the relatively local sledging journeys of the summer. A trip along the southern coast of Ross Island undertaken by Wilson, Hodgson and Croucher found tide cracks along the edge of the Barrier, providing further evidence to show that the Barrier was afloat. Wilson had also returned to Cape Crozier with Cross and Whitfield for a 23 day trip to investigate the Emperor Penguin rookery further. Here he had become the first man to witness the post-breeding migration of these birds out to sea on ice floes, thus securing another important piece of the puzzling breeding cycle of these remarkable birds. Wilson also travelled with Armitage and Heald to explore the area around the Saddle Mountain (Koettlitz) Glacier and so to fill in one of the last gaps on their map of the local McMurdo Sound area.

As Scott mused over his Christmas dinner on the sledging reports that he had received when he returned to the ship, he had every reason to be pleased. The second sledging season had been a great success.

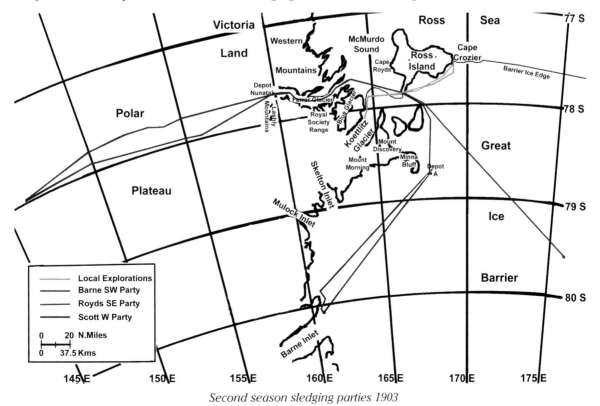

Second season sledging parties 1903

Cape Crozier: 7 September - 17 September 1903

"Blowing and drifting hard from southeast when we got up, and on into the forenoon. Everything was ready for a start, and during a lull about 11 a.m. we got off with our flags flying, cheered by the ship as we left and cheering them in return. The party consists of Lieut. Royds, myself and Williamson A.B. in one tent, Cross, first class Petty Officer, Whitfield, Leading Stoker and Blissett, Lance Corporal Royal Marine Infantry in the other tent." Mon 7 Sep EAW

"For this journey we are in three-man sleeping bags, for warmth's sake, not comfort, for I can imagine nothing more uncomfortable." Mon 7 Sep EAW

"If however one hurries the bird's movements at all, down he goes on his breast, and drawing his feet close in under the belly, he holds the chick there and hardly using his feet at all, shoves himself along with his wings and beak, digging them alternately into the snow. In this position it is not long before the chick slips out behind and is left helplessly whistling for a new nurse, an appeal answered like a shot by two or more of the nearest birds unoccupied, who get close up to the deserted chick and seizing it anyhow in their beaks try to shove it into their laps." Sun 13 Sep EAW

"...we found in all about 30 young dead chicks. Fifteen of these I brought home." Sun 13 Sep EAW

"Spent all the forenoon painting the frozen Emperor chicks in their quaint and life-like attitudes. How they can freeze in the attitudes they have is a puzzle, for many of them are standing, perfectly balanced. One can stand them up and leave them." Sat 26 Sep EAW

Frozen Emperor Penguin eggs and chicks from Cape Crozier. Sep 1903

Western Depot Journey: 9 September - 20 September 1903

Looking up the Great Western (Ferrar) Glacier from New Harbour entrance. 16 Sep 1903

"The object of the journey was to place a depôt at a convenient spot, - say Cathedral Rocks, in the glacier, on the way to the inland ice, - and so facilitate the later extended journey on to the mainland ice, - 21 days were allowed; but the object was as a matter of fact achieved in 12, and a depôt of 3 weeks provisions for six men, besides several details, amounting altogether to 43 lbs. made, instead of a depôt only of 2 weeks for six men. The party consisted of Captain Scott, - myself, - Mr Dailey the Carpenter, - in one tent, with Lashly Ldg Stoker - Evans PO 2cl, and Handsley AB in the 2nd tent, - originally Mr Feather the boatswain was coming, but the Doctor pronounced him unfit, so Mr Dailey came in his place." undated RWS

"...the depôt was made alongside a fairsized Quartzite boulder on the left side of the medial moraine going up, with Descent Pass full in view and Cathedral Rocks just about to shut off the view of the Western Mountains; can't fail to find the place again." Thu 17 Sep RWS

"Total increase of weight on gear, due to condensation and accumulation of snow estimated at 81.5 lbs. or 13.6 lbs. per man." Sun 20 Sept RWS

Looking up the Great Western (Ferrar) Glacier

At the Ship: Spring and Summer 1903

Weller, waiting by a fish trap hole to harpoon a seal

"While they were skinning the seal I went out clearing the hole of blood and ice crystals, and after about 20 minutes shovelling saw something waving about in the water which I pulled up, and found to be an enormous fish; so that Weller was not wrong after all, he had harpooned a fish, and the seal at the same time, but the fish's head had been broken off, when we hauled the seal up, - a great pity. We immediately brought it inboard, where it caused much excitement, the remains were 3 ft 10 ins long and weighed 39 lbs., a beautiful fish, it must have been nearly 4 ft 6 ins long complete and weighed 45 lbs. Hodgson decided not to pickle it as it was a spoilt specimen, and would take so much spirit, 10 gallons - but to take all necessary measurements, preserve the skeleton and stomach, and we could eat the flesh." Thu 1 Oct RWS

"A nasty light, no horizon visible, snow falling. Michael Barne started off in the afternoon with a party of six and a supporting party also of six under Dellbridge, 2nd. Engineer. Mulock has gone with Barne...the object is to explore one of the openings in our new land discovered last year to the south, to see whether it is a strait or merely a fjord." Tue 6 Oct EAW

Weller's headless fish

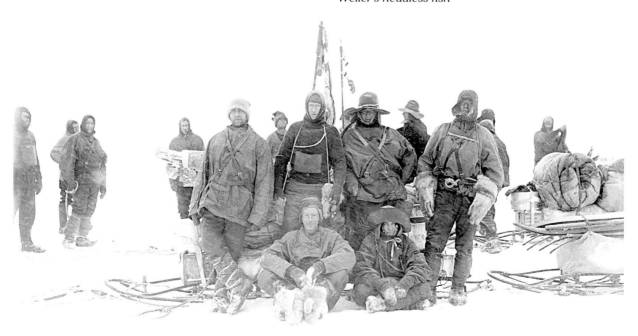

Barne's South-west Party about to depart: L-R (back) Joyce, Smythe, Crean & Quartley; (front) Barne, Mulock.
Well-wishers and members of the South-west Support Party (Dellbridge, Pilbeam, Wild, Allan, Croucher and Heald)
are milling around in the background

Cape Crozier: 12 October - 5 November 1903

L-R: Cross, Wilson and Whitfield, about to depart for Cape Crozier

"My party included myself, J. Cross, 1st Class P.O., R.N. and T. Whitfield, Leading Stoker, R.N. We took one eleven foot sledge with tent, equipment and food for three weeks, each weekly bag averaging 40 lbs besides biscuit, and two gallons of oil." Mon 12 Oct EAW

"...there seemed to be far fewer chicks than when we were here in September. There were dead ones all round, but all so filthy as to be useless for skinning, many worn naked of down and rotten, through having been nursed and fondled long after they were dead." Sun 18 Oct EAW

Whitfield and Cross pulling the sledge for Cape Crozier

"...got a shelter built up for our blubber stove, which I hoped to use often and so economize our very spare allowance of oil. For I had but three gallons for the whole journey, which I hoped to extend to a month." Wed 21 Oct EAW

Digging out the blubber stove at camp,
after a blizzard, Cape Crozier

Emperor penguin rookery, Cape Crozier, looking east along the Ice Barrier

Local Wildlife: Spring and Summer 1903

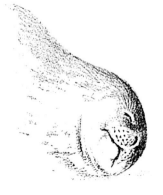

"...spent the day again painting... during the afternoon a fish of a new kind which was taken from the stomach of a seal. It had to be painted at once or not at all so I lost my sleep, but it was worth it. A very queer shaped beast. The seal was a yearling, the first killed with a harpoon as it rose in the fish hole, Skelton having conceived the notion of killing them in this way. He was easily hauled out and there seems to have been very little difficulty about the whole thing. The stomach was crammed with this new fish, quite freshly swallowed and excellent specimens." Sun 27 Sep EAW

"...went with Muggins to Pram Point...There were many Weddell seals there and seven of them had recently born calves. Made notes on them and tied tin labels to their hind flippers, so as to know their respective ages." Tue 10 Nov EAW

Seal and calf near Pram Point

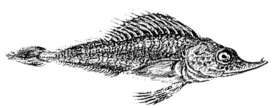

McCormick's (or South Polar) Skuas, nesting near Winter Quarters Bay

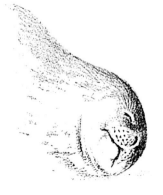

"In every little valley was a skua sitting on two eggs laid in a saucer-shaped hollow in the gravel. Nothing but the eggs lay in the nest, there was no lining whatever. The birds attacked us vigorously as usual." Fri 11 Dec EAW

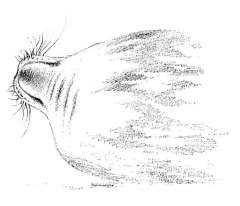

JAEGER
PURE WOOL

The Safest Wear for Travellers in all Climates.

The Jaeger Co. have fitted out many Expeditions, Arctic and Antarctic, including :—

Nansen, 1893.
Jackson-Harmsworth, 1894.
Wellmann, 1898.
Borchgrevink, 1898.
Duc D'Abruzzi, 1899.
National Antarctic (Discovery), 1901.
Ziegler (Baldwin), 1901.
National Antarctic Relief.
Ziegler (Fiala), 1903, (Morning) 1902.
Argentine, 1903.

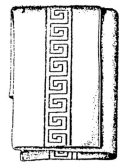

Camelhair Blankets.

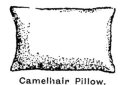

Camelhair Pillow.

Please write for complete Illustrated Jaeger Price List (No. 40) and pattern—sent free.

Fixed Moderate Prices.

London Jaeger Depots:—

126, Regent Street, W.
456, Strand (Charing Cross), W.C.
30, Sloane Street, S.W.
115, Victoria Street, S.W.
85 & 86, Cheapside, E.C.

Fleecy Knitted Travelling Cap (Turned down).

Sleeping Bag.

N.B.—The JAEGER Natural Wool Under= wear is GUARANTEED against Shrinkage.

It is made in various textures to suit all climates--- and in a large number of sizes to suit all requirements.

Short Spencer.

Shoulder Warmer.

Undervest.

Men's Pants.

Pyjama Jacket

Pyjama Trousers.

- 119 -

Sledging: Spring and Summer 1903

"Started away again for the west. We are to explore the corner by Mount Discovery and find out all we can about the old dirty so-called penknife ice. No one has yet been in this corner of the strait. It is my first visit to the west coast and I hoped to get sketches among the mountains there." Sat 28 Nov EAW

"Ferrar had returned all right and had made a great find in the western mountains of fossil plants in some coal shale beds, which means that the South Pole has at one time had an abundant vegetation." Sat 12 Dec EAW

"Royds made a successful trip over the Barrier getting out 155 miles and averaging 10.2 miles per day." Sat 13 Feb RWS

The commencement of pinnacle ice on part of the Saddle Mountain (Koettlitz) Glacier, showing the north face of Saddle Mountain (Mount Morning) 7 Dec 1903

"Barne had been out about 68 days but had experienced terribly bad weather, and had only been able to get to the mouth of one of the Fiords." Sat 13 Feb RWS

The Western Journey:
12 October - 21 October & 26 October - 12 December 1903

"Leave for the West tomorrow, a total party of 12, - in two hauling parties of 6. - The extended party consisting of The Skipper, myself, Boatswain, Lashly, Evans, and Handsley, - The supporting party of Ferrar, The Carpenter, Kennar, Williamson, Plumley and Weller. - The former for 65 days out, The Carpenter, Williamson, and Plumley for 35 days out and Ferrar, Kennar and Weller to come as far as our last depôt and then return to investigate the glacier and stop out as long as he likes up to Dec 15th." Sun 11 Oct RWS

About to head West: L-R: Skelton (sitting), Evans, Scott, Handsley (sitting), Feather, Lashly. 12 Oct 1903

"After breakfast the Captain called Lashly and myself into his tent to tell us that he had decided to push on with 3, the remainder to return, - as he was anxious about Handsley. He said he had spoken to the Boatswain about it and he had taken it very sensibly and of course I must go back in charge of the party. Evans and Lashly apparently being the fittest, he would go on with them." Sun 22 Nov RWS

Just off: Lashly, Handsley, Scott, Feather, Evans, Skelton. 12 Oct 1903

"I took 3 photos, - one of the rocks in situ, one of the trench looking up, and one of a section of the glacier side...After my photos I gathered one or two decent stones...On mounting the moraine, I noticed 2 or 3 handy icicles for filling the Doctor's Bacteria bottle." Wed 9 Dec RWS

"I took a photo of the hanging glacier and the obelisk...Handsley carried the camera back for me, - for which I was very thankful, - as it is no light weight to carry 8 miles or so." Wed 9 Dec RWS

"After breakfast I took the camera up a rise about ¼ mile past and above Xmas camp and took a round of 4 photos from the entrance of Northern Fiord to Windy Gully, and including Isolated Rocks and falls." Thu 10 Dec RWS

The side of the Western (Ferrar) Glacier, with Handsley. 9 Dec 1903

Western (Ferrar) Glacier, Cathedral Rock Ice fall, Windy Gully visible. 10 Dec 1903

11: The Return to Civilisation
26 December 1903 - 1 April 1904

Whilst the results of the second season were pleasing to all concerned, it was a considerable worry that the sea ice was, once again, showing no sign of leaving McMurdo Sound. Scott began to worry that they might have to face a third season trapped in the ice. Before sledging westward he had left instructions to start sawing and blasting the ice in an attempt to create a channel through which the ship might break out. The first reports that Scott received from Armitage relating to this work were promising. Dell brought the dispatches. Due to injury his summer had been spent at the ship working the previous year's husky puppies into a viable sledge team. Dell's success meant that he was now running a daily 'dog post' service from the ship to the 'sawing out' camp. The positive tone of these dispatches meant that Scott was confident that some progress was being made. When Scott inspected the work himself on 31 December, however, he rapidly saw what the majority of his officers believed to be the case - the sawing operation was having such a negligible effect as to be a waste of time. He soon called it off and moved the sawing and blasting operation to the area of Winter Quarters Bay to loosen the ice around the ship itself. Three men remained in the area of the sawing out camp to kill Adelie Penguins for the larder against a possible third winter.

Scott, meanwhile, asked Wilson to go on a short camping trip. Wilson and Scott had developed a deepening friendship over the course of the Expedition and Scott wanted time to talk things over. The two friends went camping at what is now Cape Royds and were delighted to discover a new Adelie Penguin rookery there, the most southerly known. As they rested in the sunshine they began to discuss the possibilities of a third season: 18 miles (33 kms) of ice still separated the ship from the ice edge and the probability of it breaking up seemed increasingly remote. The main drawback to another season was the lack of sledges and the other equipment needed for major sledging journeys but there was still plenty of work that could be accomplished. On 5 January, Scott looked out of the tent and saw *Morning* sail into view. A few minutes later they saw a second ship. This was a considerable surprise and it wasn't until they approached the relief ships that they ascertained the real reason for the presence of the second ship, *Terra Nova*. They were greeted warmly by Captain Colbeck, who then presented Scott with orders from the Admiralty to return home immediately and to abandon *Discovery* if she could not be freed. The failure of *Discovery* to break out of the ice the year before had given Sir Clements Markham's opponents their chance and the government wrested control of the National Antarctic Expedition from Markham and the Royal Geographical Society. It was the Admiralty who had sent the second ship and orders to abandon *Discovery*. The order was a considerable shock to all aboard and was one which Scott had to obey despite its obvious vindictiveness. Two days later Scott gave the instructions to transfer all of the scientific collections and equipment from *Discovery* to *Terra Nova*. He also gave the order for Royds to resume the ice blasting operations; *Terra Nova* had brought the fresh supply of gun cotton which Scott had requested against this event. *Terra Nova* was a stronger ship than *Morning* and under one of the most experienced of the Dundee whaling Captains, Harry McKay. He used every opportunity to push through new leads or channels opened up by the blasting to edge ever closer to *Discovery*. It was not, however, closing the distance fast enough to have any prospect of success. McMurdo Sound is of such a nature that to this day only one force is strong enough to break the ice out, and that is an ocean swell. As the time for their departure grew nearer, all aboard *Discovery* became gloomier. Even as the scientific collections were being transferred to *Terra Nova*, however, the scientific programme carried out aboard *Discovery* was continuing. The Cape Royds camp was proving very popular with the officers of the *Morning* and Wilson often stayed there to make wildlife observations. He was delighted to capture an Elephant Seal with Ferrar and Davidson (of the *Morning*), still amongst the most southerly observations made for this species.

On 28 January, when they had all but given up hope, the men awoke to find *Discovery* riding 18 inches (45cm) on the swell that they had all been waiting for. The swell lasted for four days; the relief ships advancing ten miles (18.5kms) with the breaking ice. When the swell stopped, so did the advance of the ships and the despondency returned, not helped by the fact that Blackwall, one of the two *Discovery* cats, was torn apart by the huskies. The swell returned on 11 February and for four days McKay led the charge, backing, ramming and rolling *Terra Nova* into every crack that appeared, to enthusiastic applause from Hut Point. As the relief ships rapidly approached, frantic preparations began to prepare *Discovery* for sea: because of the Admiralty's orders preparations for abandonment had previously taken priority. It meant twice as much work for Skelton and his team in the engine room and nearly cost the ship. All that now imprisoned *Discovery* was a small amount of Bay ice. On 16 February, to wild cheering from all three ships, a final detonation of gun cotton allowed *Discovery* to float free. Later that afternoon, a small cross was erected on Hut Point to the memory of AB Vince and dedicated with a short service. During the evening a storm blew up, threatening to drive *Morning* and *Discovery* onto the shore of Observation Hill. The following day the storm was worse than ever; *Discovery* started to drag her anchors and be driven onto the lee shore. Frantic work in the engine room meant that steam could now be raised but in one boiler only. Scott gave the order and saved the ship from being smashed against the icy shore of Observation Hill but as they tried to steam out of Winter Quarters Bay they were thrust instead onto a small shoal off Hut Point. There *Discovery* sat, grounded amidships, whilst hurricane force winds and waves pummelled her. Later that evening the prevailing current around the Point changed and *Discovery* was freed as suddenly as she had been cast aground. Fortunately there was little damage but the Admiralty's orders had nearly cost the ship several times over.

The scattered ships were relieved to find each other still in one piece the following day and both relief ships proceeded to transfer coal supplies to *Discovery* at the Erebus Glacier Tongue, along with the previously transferred collections. Nevertheless, they had not finished taking on water when another storm blew up. Fortunately *Discovery* could now maintain full pressure in both boilers and the three ships sailed out of McMurdo Sound and headed north, *Morning* and *Discovery* making running surveys of the coast of Victoria Land where they could. *Discovery* was finally prepared for sea when she was able to anchor in Wood Bay to finish watering ship. Shortly thereafter it was found that the rudder was badly damaged and *Discovery* and *Terra Nova* put into Robertson Bay off Cape Adare in order to change it. Scott then sailed as far west as ice and his coal supplies permitted in order to try to join up the discoveries around Adelie Land with Victoria Land and the sighting of lands claimed by Wilkes in between the two. He had not got nearly as far as he had hoped when he was obliged to turn north on 4 March having once again disproved some of Wilkes' claims. Scott however, was not happy, believing that he had achieved nothing but renewed controversy when he would rather have solved the puzzle.

Discovery sailed north-eastward through the Southern Ocean, heading for the Auckland Islands, where the three ships had agreed a rendezvous. For Wilson it was a time to re-acquaint himself with the seabirds; for Skelton it was a busy time in the engine room. It was late in the season to be sailing so far south and all three of the ships were buffeted by storms and mountainous seas. *Discovery* reached the rendezvous at Port Ross in the Auckland Islands on 15 March. The joyous shock of seeing green vegetation after two years can only be imagined. Everyone enjoyed time ashore, hunting, walking, or simply enjoying the phenomenon of bird song. Wilson made a substantial collection of wildlife specimens. The time was also spent in re-painting *Discovery* for her anticipated arrival back in New Zealand. *Terra Nova* arrived on 19 March and *Morning* the following day. The three ships sailed for New Zealand on the 29th.

On Good Friday, 1 April 1904 the three ships were sighted from Lyttelton. Oriana Wilson ran over the Port Hills to Lyttelton when she heard the news and sailed out to greet her husband in a tug. She had spent the last year in New Zealand awaiting the ship's return and finally the day had come. By the time the ships arrived in port the docks were lined with cheering crowds. *Discovery* had returned to civilisation.

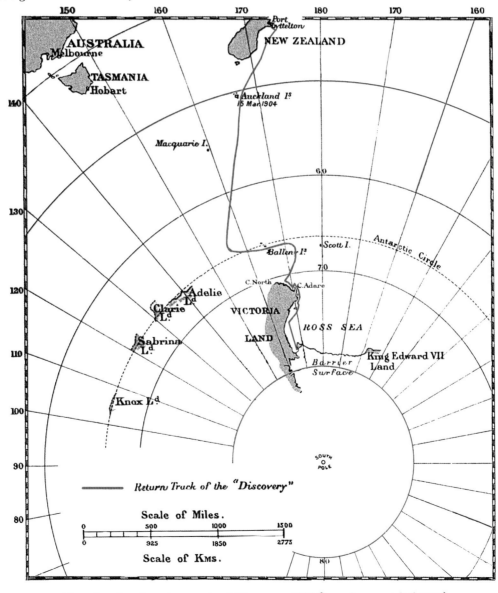

Map showing the return route of Discovery. 1904 (based on a period map)

Sawing Out Camp: 16 December 1903 - 2 January 1904

Sawing out Camp

"At 5 a.m. Bernacchi came in and reported that it was 'all up with the sawing', as the forces of nature had stepped in and everything was frozen up again and the saws couldn't be budged. At 10 a.m. we breakfasted and were at the saw by noon. It took us 2 hours to free the saw, straighten one of the iron tripod legs and explode 16¼ lbs guncotton. We then had 2 hours' sawing and did 30 ft in all. There is no open water to be seen from where we are sawing, only unbroken floe. The ice is 7 ft thick - and the cracks freeze up again as soon as we saw them. It will take at the rate we are going now just about 40 weeks to cut a canal to the ship! And we must be out and away before the beginning of March." Sat 19 Dec EAW

"The sawing tent was pitched about ¼ mile South of the 1st Erebus [Dellbridge] Island North of the glacier snout, and about 1½ miles North of the glacier. - It was also more than a mile from the saws, so that besides a 4 hours watch on the saw we had a ½ hours walk each way. We were divided into 3 watches and had a meal before and after each watch and then turned in. The small cooking range from the Hut, which has been on the mess deck all the winter, did the cooking and worked very well, - everybody had tremendous appetites and during the fortnight we were there, something between 30 and 40 seals were killed for food and several Adelie Penguins." Mon 21 Jan RWS

Weddell Seal

Sawing out Camp

"There never was a healthier crowd of ruffians than the 30 unwashed, unshaven, sleepless swearing, grumbling, laughing, joking reprobates that lived in that smoky Saw Camp." Thu 31 Dec EAW

"...the Captain put all hands on the saws for half an hour just to see how they worked. Then shear legs, saws and all were packed up and taken to the glacier and finish all sawing out here. He is going to try a bit round the ship to see if she can be got loose at all there." Sat 2 Jan EAW

"Dell makes a trip from the ship to the tent one day and back the next, - he has succeeded in making a fine dog team out of six first year's puppies." Sat 2 Jan RWS

Cape Royds and the Arrival of the Relief Ships: 2 January - 5 January 1904

Adelie Penguins

"Wilson and the Skipper arranged to go on towards Cape Bird, make a camp, wait for the relief ship, and explore the place a little. 5 hands remained in the [sawing] camp to kill Adelie penguins for storing in case of another winter and erect a signal station on top of the island, to communicate arrival of relief ship to winter quarters. They were Lashly, Evans, Handsley, Heald and Clarke." Sat 2 Jan RWS

"We reached the open water at last and a prominent cape [Royds] of rocky volcanic stuff with but little snow. Here we were delighted to find a small Adélie Penguin rookery...We pitched our camp on a gravelly spot on the top of the shore rocks, a position from which we had an excellent view all over the strait and its entrance - from which therefore we could watch the doings of the pack ice, on which our eventual liberation depended - and from which we should see the 'Morning' when she first hove in sight." Mon 4 Jan EAW

"The Captain and I were writing in the tent - it was a beautiful warm sunny morning and we sat there on our sleeping bags with the tent door tied open. He suddenly looked out and said 'Why, there's the 'Morning'.'...I looked out again to feast my eyes on the welcome sight, when lo and behold, there before us lay a second ship like the first. We were dumbfounded and a host of surmises arose...It was a thrilling moment approaching the ships. No one was expected and everyone was below...at last four Dundee whaling men from the 'Terra Nova' spotted us as strangers and came out to meet us. They spoke such perfect Dundee that we could hardly understand a word they said for a bit. Then we gathered that the Government had stepped in and were responsible for the 'Terra Nova'." Tue 5 Jan EAW

"There had of course been many theories to account for the second ship, - that it was the German, an Australian or some other separate expedition, a service gunboat. I think one or two did actually suggest that the government had taken the matter in hand. It was of course a tremendous surprise to us, especially the order that we were to return anyhow." Wed 6 Jan RWS

THE COMING OF THE RELIEF SHIPS. 1904.

Preparing for Departure: January 1904

"Transporting collections and gear to the relief ships started on the 14th Jan, - the system being for us to take a load to the tent at the end of the glacier snout one day, and parties from the relief ships to take it on the next day, so that each party sleeps in the tent on alternate nights." Thu 14 Jan RWS

"I had to set to work at once packing up all my collections of bird skins, birds' eggs, and seals." Fri 22 Jan EAW

Dog team and Mount Erebus

"Everybody busy packing up collections and instruments. I packed up all the camera gear and the negatives." Thu 14 Jan RWS

"Sent 3 cases and 6 casks to the 'Morning' by sledge. Packing all the forenoon. Finished blowing some Adélies' eggs from Cape Royds rookery and 3 Emperors' eggs, all frightfully rotten." Mon 25 Jan EAW

"Well the beast was a young male Sea Elephant and to find one down here is quite a new thing, so we were very pleased indeed. Total length was about 12 feet and his girth was enormous, just on 10 feet, at the shoulders. There was from 2 to 3 inches of blubber on him." Mon 11 Jan EAW

"The skuas proved a trouble, for I had put the beast's tongue on one side and his eyes, which were remarkably large. I buried them in sand, as I wanted the tongue to cook. The skuas not only unburied these tit-bits, but carried them off to sea and eat them. They also carried off my jacket several yards and I saw one fly off with a long seal skin knife sheath of about 18 inches in his bill. When I left the skin for the night I buried it in a big sand heap, but the brutes got it out and made several bare patches by pecking all the horny hair off." Mon 11 Jan EAW

View from Hut Point towards the Gap. The black bulb thermometer stand with the magnetic variation study hut behind

Wilson (left) with Ferrar, collecting the most southerly Elephant Seal then recorded

Winter Quarters Bay: January - February 1904

"Sawing a canal from Hut Point to the ship was started about the 5th Jan, but was soon given up as useless, and digging out the snow round the sides of the ship started." Sun 10 Jan RWS

"On the 12th I took the first photos with my new camera of the men sawing, and got a most excellent negative." Tue 12 Jan RWS

"Whenever the stores party returns from the tent, they bring a quarter of beef and some potatoes - so we are living well." Mon 18 Jan RWS

"Brought my new camera down and took several photos. - Royds was exploding 3 gun cotton charges abreast, but it wasn't doing much good, the ice itself going out with the swell; however, the blasting does crack the ice, and may be of great use later on; - I believe the relief ships have each brought down about 7 tons of gun cotton." Mon 25 Jan RWS

"It was today that we first felt the ship working with the swell under the ice. The fittings in the ward-room were creaking off and on all day." Thu 28 Jan EAW

Guncotton explosions were going all day, the Captain superintending. The 'Morning' is now in the same position as when she left McMurdo Strait last year, on March 2nd." Fri 5 Feb EAW

Using the ice saw to break up the ice around Discovery - Observation Hill and the Gap in the background

Dell and the dog-team, posing in front of Discovery - Ski slopes in the background

"Guncotton charges are now being exploded at Hut Point, as well as at the relief ships." Wed 10 Feb EAW

Breaking the ice - a gun cotton explosion, Winterquarters Bay by Hut Point - looking towards Arrival Heights

The Relief Ships Approach Winter Quarters: 14 February 1904

Terra Nova (left) and Morning approaching Winter Quarters Bay as the ice breaks out of McMurdo Sound: 10pm

"Much ice breaking away and going out. The ships are now only 4 miles from us." Thu 11 Feb EAW

"Blasting here at Hut Point and day and night at the ships, as there is a swell. Two miles have gone out since yesterday morning." Fri 12 Feb EAW

Cheering the approach of the relief ships from Hut Point

"About 6 p.m. the ice began breaking up in a marked and rapid manner with a southerly breeze. Everyone was watching the relief ships working their way in, from 7 o'clock onwards when they were within a half or ¾ of a mile from Hut Point. There was no halt in their progress, and they were both backing and ramming again and again and working in to the cracks as they appeared. The 'Terra Nova' of course, being the strongest ship and having the more powerful engines did most, and MacKay made all hands 'sally' the ship, i.e. run from side to side to give her a good roll, which was a great help. It was about 11 p.m. when the two ships at last broke through and reached Hut Point basin and tied up, the one to the ice in our bay, and the other to our very foc'sle. Such a cheering and general all round congratulation there was, and festive rejoicing till nearly 3 a.m." Sun 14 Jan EAW

"Doorly came up from 'Morning' on evening of 11th Feb, and reported ice going out fast; and request for assistance, so after dinner Royds went down with most of the hands. Barne and myself dug holes at Hut Point and made 2 or 3 blasts on the 12th with fair effect. Ships came in gradually on the 12th and 13th and 14th and on the evening of the 14th while we were at dinner, we got a report that the ice was breaking away everywhere, ships less than a mile off and 'Terra Nova' charging and rolling the fast ice; everybody clustered on Hut Point to watch them, - very stirring sight, - they both got in and made fast to ice in our bay about 11 P.M. of the 14th." Sun 14 Feb RWS

Terra Nova (left) and Morning approaching Winter Quarters Bay as the ice breaks out of McMurdo Sound: 11pm

The Release of *Discovery*: 14 February - 17 February 1904

Winter Quarters Bay, looking south-west from Hut Point/ski slopes, the Relief ships arrived, about midnight 14-15 Feb 1904.
L-R: Morning, Discovery and Terra Nova

Vince's Cross

"A last charge of guncotton on the port quarter freed the ship. She rose a lot in the stern and floated level once again in excellent trim, amid cheers from the other two ships and dipping ensigns...The 'Discovery' swung round on her two cables and finally left her ice bed, which was very soon floating away in large blocks, leaving the impress of all her planks and seams." Tue 16 Feb EAW

"On the 15th we raised steam in the Donkey boiler, and working parties from the 'Terra Nova' and 'Morning' came soon after noon to bring ice alongside for us to melt; by midnight we had the Starboard boiler filled and lit up and the Port boiler during the forenoon of the 16th. I had taken several photos of the three ships and various incidents."
Tue 16 Feb RWS

Discovery breaks free, the ice pack that surrounded her floating away. Morning is also visible. 16 Feb 1904, looking across Winter Quarters Bay from Hut Point to the Gap

"...all went on shore in a whaler and Captain Scott read a short service at the big cross, which was put up on Hut Point yesterday to the memory of Vince A.B." Tue 16 Feb EAW

"A wooden cross was erected on Hut Point in memory of George Vince AB who was lost in March '02 while sledging." Wed 17 Feb RWS

"...on the morning of the 17th in trying to come out of harbour we grounded at Hut Point and remained there for 7 hours, the ship coming off when we went astern...Elms, Dr Souter, and a party of men from the Terra Nova were on board us when we went aground and gave us a lot of help. At one time the main inlet got choked, and things generally looked very bad for us." Wed 17 Feb RWS

Leaving McMurdo Strait: 18 February - 19 February 1904

"On the forenoon of the 18th Feb we proceeded with the 'Terra Nova' to the glacier snout, the object being to find a sheltered cove for coaling, transferring stores, and filling the ship's tanks. We had a great deal of trouble to do this, as the ice anchors continually dragged. We got 50 tons of coal from the 'Terra Nova' and about 700 cases of provisions, then went round to the South side of the glacier and took in 25 tons of coal from the 'Morning', tried also to get in water (ice) and the whaler left on the glacier, but a strong southerly breeze springing up, we were prevented and finally steamed away to the North about 5 P.M. 19th Feb; picked up the 'Terra Nova' at the entrance of the bay, and lost sight of our winter quarters after being a fixture there for over two years etc...no sail was set although it would have done very well, but none of it is ready to set...The 'Morning' could not keep up with us and gradually dropped almost out of sight."
Fri 19 Feb RWS

Discovery taking aboard coal and other supplies from Terra Nova, Erebus Glacier Tongue. 19 Feb 1904 (Dellbridge Islands behind)

"I shall not soon forget the last view we had of our strait as we last saw Mount Discovery in the midnight sunset. It was a blaze of colour astern of us, a glowing orange fire and standing out black on our starboard quarter was the 'Terra Nova' under sail and farther astern on our port quarter, the 'Morning'." Sat 20 Feb EAW

Emperor Penguins on the Erebus Glacier Snout. 19 Feb 1904

Midnight, the last sight of Mount Discovery: SS Morning and Terra Nova following Discovery out of McMurdo Strait. 19 Feb 1904

At Sea: the Coast of Victoria Land 20 February - 24 February 1904

"Steaming along the coast all day, making a running survey; - Ross's survey of this part is rather incomplete owing to the great distance he was off it. 'Terra Nova' keeping company but 'Morning' a long way astern." Sat 20 Feb RWS

"Erebus dropped below the horizon before noon." Sat 20 Feb RWS

Tabular iceberg - much worn

Terra Nova passing through bergs, from the deck of Discovery

"Turned out at 7 a.m. with a glorious view ahead of the very fantastic Possession Islands, discovered by Ross. There are nine of them, all sorts of shapes, of columnar basalt like Giant's Causeway. All the forenoon and afternoon I spent in sketching them." Wed 24 Feb EAW

The Possession Islands.
24 Feb 1904

"Passed through Possession islands, of which I took photos, and also some of large bergs." Wed 24 Feb RWS

Sailing through the Possession Islands

Cape Adare: 24 February - 25 February 1904

Skua

The Southern Cross Hut and Cape Adare from port side of Discovery

"During the day it was discovered that our rudder was badly damaged, the shaft being shattered, - I think I know when it was done, because I heard it crack and splinter at the time, we were going astern from Erebus Glacier on the 19th Feb and ran into a very heavy floe. The Captain decided to anchor in Robertson Bay and ship spare rudder." Wed 24 Feb RWS

"At 5 p.m. we were anchored in Robertson Bay and a boat from the 'Terra Nova' fetched us and landed us on the 'Southern Cross' camp ashore. Ferrar, Bernacchi and self went on shore with Jackson, Elms, Day, Souter and Smith. I took a gun and shot a dozen skuas, 3 or 4 of which were just fledged, learning to fly." Wed 24 Feb EAW

"Wilson brought me off an Adelie Penguin to skin and Ferrar 3 large bars of tool steel which were lying there. About 40 Adelies were brought off for fresh meat. Magnetic observations were taken ashore by Bernacchi, who also took my camera." Wed 24 Feb RWS

"...the new rudder, a 3½ ton one instead of 4 tons, was shipped by 10 p.m. when it was already too dark to work any more and all hands were knocked off to turn to at 6 a.m. We were blessed with a flat calm and beautiful weather or the thing could not have been done." Wed 24 Feb EAW

Discovery (left) and Terra Nova in Robertson Bay, from the beach

"...sketched for 2 hours. It was a bright sunny morning, but rapidly became overcast. We had the whole of the fine Admiralty Range of mountains in sight, Mount Sabine, Minto, Adam, Whewell etc." Thu 25 Feb EAW

Mount Sabine and Admiralty Range, Robertson Bay, from starboard side of Discovery

The Two Sisters, Cape Adare

At Sea: Cape North to the Auckland Islands 26 February - 14 March 1904

Sturge Island, one of the Balleny Islands. 2 Mar 1904

"Caught a snow petrel for Wilson. Have also caught 2 Antarctic petrels." Mon 29 Feb RWS

"Was called 7 a.m. to see one of the Balleny Islands, but all the top was cloud covered. A steep cliffy shore, heavily glaciated, with a steep ice cliff foot extending the whole length, was all one could see." Wed 2 Mar EAW

"We are now between the Balleny islands and the mainland, - a part never successfully negotiated before." Thu 3 Mar RWS

"I reported to the Captain that we only have now 60 tons of coal on board, so at 8.0 P.M. a NW course was set, and we have at last commenced our journey home; or rather to Auckland Islands and thence to New Zealand: It would be foolish to go further from safety with a less amount of coal, - it is little enough as it is." Thu 3 Mar RWS

"Trawled in the evening, and got a good catch of stones, but very few biological specimens." Fri 4 Mar RWS

"Crossed the Antarctic circle just before noon, having over 2 years and 2 months inside it." Sat 5 Mar RWS

Thalassœca antarctica

Balleny Islands. March. 2. 1904

" The Antarctic Petrel "

"A roll of 48° to starboard rather upset things at dinner. There were wonderful crashes. I saw one man's lap receive a bowl of brown sugar, a plate of stewed plums, a glass of port and a cup of coffee." Sun 6 Mar EAW

"We have seen the last Snow Petrel and thank God, the last iceberg." Mon 7 Mar EAW

Snow Petrel

The Auckland Islands: 15 March - 29 March 1904

"Turned out 6.30 a.m. to see the green land. What a rest! And what a beautiful sight! The whole island is clothed with bright green and russet scrub to the water's edge, and what bright yellows and reds and whites and blacks there were on the beach. It was a lovely sight and we all enjoyed it to the full in the sunshine." Tue 15 Mar EAW

"Ah! The sight of the green scrub and the warm breezes carrying shadows over it all as over a wheat field, the joy of the warm air and the novelty of some blue-bottle flies that found their way on board and were soon buzzing round the ward-room. We seemed to have plunged all at once back into life again out of the Antarctic." Tue 15 Mar EAW

NZ government supply station for castaways, Enderby Island (with Dellbridge)

"Anchored in Laurie harbour well up before 9.0 A.M. We were much surprised to find no sign of either of the relief ships, - can only suppose they have been driven to leeward in the general bad weather that has prevailed and will take time to get up again to this longitude." Tue 15 Mar RWS

"I had but little time to note the Sea Lions properly, as I am spending my energies chiefly on the Auckland Island birds." Sat 19 Mar EAW

"There were some calves. One I saw among a group of females as big as a large terrier and of a reddish chestnut colour, very active." Sat 19 Mar EAW

Hooker's Sealions, Enderby Island

The first trees seen for two years

"On the way up in the morning, we saw the 'Terra Nova' come in, - 5 days after us, - but could see no sign of the 'Morning'. On arriving on board we heard from the Enderby Island party that they had seen a ship's light; and surmised it was the 'Morning' waiting outside for day light." Sat 19 Mar RWS

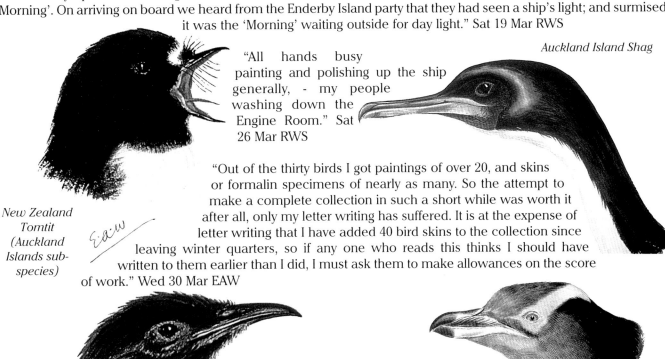

Auckland Island Shag

"All hands busy painting and polishing up the ship generally, - my people washing down the Engine Room." Sat 26 Mar RWS

"Out of the thirty birds I got paintings of over 20, and skins or formalin specimens of nearly as many. So the attempt to make a complete collection in such a short while was worth it after all, only my letter writing has suffered. It is at the expense of letter writing that I have added 40 bird skins to the collection since leaving winter quarters, so if any one who reads this thinks I should have written to them earlier than I did, I must ask them to make allowances on the score of work." Wed 30 Mar EAW

New Zealand Tomtit (Auckland Islands sub-species)

Yellow-eyed Penguin

Auckland Island Teal

Tui

Return to Civilistation: Lyttelton, New Zealand 1 April 1904

L-R: Morning, Discovery and Terra Nova at Lyttelton, New Zealand

"...are this evening right abreast of Akaroa. Last night at midnight we were up to Cape Saunders. We have been rather far out all along to be sighted and signalled, but I rather suspect they have guessed who we are. We ought to be in Lyttelton first thing tomorrow morning." Thu 31 Mar EAW

"'Good Friday', and a good Friday indeed! We were all off the 'Heads' early in the morning - 'Discovery', 'Morning' and 'Terra Nova', when the pilot came out in a tug. I soon saw that Ory was not on board. We were all clean and dressed in white shirts and collars today, the first time for more than two years. We took the pilot on board and went in towards harbour and before long out came a crowded tug to meet us. And there was Ory, looking not a day older than when I left her, and far more beautiful." Fri 1 Apr EAW

Morning dressed overall, Lyttelton

12: The Journey Home and Thereafter
2 April 1904 -1907

Arriving in civilisation was something of a shock. Once the cheering crowds of welcome had faded away, the officers and men of the Expedition were wined, dined and feted by the warm hearted New Zealanders. In turn they held their friends spellbound with tales of the frigid south. It was quite a change after two years of isolation. Reginald Skelton was too busy paying court to Miss Sybil Meares to write a single word in his diary during this period. For Edward Wilson it was time to re-acquaint himself with his wife, Oriana. They escaped the endless round of parties to spend three weeks travelling together in the North Island, taking the honeymoon that they had been unable to have before the Expedition sailed. Other members of the ships' companies were also succumbing to romance, amongst them Isaac Weller and Lt. Evans (of *Morning*) who soon married New Zealanders. The principal aim of the ten week New Zealand visit was not social, however. Expedition funds were now low and so the utmost economy had to be exercised in re-fitting the ships. Much of the work on *Discovery* was done by the crew. The scientists too were busy organising the delivery of their important collections to appropriate museums. Wilson was often to be found working at the Canterbury Museum in Christchurch. Before they could sail, the magnetic work also had to be correlated with the readings from the Christchurch magnetic station. The wild parties and romances were interspersed between long periods of hard work. *Terra Nova* sailed from Lyttelton in mid-May. She had not been hired for scientific work and had little to do beyond refitting. Many of those involved in the Expedition thought that her voyage had been an unnecessary waste of public money. *Morning* and *Discovery* remained for another fortnight, completing their work and becoming caught in a final frenzy of 'farewell' parties. They finally set sail for England on 8 June.

The officers and crew of *Discovery* had little time to re-adapt to shipboard routine; they were soon sailing through the South Pacific in fierce storms. Once the weather had calmed they resumed the steady pace of the outward voyage. Wilson was occupied painting and sorting collections, whilst his eager assistants were trying to catch seabirds. Skelton was busy in the engine room or writing letters to Sybil. On 6 July they sighted the coast of Chile, soon entering the Straits of Magellan. The sharp snow-clad peaks of Tierra del Fuego, fringed by gnarled green trees, formed an impressive backdrop to their passage. *Discovery* dropped anchor in Punta Arenas on 8 July. Most of the officers and crew went ashore. The Expedition was relatively unknown in Chile and their reception was muted. Skelton thought that it was a "good thing" for one or two of his contemporaries to experience. He spent most of his time doing necessary maintenance in the engine room. Wilson had never much enjoyed the lionising and was more than content to wander around in comparative anonymity.

Discovery sailed on 9 July and headed down the Straits towards the Atlantic Ocean, which they entered the following day. They arrived at Port Stanley in the Falkland Islands on 12 July and proceeded to re-coal the ship. They were "expecting wonders" at Port Stanley, according to Wilson, but were to be bitterly disappointed. Port Stanley was a town of "about a hundred shanty huts" and whilst everyone turned out to greet them, arriving there was an anti-climax. The coaling proceeded apace. Wilson and other officers spent a good deal of time ashore adding specimens of wildlife to the Expedition's collections. *Morning* arrived on 17 July, having sailed around Cape Horn; an excited reunion taking place between the ships that night. The men of *Morning* were no more impressed by Port Stanley than the men of *Discovery* had been.

Discovery sailed from the Falklands on 20 July, and tossed her way through the 'roaring forties' of the South Atlantic. They were soon into the tropics, the searing heat having become an almost novel experience. Wilson packed and re-packed his collections. Deck cricket became a popular pastime along with other deck sports, such as wheelbarrow racing and spar fights over sail baths. Seabirds and fish continued to be at risk to scientific collecting. They crossed the line on 13 August. Increasingly thoughts turned to home and what might happen to them after the Expedition. There had been radical reforms in the armed services whilst they had been away. Reginald Skelton, who as a support officer had had no official rank as such, now found himself with the rank of Engineer-Lieutenant RN. They were returning to a changed world from the one that they had left in 1901 for three years of glorious isolation and they could but wonder what it would hold for them. Of additional concern was the amount of coal that was being used in windless conditions and it was finally decided to put into the Azores to take on further supplies. *Discovery* arrived off Delgada on 31 August. In port they also found the oceanographic yacht of the Prince of Monaco, *Princess Alice*. The Prince was a marine scientist of some note and was much interested in the Expedition and its findings. They departed on 2 September.

As they sailed towards home shores, Skelton and Wilson sorted the fixtures and fittings of the ward room for distribution amongst the officers, a naval tradition which ensured a fair share of souvenirs all round. Both men stopped writing their Expedition diaries on 8 September, although Wilson made no entry beyond the date. This was the day that the Bishop's Rock lighthouse was sighted. They were home. On the 9th the southern English coast was in full view as *Discovery* slowly steamed up the channel. She arrived at Portsmouth on 10 September 1904, cheered from every ship and by the huge crowds lined up on the wharves to greet her. Sir Clements Markham was the first to board and welcome them home: it was a proud moment.

A royal aide-de-camp arrived the next morning bearing a message of congratulation from the King. Commander Scott was promoted to the rank of Captain. It was the start of a long social whirl to acknowledge the Expedition's achievements and the bravery of all who had served upon it. A large banquet was hosted by the Mayor and City of Portsmouth. *Discovery* was soon under way, again, however, sailing round to London on 14 September where Shackleton and many of the men's families met the ship. It had been a long separation from friends and loved ones. Here the officers, crew and collections were discharged by the end of the month and the ship was briefly opened to the public before eventually being sold. The feasts, dinners and applause for the Expedition's achievements continued. Scott left for Balmoral on 26 September to report in person to the King, at His Majesty's request. A new medal was struck and awarded to many who had been on the Expedition; the reverse of the new Polar Medal was based on one of Skelton's photographs.

Amidst the invitations and celebrations Skelton and Wilson were still working hard. Being the principal photographer and artist to the Expedition they were asked to arrange the Expedition Exhibition which opened at the Bruton Gallery in London in November 1904. The exhibition was an astonishing success, reaffirming public interest in the National Expedition. Crowds lined up to gain entry to it and it later had a successful tour of many provincial towns. Captain Scott, too, was busy. On 7 November he addressed a packed Royal Albert Hall at the start of a long lecture tour. During the proceedings, Sir Clements Markham and many of the officers and men of *Discovery* and *Morning* were presented with gifts or RGS medals, to acknowledge their important contributions to the success of the Expedition. The 7,000 people packed into the Hall enthusiastically applauded all. As life settled back towards normal routine, however, Wilson and Skelton still received numerous requests for lectures, for lantern slides, or to illustrate books on the Expedition. The *South Polar Times* was published. As did all the scientists, Wilson worked hard on the Expedition Scientific Reports. He also worked with Skelton on publication of an official photograph album. These volumes finally started appearing in 1907 but weren't completed until 1913. It is rarely acknowledged how much work occurs after an Expedition, particularly one where scientific reports need to be published; the post-Expedition work for *Discovery* took some years and considerable effort on the part of those involved.

In addition to work, however, Skelton's life was about to change as a result of his voyage. In early January 1905 a young New Zealand woman stepped off a ship and onto Britain's shores; it was Miss Sybil Meares. Reginald Skelton and Sybil Meares married within a few days of her arrival. Sadly, no photographs of the Expedition photographer's wedding seem to exist.

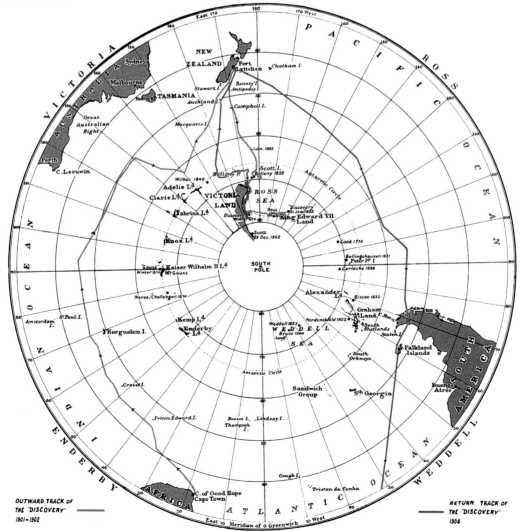

Map showing the outward and return route of Discovery through the Southern Ocean and known Antarctic lands and discoveries. 1904 (based on period map)

New Zealand: 2 April - 8 June 1904

"We saw the most luxuriant bush and forest, tree ferns and Nikau palms, Maori settlements, Maori canoes, long dug-outs, 40 to 50 ft. of one long tree trunk. We saw Maoris' graves, a little enclosure of paling on a mound in the midst of the wildest bush. There were Maori whares and storehouses, built of stake and withy and reed on four posts, which raised the whole thing 4 ft. off the ground. The scarlet Rata in places was flowering and there were a wonderful number of birds. We saw the Maori women washing their clothes in the river, kneeding them on an old tree trunk." Thu 5 May EAW

Crow's nest Geyser, Taupo. May 1904

Carved Maori building

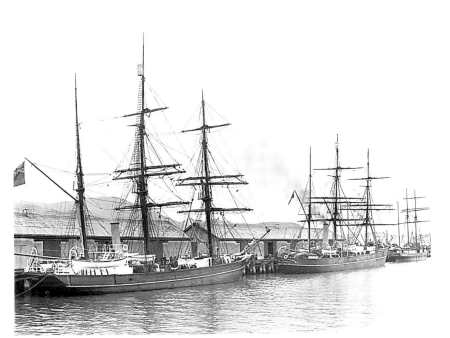

"Preparations in town for a dance we are giving to the people of Christchurch. Decorating the supper room. Ory and Morrison of the 'Morning' were given charge, and the decoration was voted an unqualified success and the room really looked very pretty indeed. The dance was in every way a grand success. Captain Scott and Ory received for the 'Discovery', Captain Colbeck and Mrs Evans received for the 'Morning'. There were 350 guests, and the dance finished up at 4 a.m." Wed 1 Jun EAW

"Big farewell dinner to 'Discovery' and 'Morning' at Coker's. We all had to speak." Fri 3 Jun EAW

"Left Lyttelton at 2 P.M. with SV 'Morning', - parted company outside the harbour." Wed 8 Jun RWS

Farewell dinner menu, Coker's Hotel. 3 Jun 1904

L-R: Morning and Discovery at Lyttelton, New Zealand

"We had a sou'westerly buster in the night and things were flying around everywhere. The ward-room was flooded, everything broke adrift that could do so, even the old pianola. For four or five hours there was pandemonium." Thu 9 Jun EAW

At Sea: South America and the Falkland Islands
9 June - 19 July 1904

"Opened Shackleton's box of gear for the Ward Room which should have come South by the relief ships; my packet contained 1 box cigarettes, sweets, Victorian mints, sardines. Got the pianola to work in the evening, - It has been repaired in Christchurch." Fri 10 Jun RWS

Wandering Albatross

"We changed our day, as we are on the 180th. meridian. Ory starts for home today." Sat 11 Jun EAW

"We have many great grey shearwaters following us, several Wandering Albatross and a Giant Petrel. Also Lesson's, Cape Pigeon and a Sooty Albatross." Sun 12 Jun EAW

"We have today come through the 'Narrows', and seen some splendid scenery. Nearly all day we have been steaming at six or seven knots along a channel averaging in breadth about three miles. Range on range of snow-covered glaciated mountain appeared on either side, and rising to meet them from the water was the same kind of rocky, brush spattered, snow-flecked foot-hill that we had on each side of us all yesterday." Thu 7 Jul EAW

In the Straits of Magellan

"Left the ship directly after breakfast with Ferrar and went for a long walk over the hills and back by the coast along the shore by the lighthouse. We got back to the ship by 5.30 p.m., pretty well tired. We saw a good many birds and got two Ringed Dotterels out of a flock. Ferrar knocked them over with his geological hammer. We got skulls and other bones and two complete skeletons of Steamer Ducks, cormorants, a penguin etc." Thu 14 Jul EAW

"...anchored off Port Stanley...went ashore before lunch to the Naval works to enquire about coal.- This place seems a pretty godforsaken place."
Tue 12 Jul RWS

Falkland Island Steamer Duck

Sunset, Southern Ocean

- 141 -

At Sea: 20 July - 17 August 1904

In the tropics: officers and scientists on deck.
L-R standing: Hodgson, Royds, Ferrar,
Wilson, Mulock, Armitage;
sitting: Scott, Skelton, Koettlitz, Barne and Bernacchi

"...we ought to be under sail alone now, - so we may have to coal at the Azores." Fri 29 Jul RWS

"Cricket after tea - sent 2 balls overboard." Wed 3 Aug RWS

"Very hot today; - wearing flannels, - everybody in different rigs, - anything for comfort and coolness." Thu 4 Aug RWS

"Photos taken of us [after church], as most of us were in clean ducks." Sun 7 Aug EAW

"We have now 150 tons of coal aboard, - will it be enough for the rest of the passage? - that is the question - we have come half way on say 100 or 110 tons of coal, and have half as much again for the remainder of the passage, - but this half of the passage is not going to be such a fair one, so that the coal will probably be a close thing." Sun 14 Aug RWS

"A steamer sighted in the evening." Mon 15 Aug RWS

Charles Royds, on the bridge of Discovery

Unidentified steam liner

In the tropics: the mess deck

At Sea to the Azores: 18 August - 2 September 1904

Sunset at sea

"Worked at arranging the fair division of the library, crockery, pantry gear and other things of the mess between the officers. Skelton and I were chosen to do this, by a general ballot. This appropriation of everything seems queer, but is apparently the usual rule at the end of a ship's commission." Fri 26 Aug EAW

"Just after dinner a large school of porpoises came up and continued to sport about under the bows. - Weller got a harpoon ready but only got in one shot before they went away that missed." Thu 18 Aug RWS

"The churches here of course are Roman Catholic, but I found only one open, funnily enough, and that struck me as being large and bare compared with continental churches. St Piedro's church this was, the largest I think, close to a triple archway near the landing place of the harbour." Thu 1 Sep EAW

A school of porpoises

"The Prince of Monaco's yacht 'Princess Alice' came in about midday, - She looked very smart. - Captain Carr, the Skipper and ADC to The Prince came aboard us to try and find our Skipper and also to say the Prince would like to come aboard. In the afternoon 5 or 6 scientists came aboard from the yacht. - they are at present busy doing this part of the Atlantic, - apparently all their scientific arrangements on board are most perfect. The Prince himself is a very notable biologist and is also interested in several other sciences. In the evening 7 of our people went aboard to dinner. The Skipper took my photographs." Thu 1 Sep RWS

St. Pedro's Church, Delgada, Azores. 1 Sep 1904

St. Michael's Church, Azores. 2 Sep 1904

Arrival Home: September 1904

"Finished up all the distribution of books etc. at a meeting after tea. Captain spoke of many things to us. One was about the names of new bits of land...[he] told me my name was being given to Cape I, the fine southernmost cape we ran against on the southern journey. He spoke also of a general present to Sir Clements Markham, from the ship." Wed 7 Sep EAW

Discovery arriving into Portsmouth. 10 Sep 1904

"The Skipper spoke about giving Sir Clements Markham a present from the ship. - also payment of servants, payment of wine bills, naming of geographical places discovered south and provisional disposal of mess property." Thu 8 Sep RWS

"Sighted flash of Bishop's rock in first watch." Thu 8 Sep RWS

Cross and Husky arrived in London. 16 Sep 1904

Officers, scientists and crew of the Discovery on arrival in London. 15/16 Sep 1904
L-R back: Private Blissett, PO Allan, AB Wild, AB Croucher, PO Kennar, AB Handsley, Lg Stoker Lashly, AB Crean, AB Dell, PO Evans, Stoker Plumley, Clarke (cook), AB Weller;
L-R middle: (three unidentified figures on far left) Lg Seaman Pilbeam, AB Joyce, AB Williamson, AB Heald, PO Cross, PO Smythe, Private Scott;
L-R front: Ch. Steward Ford, PO Feather, Lt. Armitage, Lt. Mulock, Lt. Shackleton, Dr Wilson, Ch. Eng Skelton, Capt Scott, Lt. Royds, Dr Koettlitz, Bernacchi, Ferrar, Hodgson, ERA Dellbridge, Carpenter Dailey

Arrival Home: The Social Whirl 1904 - 1905

Cakes for Edward Wilson's 'at home' reception on return to Cheltenham. 26 Sep 1904

"At a meeting of the Norwich Council of the Mayor, Aldermen, and Citizens of the City of Norwich, held on the seventeenth day of January one thousand nine hundred and five

Resolved on the report and recommendation of the Castle Museum Committee, that the thanks of the Council be given to Engineer Lieutenant R W Skelton R.N. for an adult female and 'chick' of the Emperor penguin, and other valuable birds' skins collected by him during the voyage of the 'Discovery' to the Antarctic Regions, and that the congratulations of the Council be offered him on the occasion of his Marriage.
By the Council
[signed]
Arnold H Miller Town Clerk"

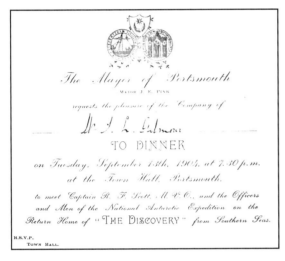

Invitation to the Mayor of Portsmouth's dinner reception. 13 Sep 1904

Invitation to Windsor Castle. 14 Jun 1905

Savage Club Welcome home dinner menu. 5 Nov 1904

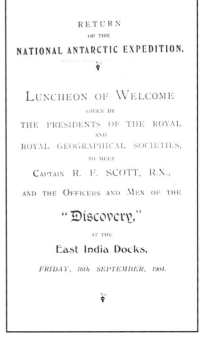

Luncheon of Welcome menu, London. 16 Sep 1904

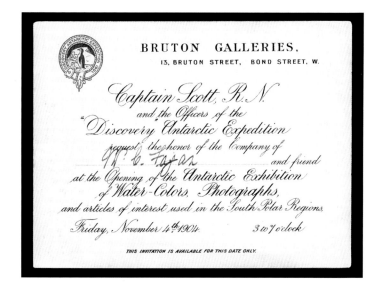

Invitation and advertisement flyers to the opening of the Expedition exhibition at the Bruton Street Galleries in London. Nov 1904

"DISCOVERY"
ANTARCTIC
EXHIBITION

(By kind permission of Sir Clements Markham, K.C.B., and Captain Scott, R.N.)

WILL OPEN AT THE

Bruton Galleries

13, BRUTON STREET, BOND STREET, W.

ON FRIDAY,
NOVEMBER 4th, 1904.

AND WILL INCLUDE

WATER COLOR SKETCHES
and COLORED DRAWINGS by

Dr. Edward A. Wilson,

AND

PHOTOGRAPHS taken by

Lieut.-Engr. Skelton, R.N.

A Model of "THE DISCOVERY"

KAYAKS,

SNOWSHOES,

SLEDGE FLAGS,

AND OTHER ARTICLES OF INTEREST
USED IN THE SOUTH POLAR REGIONS.

The EXHIBITION will be on view daily, 10 to 6
(including Saturdays).

The Bruton Galleries, 13, Bruton Street, Bond Street, W.

Discovery in the pack ice: Wilson's frontispiece for Scott's 'The Voyage of the Discovery' 1905

The world's first photograph of an Emperor Penguin chick, taken by Skelton. Photographs such as these had an enormous public impact upon being shown in the exhibition

"I am still lecturing here and there for what shekels I can get, and doing much painting and drawing for two books on the Antarctic - as well as writing myself and illustrating the first volume of the museum publication, a large quarto." EAW, letter to John Fraser, 9 May 1905

Discovery in Winter quarters 1904. Wilson spent many months painting water colour orders from the exhibition, based on his Expedition paintings and sketches

Weddell Seal and pup, proof plate

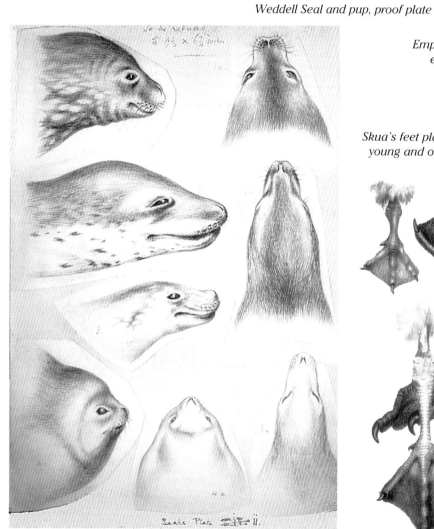

Seal heads, preparatory plate

Emperor Penguin eggs, plate

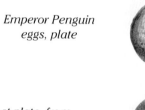

Skua's feet plate, from young and old birds

13: Epilogue
One Hundred Years On 1901-2001

The British National Antarctic Expedition of 1901-1904 achieved considerable advances in the field of Antarctic exploration and scientific knowledge: it discovered the Polar Plateau, hundreds of miles of new coastline and amassed large collections of scientific specimens and data. Along with the important geological specimens collected by Ferrar and Barne were the geographical discoveries of the Western, Southern and South-western parties: all provided convincing evidence of the existence of an Antarctic continent. The magnetic work carried out during the course of the Expedition by Armitage, Barne, Bernacchi and Scott, permitted the location of the South Magnetic Pole to be determined; as a part of the first major international scientific programme to be carried out in Antarctica, this data also contributed greatly to new maps of magnetism for the Southern Hemisphere, so vital to the navigation of shipping in the southern seas. The primary aims of the Expedition were therefore met; in carrying them out, the first major exploratory sledge journeys to penetrate towards the heart of Antarctica were made. Other important results were also obtained. The meteorological data collected by Royds, Koettlitz, Wilson and others, uncovered the existence of the 'coreless' Antarctic winter, one of the great keys to Southern Hemisphere weather patterns. Although this data was at first publicly criticised by the Meteorological office it was later forced to retract much of its criticism when it was shown to be in error. The Expedition also determined the nature of the Great Ice Barrier and showed that it was afloat, a question that had caused considerable puzzlement to many scientists. Scientific knowledge of the wildlife of the southern region of our planet was also augmented by Hodgson and Wilson: new species were found and others studied in greater depth. The discovery of the first breeding colony of Emperor Penguins and the commencement of the unravelling of its remarkable breeding cycle was of particular note.

Nevertheless, a mere one hundred years after the Expedition its achievements have, perhaps inevitably, become obscured by the layering of time. In part, this is the fault of those academic historians and journalists who, in recent decades at least, seem more interested in psychological profiles and other mixtures of mischief than in human achievement. In part it is due to the fact that with this Expedition the Heroic Age of Antarctic exploration is set alight in the popular imagination. It launched many of the big names of the Age from Scott and Shackleton to Wilson, Evans, Wild, Joyce, Lashly and Crean, who in turn launched names like Mawson, Worsley, Priestley, and Cherry-Garrard through their further Antarctic work. This Expedition is thus the foundation stone of many of our modern epic tales which still exert a hold on the public imagination. Yet it is the very nature of the great epics that they overshadow that which preceded them and there is no doubt that the achievements of *Discovery* seem to pale beside the dramatic stories of the so called 'Race to the Pole' which followed (among which it is often mistakenly included), or the monumental failure of Shackleton's Trans-Antarctic Expedition with its near miraculous tale of rescue. Nevertheless, the scientific and geographical accomplishments of the National Expedition were solid ones and underlie important and subtle influences in our everyday lives. Of the many hundreds of thousands of fans of penguins, for example, who now remembers the men that helped to unravel their mysteries and brought them to the public eye? Or the sufferings and hardships that they underwent to do so? And yet these achievements bring a great deal of pleasure to many. Less commonly recognised is the fact that many of the officers and men of *Discovery* went on to long and glittering careers in public service, rather than exploration, the Expedition having been the very training ground for the brightest and best of the British Navy that Sir Clements Markham had hoped. Through these men and their achievements the Expedition became a force for incalculable good. Of the officers, no less than four were eventually knighted (Royds, Shackleton, Skelton and Scott [posthumously]), and many of the men and officers amassed large collections of other public honours. Many of the scientists too, went on to contribute greatly to the sum of our human knowledge.

There has, however, been a new and exciting twist to the story in recent years, which would delight those who sailed in *Discovery*. The British National Antarctic Expedition gripped the public imagination one hundred years ago, just as the space age expeditions would grip our modern era nearly 70 years later. Some have drawn parallels between the two but there are important differences. When humans finally set out for Mars they will know more about where they are going than the men who sailed for the Southern portion of our planet one hundred years ago. They will also have faster communications to the rest of the world, a time lag of never more than mere hours, as compared to a minimum of one year for the men of *Discovery*. What still holds true (and even here certain things, such as computer software malfunctions, can probably be corrected from central control) is the fact that if anything were to go badly wrong no one on Earth could do much to help. It is hard to see how the two eras of exploration truly have much in common, except for their grip on the public consciousness. Nevertheless, when the National Aeronautical and Space Administration of the United States chose to name one of its Space Shuttles *Discovery*, they deliberately selected a name with a long and illustrious association with vessels of scientific exploration. It brought the historic name straight into the modern era. Nor do such associations between space and things polar end with the name. Considerable quantities of data relating to the nature of Antarctica have been collected from the space programme whilst Antarctica itself helps to contribute to the continued expansion of space exploration. NASA uses the Antarctic to test some types of new equipment and on this level at least the continued scientific and exploration work there has become intricately intertwined with the continued scientific and exploration work in space. Sir Clements Markham would laugh.

Despite, or perhaps because of, these complexities of historical layering, the centenary of *Discovery* is generating a new interest in both the ship and in the British National Antarctic Expedition itself. The stories and accomplishments of the Expedition are of such interest in and of themselves that they are increasingly being retold. Scott's historic ship *Discovery* lies today in the port of Dundee, close to where she was built and launched one hundred years ago. *Discovery* had a long and illustrious career in both the Arctic and Antarctic after the National Antarctic Expedition and some modifications were made, particularly for Mawson's B.A.N.Z.A.R.E Expedition (1929-31). Nevertheless, she would still be instantly recognisable to Scott and his companions. *Discovery* finally returned to Dundee in 1986 providing a renaissance for the ship, its stories and for the city. She is now the core of one of the most important Polar Museums in the world, which continues to tell the tale of the historic ship and her expeditions to delighted visitors. She has also increasingly become a focal point for the descendants of members of the Expedition, keen to share their family stories with the general public. August 2001 saw a large gathering of descendants at the ship for the centenary of the Expedition's sailing. The ongoing restoration and maintenance costs on the historic ship are unfortunately considerable but amongst other innovative fundraising ideas is the provision of fine dining (by reservation only) in the ward room. Although modern menus do not permit the inclusion of seal or penguin steaks, it is a deeply evocative way to spend an evening.

Other British museums also have fine collections of material from the British National Antarctic Expedition on display to the public and so continue to tell the story of the Expedition and its accomplishments. The Scott Polar Research Institute in Cambridge is amongst the world's top polar archives and has a small museum which includes material from the Expedition. The Cheltenham Art Gallery and Museum has a display relating to Edward Wilson (who was a native of the town) which includes *Discovery* material. Further afield, the Canterbury Museum in Christchurch, New Zealand, with its historic links to the Expedition, also has a fine collection of material on public display. Further even than this, are the Antarctic sites themselves. The Ross Sea and McMurdo Sound are increasingly a destination for cruise ship tourists who wish to visit the historic sites connected with Captain Scott or Sir Ernest Shackleton. The huts which remain, including 'Professor Gregory's Villa' at Hut Point, perhaps contain the best of all the collections of historic material. These are conserved today by the Antarctic Heritage Trust and the New Zealand Government. The increasing number of visitors is starting to cause extra conservation difficulties but, at the same time, the visitors help to pay for the preservation of these great historic monuments. As with many of the decisions on the original expeditions themselves, it is a difficult balance. So also is the fact that Winter Quarters Bay itself has now largely been overtaken by the metropolis that is the United States' McMurdo Station, controversially blighting many historic views but at the same time providing remarkable facilities to scientists. The exploration of Antarctica has always excited controversy and no doubt will continue to do so for many more years to come.

For as long as there are human beings interested in the history of exploration, it seems likely that those who sailed on the British National Antarctic Expedition 1901-1904 will be remembered. Some have specific memorials: statues and stained glass windows to commemorate their achievements. Many have features named for them on the Antarctic landscape that they were the first to explore; some do not. It is, however, the ability of their story to inspire the lives of others which has, perhaps, been their greatest legacy. They were human beings, like all of us, and rose to the challenge of difficult circumstance to achieve much for the greater good. One hundred years on, it is right that we remember and salute them all: the dogs, the men and the officers of the ships *Discovery*, *Morning* and *Terra Nova*.

One Hundred Years on: *Discovery* Today

During an Expedition centenary dinner in the Ward room of Discovery, David Wilson and Judy Skelton enjoy a glass of Dewar's whisky, just as their ancestors had done one hundred years before. The Ward room is still frequently used for such purposes

Today, *Discovery* is open to the public at Dundee in Scotland where it is looked after by the Dundee Heritage Trust. Many 'Expedition families' maintain their links with the famous ship on which their forebears sailed, particuarly in her centenary year.

Discovery anchored at Discovery Point, Dundee, the floating platform is used for maintenance and restoration work

Aboard Discovery at Dundee. The heads (or toilet blocks) are no longer in their original position, having been moved during refits for subsequent exploration work

Discovery anchored at Discovery Point, Dundee

One Hundred Years on: Continuing to Tell the Story

A hip flask donated by Reginald Skelton; on display at Discovery Point, Dundee

Edward Wilson's Officer's furs, an ice axe and snow shoes, donated by the Wilson family, with an Adelie Penguin, donated by the Dell family; on display at the Cheltenham Art Gallery and Museum

Several British Museums have fine collections of material relating to the British National Antarctic Expedition 1901-1904, much of which is on public display. Such exhibitions continue to tell the story of the Expedition's remarkable achievements.

A rum barrel, or grog tub, donated by the Wilson family; on display at Discovery Point, Dundee

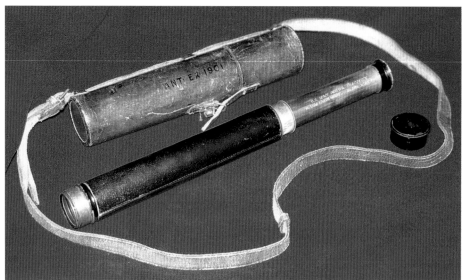

A telescope that displays the continuing inheritance of the name Discovery as a name for vessels of exploration is on display at the Scott Polar Research Institute, Cambridge. First used by Nares aboard his ships Alert and Discovery on the British Arctic expedition (1875-76), the telescope was then used by Scott aboard the new ship Discovery during the British National Antarctic Expedition 1901-1904, it was then also taken aboard the United States Space Shuttle Discovery in 1984. The case is inscribed 'Ant: Ex: 1901' and the telescope inscribed 'U.S. Space Orbiter Discovery 96 low earth orbits 30 Aug. - 5 Sep. 1984'

One Hundred Years on: the Ross Sea and McMurdo Sound

View over the Great Ice Barrier, now known as the Ross Ice Shelf, looking through the drifting snow towards Mount Terror and Ross Island

The Ross Sea and McMurdo Sound region of Antarctica would still be recognisable to the participants of the Expedition one hundred years on. What for them was a challenging voyage towards isolated exploration of the unknown is, however, increasingly a destination for cruise ship tourists today.

Mount Erebus from McMurdo Sound

Looking across the Sea Ice to the Western Mountains, now the Royal Society Range of the Trans-Antarctic Mountains, McMurdo Sound

One Hundred Years on: Hut Point and Winter Quarters Bay

Looking across Hut Point (where Professor Gregory's Villa is just visible) towards Crater Heights, the Gap and Observation Hill

Looking towards Professor Gregory's Villa, the Ski Slopes and Crater Hill from Hut Point

The last remaining Expedition Hut, Professor Gregory's Villa still standing 100 years on

A century later, the familiar landmarks of the Expedition's winter quarters, whilst still recognisable, have been overwhelmed by the urban sprawl of the United States' McMurdo Bay Station. Whilst providing research facilities that would have been the envy of *Discovery* scientists, the environmental consequences of such large scale occupation have been questioned by many. The historic site around the hut itself is maintained by the New Zealand Government and the Antarctic Heritage Trust.

The memorial cross to AB Vince, Hut Point

The remains of stores in Professor Gregory's Villa. Used by many subsequent expeditions, the hut is a popular visitor site - but the condensing fog of visitor's breath on artefacts is of concern to conservators

One Hundred Years on: *Discovery* Enters the Space Age

The Aurora Australis viewed from space aboard the space shuttle Discovery, during mission STS-39. May 1991

The name *Discovery* continues to be associated with vehicles of scientific and geographical exploration. When the United States' National Aeronautical and Space Administration named one of their space shuttles *Discovery*, they continued a centuries old tradition. The Space Shuttle *Discovery* first flew in August 1984. Many new aspects of Antarctic science have been uncovered by the space programme and McMurdo station is often the base used for the Antarctic field trial programmes of future space-bound equipment. Antarctic environments are thought to be the closest earth-bound conditions to those on some moons and planets.

The space shuttle Discovery blasts off on mission STS-70. 13 Jul 1995

The space shuttle Discovery blasts off on mission STS-26. 28 Sep 1988

One Hundred Years on: the Men of *Discovery* Remembered

The Skelton Glacier flows down the valley that opens on to the Ross Ice Shelf through Skelton Inlet. Many of the geographical features of the Ross Sea region stand as landmarks to the participants of the British National Antarctic Expedition 1901-1904

The memorial window to Admiral Sir Reginald Skelton R.N. in Aldingbourne Church, W. Sussex

One of the many statues of Captain Scott stands in Christchurch, New Zealand

The statue of Dr Edward A. Wilson FZS which stands on the promenade in his native town of Cheltenham

Wilson

Discovery Ship's Company when She Sailed from New Zealand for the Antarctic on 24 December 1901

Skelton

Ward Room

Officers		Scientists	
A B Armitage 'The Pilot'	Lt MM	L C Bernacchi 'Bunny'	Physicist
M Barne 'Mr Frostbites'	Lt RN	H T Ferrar 'Our Junior Scientist'	Geologist
C W R Royds 'Our Charlie'	Lt RN	T V Hodgson 'Muggins'	Biologist
R F Scott 'The Skipper'	Cdr RN	R Koettlitz 'Cutlets'	Surgeon/Botanist
E H Shackleton* 'Shackles'	Lt MM	E A Wilson 'Billy'	Surgeon/Zoologist/Artist
R W Skelton 'Skelly'	Ch Eng RN		

G F A Mulock, Lt RN, transferred from *Morning* to *Discovery* in March 1903 to replace Shackleton in the Ward Room

Warrant Officer's Mess

F E Dailey	Carpenter RN	J H Dellbridge	2nd Engineer RN
T A Feather	PO 1cl RN (Bosun)	C R Ford	Chief Steward RN

Mess Deck

D S Allan	PO 1cl RN	Thomas Kennar	PO 2cl RN
A H Blissett	Pte Royal Marines	William Lashly	Lg Stoker 1cl RN
H Brett**	Cook	W Macfarlane*	PO 1cl RN
H Buckridge**	Lab Asst	W Page**	Stoker RN
C Clarke	Cook	W Peters**	AB RN
T Crean	AB RN	A Pilbeam	Lg Seaman RN
J Cross	PO 1cl RN	F Plumley	Stoker RN
G B Croucher	AB RN	A L Quartley	Lg Stoker 1cl RN
J W Dell	AB RN	G Scott	Pte Royal Marines
J Duncan**	AB MM	W Smythe	PO 1cl RN
E Evans	PO 2cl RN	G T Vince+	AB RN
J Handsley	AB RN	J D Walker**	AB MM
C H Hare**	Steward	W I Weller	AB MM
W L Heald	AB RN	T Whitfield	Lg Stoker 1cl RN
W Hubert**	Donkeyman MM	J R F Wild	AB RN
E E M Joyce	AB RN	T S Williamson	AB RN

Abbreviations:

AB	Able Seaman	MM	Merchant Marine
Cdr	Commander	PO	Petty Officer
Lg	Leading	Pte	Private
Lt	Lieutenant	RN	Royal Navy

*   Invalided home with *Morning* in March 1903

**   Returned to New Zealand with *Morning* in March 1903

\+   Died at Danger Slopes during a blizzard in March 1902 while returning from spring sledging attempt to reach Cape Crozier. A cross was erected at Hut Point in his memory just before *Discovery's* departure from Winter Quarters in February 1904. (See Chs 5 & 11)

Select Bibliography and Further Recommended Reading

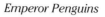

Emperor Penguins

ARMITAGE, A.B.   *Two Years in the Antarctic* London, Edward Arnold, 1905

BERNACCHI, L.C.   *Saga of the 'Discovery'* London, Blackie and Son, 1938

BRITISH NATIONAL ANTARCTIC
EXPEDITION 1901 - 1904   *The South Polar Times* London, Smith, Elder and Co. 1907

DOORLY, G.S.   *The Voyages of the 'Morning'* London, Smith Elder & Co., 1916
The Songs of the 'Morning' Melbourne, Bread and Cheese Club, 1943

HUXLEY, E.   *Scott of the Antarctic* London, Weidenfeld & Nicolson, 1977

MARKHAM, A.H.   *The Life of Sir Clements Markham* London, Smith Elder & Co., 1917

MARKHAM, C.M.   *Lands of Silence* Cambridge, Cambridge University Press, 1921
Antarctic Obsession (Ed. C. Holland) Huntingdon, Bluntisham Books, 1986

SAVOURS, A.   *The Voyages of the 'Discovery': The Illustrated History of Scott's Ship*
London, Virgin Publishing Ltd, 1994

SCOTT, R.F.   *The Voyage of the 'Discovery'* Vols I & II. London, Smith Elder & Co., 1905

SEAVER, G.   *Edward Wilson of the Antarctic, Naturalist and Friend* London,
John Murray, 1933
Edward Wilson, Nature Lover London, John Murray, 1937
The Faith of Edward Wilson London, John Murray, 1948

WILSON, D.M. & ELDER, D.B.   *Cheltenham in Antarctica: The Life of Edward Wilson* Cheltenham,
Reardon Publishing, 2000

WILSON, E.A.   *Edward Wilson Diary of the Discovery Expedition* (Ed. A. Savours)
London, Blandford Press, 1966

YELVERTON, D.E.   *Antarctica Unveiled: Scott's First Expedition and the Quest for the Unknown
Continent* Boulder, University Press of Colorado, 2000

Discovery in Winter Quarters

Arrival Heights   Ski slopes   Crater Hill   Crater Heights   The Gap   Observation Hill   Cape Armitage

Arrival Bay   Hut Point   Scientific study huts   Professor Gregory's Villa   Discovery   Winter Quarters Bay

List of Illustrations and Copyright Acknowledgements

Frontispieces.

- E.A.Wilson. Wandering Albatross Sketches. Field Sketch Book. *Discovery* 1901. (c) SPRI 1636
- E.A.Wilson. The toboggan race. *South Polar Times*, April 1903. (c) DHT

- E.A.Wilson. Skis. c1905 (c) SPRI Box 52
- E.A.Wilson. Polar hieroglyphs. *South Polar Times, Aug 1903.* (c) DHT
- E.A.Wilson. Emperor Penguin, Pack Ice, Roff Sea. Jan 1902. (c) SPRI 1479

- D.M.Wilson. *Discovery* Expedition Crest in centenary motif. (c) D.M.Wilson
- E.A.Wilson. The Flags of the SS *Discovery. South Polar Times,* Aug 1902. (c) DHT

- C.R.Ford. Stern View of *Discovery* after the first winter. Nov 1902. [Fo182]. (c) SPRI LS2000-42-40

"Fortitudine Vincimus"
E.H. Shackleton

Preface

- M.Barne. 'Skelly', cartoon of Ch. Eng. Reginald Skelton. *South Polar Times*, Aug 1902. (c) DHT
- M.Barne. 'Billy', cartoon of Dr Edward A. Wilson. *South Polar Times*, Aug 1902. (c) DHT

Chapter One: Introduction

- George Henry ARA. Sir Clements Markham, President of the Royal Geographical Society. (c) Royal Geographical Society

- Map showing the proposed routes of the European Antarctic Expeditions with projected geographical features of an Antarctic continent. From a paper given to the Cheltenham Natural Science Society by Dr E.T.Wilson, (father of Dr Edward A. Wilson) 1901/02. (c) CAGM 1990.550.173

- The Dundee Shipbuilders Company Ltd. Advertisement from the Bruton Gallery Catalogue 1904. (c) DHT

Chapter Two: Expedition Preparations

- Photographer unknown. Ch. Eng. Reginald Skelton RN Photographic Portrait. (c) SPRI P58/77/25
- Photographer unknown. Dr Edward A. Wilson FZS. Photographic Portrait. (c) CAGM 1995.550.195

- Photographer unknown. SS *Discovery*. View of Stern, Keel and After Frame being worked. Panmure Shipyard, Dundee. (c) SPRI P58/77/12/02
- Photographer unknown. SS *Discovery*. View of Stern with part of the outer planking worked. Panmure Shipyard, Dundee. (c) SPRI P58/77/12/05
- Photographer unknown. SS *Discovery*. View of the Fore-end with outer planking completed. Panmure Shipyard, Dundee. (c) SPRI P58/77/12/08

- Photographer unknown. The naming of the SS *Discovery* by Lady Markham. 21 Mar 1901. Dundee. (c) SPRI P58/77/12/11
- Photographer unknown. *Discovery* glides towards the Tay, Dundee. 21 Mar 1901. (c) SPRI P58/77/12/14
- R.W.Skelton (prob). Safely launched. *Discovery*, on the Tay at Dundee. 21 Mar 1901. (c) SPRI P58/77/12/18

- R.W.Skelton (prob). *Discovery*, not long after launching, at the Quayside in Dundee. Mar 1901. (c) SPRI P58/77/12/19
- R.W.Skelton (prob). The boilers being lowered into *Discovery*. Mar 1901. (c) SPRI P58/77/12/25
- E.A.Wilson. Discovery's Trial Trip. *South Polar Times*, Jun 1903. (c) DHT
- C.W.Royds. Armitage at the compass during *Discovery's* trip from Dundee to London, 3-5 Jun 1901. Cdr Scott and Sir Clements Markham may be seen in the background with an unidentified third figure, possibly George Murray. [R3]. (c) SPRI P83/6/1.1

- E.A.Wilson. *Report on the Collections of Natural History made in the Antarctic Regions during the Voyage of the Southern Cross.* Seal Plate II. Weddell Seal. (c) Private
- E.A.Wilson. *Report on the Collections of Natural History made in the Antarctic Regions during the Voyage of the Southern Cross.* Seals, opening text. (c) Private
- E.T.Wilson. (prob.) Dr and Mrs Edward Wilson on their wedding day. L-R: Miss Polly Wilson, Dr E.A.Wilson, Mrs Oriana Wilson, Miss Constance Souper. (c) CAGM 1990.550.186
- E.T.Wilson. Edward Wilson Trying on Officers' furs for the forthcoming expedition in the garden at Westal, Cheltenham. (c) CAGM 1990.550.186

- Pass for a visit to view *Discovery* whilst berthed at the East India Docks, London. (c) SPRI BNAE MS366/17/ER.
- E.T.Wilson (prob). Ford (?), the Chief Steward, working below decks with two u/d men. (c) CAGM 1990.550.186
- Savage Club Farewell Dinner Menu for the Officers of *Discovery*. 6 Jul 1901. (c) SPRI BNAE MS366/17/ER. p22
- Photographer unknown. Officers and Scientific Staff of the SS *Discovery*. 17 Jul 1901. L-R rear: Dr E.A.Wilson; W.Shackleton; Lt. M.Barne; Cyril Longhurst (Expedition Secretary); Lt. E.H.Shackleton; Ch. Eng. R.W.Skelton; T.V.Hodgson; Dr R.Koettlitz. L-R front: George Murray; Cdr R.F.Scott; Lt. A.B.Armitage; Lt. C.W.Royds. (c) SPRI P58/77/12 p26 - Note: W.Shackleton did not, in the end, sail with the Expedition.
- C.W.Royds. *Discovery* being cheered by the Worcester on her way down the Thames. [R4]. (c) SPRI P83/6/1.3 p38
- C.R.Ford. *Discovery* Leaving London. *South Polar Times*, Aug 1902. (c) DHT

- S.Begg, for the *Illustrated London News.* Cdr Scott is presented by Sir Clements Markham to King Edward VII, accompanied by Queen Alexandra and the Princess Victoria. (c) *Illustrated London News* Library.
- C.W.Royds. After the King's departure. L-R: Dr Wilson; Ch. Eng. Skelton; Lt Shackleton; Dr Koettlitz; Cdr Scott (Wearing the Royal Victorian Order presented by the King); u/d lady (possibly Lady Markham); Sir Leopold McClintock; Admiral Markham (behind); Mr Llewellyn Longstaff. [R6]. (c) SPRI LS2000-42-211
- G.M.Burn. The Departure of *Discovery* from Cowes. 6 Aug 1901. The Royal Yacht, *Osborne* is shown flying the Royal Standard to the port side of *Discovery* with the Royal Party on deck watching the departing ship. The Royal Yacht *Victoria* and *Albert* is shown astern. Many other prestigious yachts were also present for the Cowes Week Regatta of the Royal London Yacht Club. (c) Dulwich College, London.
- E.A.Wilson. Alum Bay, the Isle Of Wight, from *Discovery*. 6 Aug 1901. (c) SPRI MS232/1 p27

- E.A.Wilson. The Bishop of London's prayer and presentation. *South Polar Times,* Jun 1902. (c) DHT

Chapter Three: The Voyage Out

- D.M.Wilson. Map showing the approximate outward route of *Discovery* from Britain to New Zealand, 1901. (c) D.M.Wilson

- E.A.Wilson. Spanish Bonito fishing boat. Bay of Biscay. 9 Aug 1901. (c) SPRI MS232/1
- E.A.Wilson. Seascape. Undated. (c) Cheltenham College
- E.H.Shackleton. Group of Officers on the bridge. L-R: Skelton; Ferrar; Armitage; Barne (holding Scamp); Wilson. [Sh02]. (c) CAGM 1995.550.186

- E.A.Wilson. His cabin. (c) CAGM 1995.550.35b
- E.H.Shackleton. "Our Wine Caterer"; Wilson. [Sh03]. (c) CAGM 1995.550.186
- E.A.Wilson. Sketch of Cdr Scott. (c) SPRI 1331

- E.A.Wilson. *Discovery* at Funchal, Madeira. (c) SPRI MS232/1p17
- E.A.Wilson. The Barracks Square, Madeira. 16 Aug 1901. (c) SPRI MS232/1 p39
- E.A.Wilson. Bridge and street scene, Madeira. 16 Aug 1901 (detail). (c) SPRI MS232/1 p42
- E.A.Wilson. Bullock Cart, Madeira. 16 Aug 1901. (c) SPRI MS232/1 p42

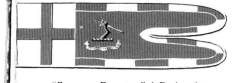

"*Semper Paratus*" A.B. Armitage

- E.A.Wilson. Small school of whales seen on this day: 22 Aug 1901. (c) SPRI MS232/1 p55
- E.A.Wilson. Sunset. 28 Aug 1901. (c) SPRI MS232/1 p57
- E.A.Wilson. Crossing the line, sketches of Neptune's Court. (c) SPRI BNAE MS 366/17ER p8
- C.W.Royds. Neptune's Court. Neptune (Allan); Queen (Mardon); and Tritons (Macfarlane, Pilbeam, Wild). [R11]. (c) SPRI P83/6/1.3 p45

- Photographer unknown. Wilson, in tropical clothing. (c) SPRI P71/35p61
- E.A.Wilson. Man of War Jellyfish. (c) NHM z88ffw
- E.A.Wilson. Small flying fish caught in townet. 13° 59´ S 34° 35´ W. 9 Sep 1901. (c) NHM z88ffw
- E.A.Wilson. Just after Sunset. Looking West. 9 Sep 1901. (c) SPRI MS232/1 p79

- E.A.Wilson. South Trinidad at Dawn. 13 Sep 1901. (c) SPRI 1322
- E.A.Wilson. Within South-west Bay, with the Monument and Landing Pier South Trinidad. 13 Sep 1901. (c) NHM DF404/61
- E.H.Shackleton. Landing on South Trinidad. L-R: Koettlitz; Ferrar; Royds; G.Murray (in Panama hat); Cross?; Wilson; Stoker Page?; Gilbert Scott; u/d; Hodgson. [Sh13?]. (c) CAGM 1995.550.186
- E.A.Wilson. The Monument (Knight), Sugar Loaf and Noah's Ark, South Trinidad. (c) SPRI MS232/1 p89

- E.H.Shackleton. Fairy Tern, South Trinidad. [Sh14]. (c) SPRI P83/6/1.4 p76
- C.W.Royds. Booby, South Trinidad. [R19]. (c) SPRI P83/6/1.3 p48
- E.A.Wilson. Trinidad Petrel. Undated. (c) SPRI 1685
- D.M.Wilson. Trinidad Petrel Eggs, Collected by *Discovery*. (c) NHM (uncatalogued)
- E.A.Wilson. Dark Phase Trinidad Petrel, sitting outside nest burrow. (c) SPRI 1649

- E.H.Shackleton. Skinning birds on deck, after South Trinidad. L-R: Dellbridge; Skelton; Wilson and Hodgson. [Sh17]. (c) SPRI P71/35 p75
- E.A.Wilson. Cape Pigeon flying sketch. (c) SPRI 1702
- C.W.Royds. Cape Pigeon, hung up abaft bridge. [R32]. (c) SPRI P71/35 p141
- E.A.Wilson. Cape Pigeon. (c) SPRI 1697
- R.W.Skelton. Dellbridge and u/d seaman holding a Wandering Albatross. [Sk2]. (c) SPRI P83/6/1.1 p1
- E.A.Wilson. Sketch of a Wandering Albatross in flight. (c) SPRI 1632

- E.A.Wilson. Table Mountain, Cape Town. 4 Oct 1901. (c) SPRI 1328
- E.A.Wilson. Between Cape Town and Simon's Bay. White Sands. 5 Oct 1901. (c) SPRI (New acquisitions)
- R.W.Skelton. (prob.) *Discovery* at Simonstown. (c) SPRI P58/77/12p27

- R.W.Skelton. Magnetic Station near Simonstown with Barne visible at door of tent. 11 Oct 1901. [Sk 7]. (c) SPRI P83/6/1.1p3
- R.W.Skelton. Lt. Michael Barne (with two u/d helpers, probably Professors Beatty and Morrison from the University of Cape Town) at work with Unifilar Magnetometer. 11 Oct 1901. [Sk 9]. (c) SPRI P83/6/1.1p3
- E.A.Wilson. False Bay. South Africa. 14 Oct 1901 (c) SPRI 427

- E.A.Wilson. Fish caught on a line, 15 Oct 1901. 35° 371/2´ S 20° 34´ E, on the Agulhas Bank, South Africa. (c) NHM Z88fw
- C.W.Royds. In the Westerlies. The Monkey Poop. u/d man at wheel. [R39]. (c) SPRI P83/6/1.3
- E.A.Wilson. Bad Weather Sketching Box. (c) SPRI MS232/1 p128
- E.A.Wilson. The Wheel. *South Polar Times,* July 1902. (c) DHT

- E.A.Wilson. White headed Petrel. 11 Nov 1901. 51° 21´ S 126° 23´ E. (c) SPRI 1680
- E.A.Wilson. Grey Petrel. 2 Nov 1901. 46° 51´ S 89° 28´ E. (c) SPRI 1708
- E.A.Wilson. Grey Headed Albatross, "Discovery 1901". (c) SPRI 1642
- E.A.Wilson. Albatross Lures. *South Polar Times,* May 1902. (c) DHT
- E.A.Wilson. Grey Petrel head. Skin 127. 2 Nov 1901. 46° 51´ S 89° 28´ E. (c) SPRI 1706
- E.A.Wilson. "Sounding". *South Polar Times*, Jun 1902. (c) DHT
- R.W.Skelton. "Sounding" - in this instance, using the Peterson water sampling bottle. Photograph probably Jan 1902 but used here as an example of a common procedure of the scientific programme carried out whilst at sea. [Sk36]. (c) SPRI P83/6/1.4p21

- E.A.Wilson. Snow Petrel. Reproduced from Scott, *Voyage of the Discovery.* (c) Private Collection.
- E.A.Wilson. Wilson's Storm Petrel. Reproduced from Scott, *Voyage of the Discovery.* (c) Private Collection.
- E.A.Wilson. Antarctic Petrel. Reproduced from Scott, *Voyage of the Discovery.* (c) Private Collection.
- R.W.Skelton. First Ice. Lane through the Pack Ice made by *Discovery.* 139° E. [Sk17]. (c) SPRI LS2000-42-158
- E.A.Wilson. Blue Petrel flying. (c) SPRI 1676.
- E.A.Wilson. Blue Petrel. Skin #8. Pack Ice. Nov 1901. "This bird was shot to bits, the sketch is rather makeshift". (c) SPRI 1674
- C.R.Ford. Dr Wilson and Asst. Eng. Dellbridge shooting birds in the pack from the bridge. [Fo5]. (c) CAGM 1995.550.186

- C.R.Ford. Dropping the anchor, Macquarie Island. [Fo16]. (c) SPRI P83/6/1.5p76
- E.H.Shackleton. Ch. Eng. Skelton photographing an Elephant Seal. [Sh22]. (c) SPRI P83/6/1.4p85
- E.A.Wilson. Sketch of Elephant Seal. (c) SPRI MS232/1

- E.A.Wilson. Head of Southern Brown (Great) Skua. (c) SPRI 1740
- E.A.Wilson. Head of Royal Penguin, Macquarie Island. Skin 22. (c) SPRI. 1501
- E.A.Wilson. Head of King Penguin, showing colour during life. Skin 13. (c) SPRI 1481
- R.W.Skelton. *Discovery* anchored at Macquarie Island, from Penguin Colonies. 22 Nov 1901. [SK23]. (c) SPRI
- E.A.Wilson. Head of Macquarie Island Shag. (c) SPRI 1727

- E.A.Wilson. Light-mantled Sooty Albatross in flight. Undated (c) SPRI 1645
- E.A.Wilson. Light-mantled Sooty Albatross head. "What a mouth, what a mouth, what a North by South". Undated. (c) SPRI 1646/2

- J.J. Kinsey? Some of the Crew at Lyttelton, New Zealand. 1901. On the Mizen Boom L-R: ABs Vince; Peters; Wild; PO Evans; ABs Walker; Heald; Sailmaker Miller; PO Macfarlane; Carpenter Dailey; 2nd Eng. Dellbridge. On the Poop deck, L-R: Cpl. Blissett; AB Sinclair; Lg. Stoker Page; ABs Dell; Weller; Lg. Stoker Quartley; PO Smythe; AB Williamson; PO Allan; Lg. Seaman Pilbeam. (c) SPRI LS2000-42-16
- J.J. Kinsey? Officers at Lyttelton, New Zealand. 1901. L-R: Dr E.A.Wilson; Lt. E.H.Shackleton RNR; Lt. A.B.Armitage RNR; Lt. M.Barne RN; Dr R. Koettlitz; Ch. Eng. R.W.Skelton RN ; Cdr R.F.Scott RN; Lt. C.W.Royds RN; L.C.Bernacchi; H.T.Ferrar; T.V.Hodgson. (c) SPRI LS2000-42-15

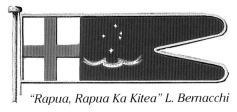

"Rapua, Rapua Ka Kitea" L. Bernacchi

- Press Photo. Miss Sybil Meares, whom Skelton thought the "prettiest girl in Christchurch", from a newspaper cutting that Skelton had with him in the Antarctic. They married in Jan 1905. (c) SPRI MS 342/1/5 BJ
- C.R.Ford. S.S.*Discovery* in dry dock. Lyttelton, New Zealand. [Fo22]. (c) SPRI P83/6/1.5
- R.W.Skelton (prob). Officers of Discovery visiting the Maori Pa at Kaiapoi. 11 Dec 1901. Visible, L-R with the Maori are; back: Barne; Hodgson; Scott; Ferrar; Wilson; Front: Koettlitz, wearing the hat and cloak with which he had just been presented. (c) DHT
- R.W.Skelton (prob). The monument on the old Maori battlefield. Near Kaiapoi. 11 Dec 1901. (c) SPRI P58/77/12 p31
- R.W.Skelton (prob). Returning from the picnic/visit to the Maori monument near Kaiapoi. 11 Dec 1901. (c) SPRI P58/77/12p33

- Photographer unkown. *Discovery* leaving Lyttelton, New Zealand. AB Bonner may be seen standing on top of the crows nest, from where he was waving to the crowds of well wishers. (c) SPRI LS2000-42-34
- Expedition Post card, "posted from the Discovery at the last port of call before sailing for the South Pole". (c) SPRI BNAE MS 366/17ER

Chapter Four: Something New Every Day
- Period map showing the outward route of *Discovery* through the Ross Sea, 1902, with additions by D.M.Wilson. (c) SPRI LS2000-42-187/ D.M.Wilson

- E.A.Wilson. Black-browed Albatross. 28 Dec 1901. 54° 54´S 171° 08´E. (c) SPRI 421
- R.W.Skelton. Black-browed and White-capped Albatross feeding astern. [Sk07]. (c) SPRI LS2000-42-127
- E.A.Wilson. Grey-headed Albatross. 29 Dec 1901. 56° 54´S 170° 27´E. (c) SPRI 1643

- E.A.Wilson. First Ice sighted after leaving New Zealand 4 Jan 1902. (c) SPRI 1765
- L.C.Bernacchi. *Discovery* in pack ice. 5 Jan 1902. [Be12]. (c) SPRI LS2000-42-48
- R.W.Skelton. Officers on ski in the pack ice. L-R: Hodgson; Koettlitz; Wilson; Bernacchi; Scott; Barne (behind); Royds; Ferrar. 5 Jan 1902. [Sk28]. (c) SPRI LS200-42-28

- E.A.Wilson. Crabeater Seal sketch. 3 Jan 1902. (c) SPRI 1429
- R.W.Skelton. Walker, with Crabeater seal on deck. 3 Jan 1902. [Sk27]. (c) SPRI LS2000-42-93
- E.H.Shackleton. Cross, Walker and Wilson, dissecting a seal on deck. [Sh29]. (c) SPRI
- E.A.Wilson. Ross' Seal sketches. (c) SPRI 1441
- R.W.Skelton. Ross' Seal on deck. [Sk29]. (c) SPRI LS2000-42-110

- E.A.Wilson. Leopard Seal, female. (c) SPRI 1424
- R.W.Skelton. On deck at last. Female Leopard Seal, 7 Jan 1902. [Sk 31]. (c) SPRI LS2000-42-112
- E.A.Wilson. Leopard Seal chasing an Emperor Penguin. (c) SPRI 67/4/3

- R.W.Skelton. L-R: Armitage, Barne and Bernacchi, taking magnetic readings. [Sk50]. (c) SPRI P83/6.1
- E.A.Wilson. The Two Sisters, Cape Adare. Undated. (c) SPRI 532
- R.W.Skelton. Exploring Borchgrevink's *Southern Cross* Hut and abandoned supplies. [Sk47]. (c) SPRI LS2000-42-25
- C.R.Ford. "Want your dinner? Why you have only just had breakfast!" Adelie Penguins. [Fo35]. (c) SPRI LS2000-42-133

- W. W. Greener. Gun and Rifle Maker. Advertisement from the Bruton Gallery Catalogue 1904. (c) DHT

- E.A.Wilson. Cape Anne, Coulman Island 13 Jan 1902. (c) SPRI (New Acquisitions)
- C.W.Royds. Cape Wadworth, Coulman Island 15 Jan 1902. [R86]. (c) SPRI LS2000-42-11
- E.A.Wilson. Cape Wadworth, Coulman Island. (c) CAGM 1964:182
- R.W.Skelton. Cape Jones ("Cape Constance"), Coulman Island 15 Jan 1902. [Sk 58]. (c) SPRI LS2000-42-99

- R.W.Skelton. Moulting Emperor Penguins, 15 Jan 1902, Lady Newnes Bay. [Sk63]. (c) SPRI LS2000-42-116
- E.A.Wilson. Sleeping Emperor Penguin, Lady Newnes Bay. (c) SPRI 67/4/2
- R.W.Skelton. *Discovery* at Lady Newnes Bay: sealing parties may be seen on the ice. [Sk59]. (c) SPRI LS2000-42-143
- L.C.Bernacchi. Mount Melbourne, Wood Bay 19 Jan 1902. [Be53]. (c) SPRI LS2000-42-146

- E.A.Wilson. Mount Erebus, 20 Jan 1902. (c) SPRI 1802
- R.W.Skelton. McMurdo Bay, 21 Jan 1902, the way south "blocked by ice". [Sk75?]. (c) SPRI LS2000-42-86
- R.W.Skelton. Sailing past Mount Terror, 22 Jan 1902. [Sk76]. (c) SPRI LS2000-42-23

- E.A.Wilson. The Great Ice Barrier. Sketch from *South Polar Times*, Jun 1902. (c) DHT
- E.A.Wilson. The Great Ice Barrier. (c) SPRI 415
- C.R.Ford. The Great Ice Barrier. [Fo37]. (c) SPRI LS2000-42-136
- E.A.Wilson. Waterworn cave in the Barrier. (c) CAGM 1930.66
- L.C.Bernacchi. A recently calved tabular berg from the Barrier, "The highest ice wall seen - 280 feet in height". [Be64a]. (c) SPRI LS2000-42-174

- E.A.Wilson. King Edward VII Land. (c) SPRI 437
- E.A.Wilson. In the Crow's nest. Undated. (c) SPRI 1338
- E.A.Wilson. Emperor Penguin, Furthest East. 31 Jan 1902. (c) SPRI 1464
- R.W.Skelton. Watering ship from a large ice floe. Farthest East. [Sk84]. (c) SPRI LS2000-42-17

- E.A.Wilson. Ballooning in the Antarctic. *South Polar Times*. Jun 1902. (c) DHT
- E.A.Wilson. Ballooning in the Antarctic. *South Polar Times*. Jun 1902. (c) DHT
- E.A.Wilson. Ballooning in the Antarctic. *South Polar Times*. Jun 1902. (c) DHT
- E.H.Shackleton. Cdr Scott (prob) being lowered from the first Antarctic flight. [Sh62]. (c) SPRI LS2000-42-65

- E.H.Shackleton. Balloon Inlet: the first aerial photograph taken in Antarctica. [Sh64]. (c) SPRI P83/6/1-4 p28
- R.W.Skelton. *Discovery* at Balloon Inlet. [Sk89]. (c) SPRI LS2000-42-131
- E.H.Shackleton. The Barrier Sledge Party preparing to depart: Armitage, Bernacchi, Cross, Joyce, Crean, Handsley. [Sh59]. (c) SPRI
- E.A.Wilson. Ballooning in the Antarctic. *South Polar Times*. Jun 1902. (c) DHT

- R.W.Skelton. Iceberg off the Great Ice Barrier. [Sk31]. (c) SPRI LS2000-42-163
- E.H.Shackleton. Looking seawards from fast ice near the Dailey Islands (Mt. Erebus in the distance), McMurdo Bay. [Sh71]. (c) SPRI LS2000-42-52

"*Semper Paratus*" C. Royds

Chapter Five: Hut Point and Autumn Sledging
- D.M.Wilson & D.C.Lawie. Map of McMurdo Sound and Hut point as known in the period of autumn sledging 1902. (c) D.M.Wilson

- R.W.Skelton. *Discovery*, newly anchored in Winterquarters Bay. Hut Point behind. [Sk95]. (c) SPRI LS2000-42-130
- R.W.Skelton. Breaking Winterquarters Bay ice with gun cotton. [Sk97]. (c) SPRI LS2000-42-149
- L.C.Bernacchi. *Discovery* in Winterquarters Bay from N.E. head of the ski slopes. Arrival Bay is to the right over Hut Point. In the distance, Black Island (left) and Mount Discovery (right) may be seen. [Be38]. (c) SPRI LS2000-42-141

- E.A.Wilson. View beyond Observation Hill and Cape Armitage, to White Island. (c) SPRI 523
- E.H.Shackleton. L-R: u/d (possibly Shackleton); Wilson and Ferrar, before leaving for White Island, flying officer's sledging flags from the Pram. [Sh88]. (c) SPRI P83/6/4.4p121
- E.H.Shackleton. Wilson (left) and Ferrar astride a blue ice mound. [Sh91]. (c) SPRI P83/6/4.4p120
- E.A.Wilson. Fractured mounds of blue ice, 4-5 feet high, NW of White Island. (c) SPRI 549
- E.A.Wilson. Beaked Whales sporting in Terror Bay. 25 Feb 1902. (c) NHM Z88ffw

- R.W.Skelton. *Discovery*, not long frozen in, with Observation Hill and the Gap in the background. [Sk104?]. (c) SPRI LS2000-42-27
- R.W.Skelton. Football match on the ice. [Sk98]. (c) SPRI P83/6/1p68
- E.A.Wilson. 'Professor Gregory's Villa', Hut Point Feb 1902. (c) SPRI (New Acquisitions)

- R.W.Skelton. Part of the Terror Party (prob. Royds, Koettlitz, Wild, Quartley, Weller and Vince) in deep snow. [Sk56]. (c) SPRI LS2000-42-221
- R.W.Skelton. Terror Party turned out in furs at Separation Camp. Showing Union Jack and four officers' pennants (Royds, Skelton, Koettlitz and Barne) with Royds, Koettlitz, Barne, Wild, Hare, Quartley, Vince, Weller, Evans, Plumley and Heald. 9 Mar 1902. [Sk60]. (c) SPRI LS2000-42-214
- L.C.Bernacchi. Danger Slope, near to where Vince fell to his death in a blizzard. [Be78]. (c) SPRI LS2000-42-13
- E.A.Wilson. Royds, Koettlitz and Skelton dragging sledge through a blizzard. Frontispiece, *South Polar Times*, Apr 1902. (c) DHT

- E.A.Wilson. The Last Skua Left Us. *South Polar Times*. Apr 1902. (c) DHT
- R.W.Skelton. Winter Quarters from above the magnetic huts on Hut Point. Crater Hill and the Gap are visible beyond "Professor Gregory's Villa" and *Discovery*. Bernacchi is standing at left. An unknown figure to the right is walking dogs. [Sk100]. (c) SPRI LS2000-42-188
- R.W.Skelton. *Discovery* in Winter Quarters, showing the windmill in commission. Observation Hill is behind the ship, showing Cape Armitage; White Island in the distance. [Sk104]. (c) SPRI LS2000-42-198
- R.W.Skelton. Five unknown men standing on the new gangplank. Seal and mutton carcasses are clearly visible hanging in the rigging. [Sk114]. (c) SPRI LS2000-42-196
- E.A.Wilson. Windmill Collapsed. *South Polar Times*. Apr 1902. (c) DHT

- E.A.Wilson. Observation Hill from the foot of Crater Hill. Looking south west. Midday. Picture appears to be dated 29 Jan 1902. This is clearly incorrect. Either it is later in 1902 or perhaps 29 Jan 1903. (c) SPRI 1280
- E.A.Wilson. *Discovery* in Winter Quarters looking towards the Western range, 28 Mar 1902 6pm. (c) SPRI 1278
- E.A.Wilson. Sunset over the Western Mountains, McMurdo Strait, 11 Apr 1902 4.30pm. (c) SPRI 522

- E.A.Wilson. Departure of Southern Depot Party. *South Polar Times*, Apr 1902. (c) DHT
- E.H.Shackleton. Wilson about to depart on the Southern Depot Party. [Sh106]. (c) SPRI P71/35
- E.A.Wilson. Three in a Sleeping Bag. (c) SPRI Box52
- E.A.Wilson. Sledging in April. (c) SPRI p62/12/6
- E.A.Wilson. A sleeping bag for three. (c) SPRI p97/190
- E.A.Wilson. Sledging pannikin and spoon. (c) SPRI p97/190
- E.A.Wilson. Finneskoe. (c) SPRI Box 52
- E.A.Wilson. Return of the Southern Depot Party. *South Polar Times*, Apr 1902. (c) DHT

- E.A.Wilson. Title for Great Emperor Penguin Hunt. *South Polar Times*, Apr 1902. (c) DHT
- E.A.Wilson. Sketch of Emperor Penguin Hunt for *South Polar Times*. (c) SPRI 1344
- E.A.Wilson. Sketch of Emperor Penguin Hunt. *South Polar Times*, Apr 1902. (c) DHT
- R.W.Skelton. Weighing the dead Emperor Penguins - men unidentified. The photograph also shows *Discovery's* boats on the ice and a live penguin chained to them. [Sk105]. (c) SPRI P83/6/1.1p75
- E.A.Wilson. Sketches of captive Emperor Penguins. 17 Apr 1902. (c) SPRI 1462

Chapter Six: The First Winter
- E.A.Wilson. Red glow on the smoke of Mount Erebus. Winter 1902. (c) SPRI 54/25/1

- E.A.Wilson. Meteorology title caption: Kew Observatory and Marine Barometer. *South Polar Times*, Apr 1903. (c) DHT
- E.H.Shackleton. Wilson, reading the thermometer at the meteorological station on Crater Hill. [Sh 155]. (c) SPRI P83/6/1.4p35
- C.W.Royds. The starboard meteorological screen, with Observation Hill and the Gap. [R124]. (c) SPRI LS2000-42-59
- Photographer unknown. The starboard meteorological screen with figure (probably Royds) looking towards the Western Mountains. (c) SPRI LS2000-42-60
- E.A.Wilson. Barograph. *South Polar Times*, Apr 1903. (c) DHT
- E.A.Wilson. Fixed Screen. *South Polar Times*, Apr 1903. (c) DHT
- E.A.Wilson. Dine's pressure-tube Anemometer. *South Polar Times*, Jun 1903. (c) DHT
- E.A.Wilson. Assman's Aspirator with Sea Surface Thermometer. *South Polar Times*, Apr 1903. (c) DHT
- E.A.Wilson. Thermograph Record. *South Polar Times*, Apr 1903. (c) DHT

- E.A.Wilson. *Discovery* in Winter Quarters, after the second major blizzard. The remains of the windmill are on the forward deck. (c) SPRI 542
There are several versions of this picture, some of which are dated 1903, presumably when they were painted. The first version appears as the

August 1902 frontispiece of the *South Polar Times*. The presence of the windmill stump clearly indicates that this scene is from the winter of 1902.
- Photographer Unknown. The Ward room stove. Probably photographed when the ship was being fitted out in 1901. (c) DHT
- H.T.Ferrar (prob). Laboratory aboard *Discovery*. Undated. (c) SPRI P75/34/55
- H.T.Ferrar (prob). Laboratory aboard *Discovery*. Undated. (c) SPRI P75/34/56
The photographer of the two laboratory photographs is unknown but is probably Ferrar, as the negatives were kindly donated to the Scott Polar Research Institute by the Ferrar family.

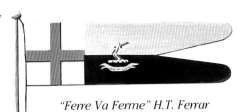

"Ferre Va Ferme" H.T. Ferrar

- The Cover, Vol I of the *South Polar Times*. (c) DHT
- E.A.Wilson. Frontispiece, *South Polar Times*, Apr 1902. (c) SPRI
- E.A.Wilson. Sea Leopard Chasing Emperor Penguins. Preparatory sketch. *South Polar Times*, Apr 1902. (c) SPRI 1426
- Artist unknown. The Cover, *The Blizzard*, 1902. (c) SPRI BNAEms366/17ER
- E.A.Wilson. Silhouette of Shackleton. South Polar Times, Jul 1902. Preparatory sketch. (c) SPRI 1335
- E.A.Wilson. Silhouette of Royds. *South Polar Times*, May 1902. (c) DHT
- E.A.Wilson. Silhouette of Barne. *South Polar Times*, May 1902 (c) DHT

- E.A.Wilson. En Route for Terror Theatre. *South Polar Times*, Aug 1902. (c) DHT
- Programme of entertainments, 1 May 1902. (c) SPRI BNAEms366/17ER
- R.W.Skelton. "Ticket of Leave: a screaming comedy in one act", The Antarctic Theatrical Company at the Royal Terror Theatre, Professor Gregory's Villa, 25 Jun 1902. L-R: standing: Pilbeam (Joe); Weller; Cross; Feather (Thos. Muggetts); Allan; seated: Buckridge (Mrs Quiver); Wild; Gilbert Scott (Mary Ann). [Sk126]. (c) SPRI P83/6/1p79
- E.A.Wilson. 25 June theatricals. *South Polar Times*, Aug 1902. (c) DHT
- R.W.Skelton. "The Dishcover Minstrel Troupe", the Royal Terror Theatre at Professor Gregory's Villa, 6 Aug 1902. [Sk130]. (c) SPRI P83/6/1p80

- E.A.Wilson. Moon over the Western Mountains, McMurdo Strait. Undated. (c) SPRI 479

- R.W.Skelton. The Ward Room (clockwise): Bernacchi; Hodgson; Wilson; Armitage (hidden); Barne (standing); Royds; (standing); Shackleton; Skelton; Ferrar; Koettlitz and Scott (Obscured by the flash). [Sk122]. (c) SPRI P83/6/1.1p37
- R.W.Skelton. The Starboard Mess (probable identities, left to right and front to back): Pilbeam, Walker; Cross, Allan, Macfarlane; Kennar, Duncan, Evans. [Sk120]. (c) SPRI P83/6/1
- R.W.Skelton. The Port Mess (probable identities left to right and front to back): Crean, Wild, Weller; Heald, Croucher, Peters; Plumley, Page, Hubert; Whitfield, Quartley. [Sk121]. (c) SPRI LS2000-42-74
- E.A.Wilson. Christmas menu and holly. *South Polar Times*, Jun 1902. (c) DHT
- E.A.Wilson. Ice King Sculpture. *South Polar Times*, Jun 1902. (c) DHT

- John Dewar & Sons, Whisky. Advertisement from the Bruton Gallery Catalogue 1904. (c) DHT With special thanks to John Dewar & Sons

- E.A.Wilson. Aurora and Moon over the Western Mountains, McMurdo Strait. Undated. (c) SPRI 1389
- E.A.Wilson. The moon shining through the Gap. undated. (c) SPRI 541
- E.A.Wilson. *Discovery* in Winter Quarters, looking north, towards Hut Point, Carmine sky. Undated. (c) SPRI 1242

- E.A.Wilson. Title, Some Physical Observations. *South Polar Times*, Aug 1903. (c) DHT
- E.H.Shackleton. Bernacchi emerging from the Magnetic variation studies hut. [Sh98]. (c) SPRI P83/6/1.4p31
- E.A.Wilson. Following the rope from Hut Point to the ship. Frontispiece. *South Polar Times*, May 1902. (c) DHT
- E.A.Wilson. Eschenhagen Magnetograph, *South Polar Times*, May 1902. (c) DHT
- E.A.Wilson. Pendulum Apparatus, *South Polar Times*, Aug 1903. (c) DHT
- E.A.Wilson. Electrometer, *South Polar Times*, Aug 1903. (c) DHT
- E.A.Wilson. Milne's Seismograph, *South Polar Times*, Aug 1903. (c) DHT

- E.A.Wilson. Mount Erebus and Castle Rock, 16 Aug 1902, midday. (c) SPRI new acquisitions
- E.A.Wilson. Return of the Sun, *South Polar Times*, Aug 1902 (c) DHT

Chapter Seven: Spring Sledging
- D.M.Wilson & D.C.Lawie. Map showing the approximate areas of McMurdo Sound covered by Spring sledging 1902. (c) D.M.Wilson

- R.W.Skelton. Hodgson with Ice Crystals on the fish trap line off Cape Armitage. [Sk147]. (c) SPRI LS2000-42-81
- R.W.Skelton. Royds by the starboard meteorological screen, with puppies playing by the ship. [Sk161]. (c) SPRILS2000-42-76
- R.W.Skelton. *Discovery*, showing the wind scoop and drift around the ship after the first winter. [Sk137]. (c) SPRI LS2000-42-171

- E.A.Wilson. Puppies. *South Polar Times*, Jul 1902. (c) DHT
- E.H.Shackleton. "Lewis the boisterous". [Sh200]. (c) SPRI LS2000-42-269
- C.R.Ford. Nell with pups. [Fo72]. (c) SPRI LS2000-42-267
- C.R.Ford. Buckridge with Vinka's puppies. [Fo67]. (c) SPRI P83/6/1.5p105
- C.W.Royds. Sledge pups. [R205]. (c) SPRI P71/35/23

- R.W.Skelton. Departure of the Southwest Reconnaissance Party: Royds; Koettlitz; Lashly; Evans; Wild and Quartley. [Sk133]. (c) SPRI LS2000-42-273
- R.W.Skelton. Harnessing dogs for the departure of the Southern Reconnaissance Party (Scott, Barne and Shackleton). Shackleton's sledging flag is being raised on the sled. Amongst the onlookers, Edward Wilson is standing to the right. [Sk138]. (c) SPRI LS2000-42-138
- A. Quartley. "Onward O'er the Snow". Sledging to the southwest. *South Polar Times*, Apr 1903. (c) DHT

- E.A.Wilson. Passing in the cooker. (c) SPRI LS2000-42-261
- E.A.Wilson. A welcome meal. *South Polar Times*, Jul 1902. (c) DHT
- E.A.Wilson. Spring sledging. (c) SPRI 508
- C.R.Ford. Captain's Southern Reconnaissance Trip returning: 'Nigger' leading. [Fo62]. (c) SPRI LS2000-42-137

- R.W.Skelton. Cow Weddell Seal. [S20]. (c) SPRI LS2000-42-106
- R.W.Skelton (Prob). Weddell Seal, on being disturbed. [Sk?] (c) SPRI LS2000-42-103
- C.R.Ford. Killing Weddell seals. [Fo83]. (c) SPRI P83/6/1.5p27
- C.R.Ford. Sealing party (Barne, Wilson, Cross, Dell, Walker & Weller) returning to ship. [Fo84]. (c) SPRI LS2000-42-274

- C.R.Ford. Spring thaw on the deck of Discovery, after removal of the awning. [F075]. (c) SPRI P75/34/8
- R.W.Skelton. *Discovery* in Winter Quarters. Note the remains of the windmill still on the forward deck. [Sk144]. (c) SPRI LS2000-42-172
- E.A.Wilson. Skiing through the Gap. Undated. (c) SPRI 62/4

- R.W.Skelton. The message post at Cape Crozier, before the return of the Adelie Penguins. [no Sk. reference?]. (c) SPRI LS2000-42-262
- R.W.Skelton. Camping under Mount Terror's Southeast slope (the man is probably Royds). [Sk199]. (c) SPRI LS2000-42-18
- R.W.Skelton. Looking east along the Great Ice Barrier from Cape Crozier. [Sk189]. (c) SPRI LS2000-42-155
- R.W.Skelton. Ice Pressure ridges at Cape Crozier. [Sk191]. (c) SPRI LS2000-42-159

- R.W.Skelton. The Emperor Penguin rookery at Cape Crozier - the first discovered. [Sk184]. (c) SPRI LS2000-42-125
- R.W.Skelton. One of the first series of photographs ever taken of Emperor Penguin chicks. Evans (left) and Quartley look on. [Sk188]. (c) SPRI LS2000-42-113
- E.A.Wilson. Emperor Penguin chick in down, taken alive from Cape Crozier, Oct 1902: the middle sized one. (c) SPRI 1473

Chapter Eight: Summer Sledging and the coming of *Morning*
- D.M.Wilson & D.C.Lawie. Map showing the approximate routes of summer sledging journeys 1902-03. Based on period maps. (c) D.M.Wilson
- C.R.Ford. Expedition cats Poplar (left) and Blackwall, enjoying the summer sunshine. [Fo187]. (c) SPRI

- R.W.Skelton. Departure of the Southern Depot Party, 30 Oct 1902. [Sk200]. (c) SPRI P71/35p62
- R.W.Skelton. Harnessing dogs for departure of the Southern Party, 2 Nov 1902. [SK205]. (c) SPRI LS2000-42-215
- R.W.Skelton. The Southern Party. L-R: Shackleton; Scott and Wilson. [Sk204]. (c) SPRI LS2000-42-204

- E.H.Shackleton. Camp on the Barrier 78º 55´S: looking north towards the Bluff. Photograph presumed catalogued under Shackleton, whose camera appears to have been used. [No Sh.reference]. (c) SPRI P71/35 p22
- E.H.Shackleton. The entire Southern Party before the return of the first supporting party under Dailey: standing L-R: Wilson? (possibly Buckridge), Barne, Scott, Shackleton, Dailey, Feather; front: Kennar, Smythe, Handsley, Weller (behind), Williamson, Joyce, Pilbeam (behind) Crean. The flags of (L-R) Shackleton, Barne, Scott, and Wilson and the Union Jack are flying. Dailey is holding his own sledging flag. Photograph catalogued under Shackleton, whose camera was used. [Sh179]. (c) SPRI P83/6/1.4p38
- E.A.Wilson. Mock suns, parhelia, perihelia and circles of light with showers of ice crystals over a dog camp on the Great Ice Barrier. (c) SPRI 54/25/4
- E.H.Shackleton. Crevasse chasm beyond Depot B, off Cape Selbourne, with Wilson standing at right. [Sh181]. (c) SPRI P71/35p70
- E.A.Wilson. Joe. *South Polar Times*, Jun 1903. (c) CAGM
- E.A.Wilson. Bismarck. *South Polar Times*, Jun 1903. (c) CAGM
- E.A.Wilson. Dog in sledge harness. *South Polar Times*, Jun 1903. (c) CAGM

- E.H.Shackleton. Christmas Day Camp. L-R: Shackleton, Scott & Wilson. [Sh184]. (c) SPRI P83/6/1.4p38
- E.A.Wilson. Farthest South Camp: Mount Markham, Shackleton Inlet and Cape Wilson. *South Polar Times*, Jun 1903. (c) DHT
- E.H.Shackleton. The ski run. Wilson stands in front of the Cape named for him. Scott is lower down, towards Shackleton inlet. Shackleton remained in camp and took the photo. Wilson's notes. [Sh189]. (c) SPRI P71/35p123
- E.A.Wilson. Mount Longstaff - farthest south land seen. (c) SPRI 1294
- E.A.Wilson. Sledging past Mount Markham, Shackleton inlet and Cape Wilson. (c) Abbott Hall Art Gallery, Kendall
- E.H.Shackleton. Impassable crevasses. The large tide crack (with Scott) which prevented land being attained. (c) SPRI LS2000-42-266

- E.H.Shackleton. "The last of the dogs" camp. [Sh193]. (c) SPRI LS2000-42-224
- E.A.Wilson. Jim, one of the two last dogs. *South Polar Times*, Jun 1903. (c) CAGM
- E.A.Wilson. Three men on ski manhauling a sledge. 1903. (c) SPRI 530
- E.A.Wilson. Camp on the Ice Barrier with fog-bow. Undated. (c) SPRI 506
- E.H.Shackleton. Camp with a view north to the Bluff. 25 Jan 1903. [Sh191]. (c) SPRI P83/6/1.4p40
- C.R.Ford. The Bluff depot (Depot A). [Fo166]. (c) SPRI LS2000-42-68 Ford took this photo whilst re-supplying the depot in early January 1903

- E.A.Wilson. 3 men on ski. (c) CAGM 1973.52 (possibly a sketch for SPRI 530)
- C.R.Ford. Return of the Southern Sledge Party, 3 Feb 1903. With Wilson's notes. [Fo189]. (c) SPRI P71/35.50b
- E.A.Wilson. Just back from the Southern Journey, with Wilson's notes [Photographer unknown but listed as W1]. (c) SPRI P71/35/50h
- L.C.Bernacchi. L-R: Shackleton, Scott and Wilson just returned from Southern Journey, with Wilson's notes. [Be140]. (c) SPRI P71/35/50c
- L.C.Bernacchi. Wilson, just back from farthest South and suffering from Scurvy. [Be141]. (c) CAGM

- International Plasmon Limited. Advertisement from the Bruton Gallery Catalogue 1904. (c) DHT

- Programme of Sports for the King's Birthday. 8 Nov 1902 (c) SPRI BNAEms366/17/ER
- E.A.Wilson. Mustard and Cress grown by Koettlitz in the *Discovery* skylight. *South Polar Times*, Apr 1903. (c) DHT
- C.R.Ford. *Discovery* dressed overall for the King's Birthday, with Observation Hill and Cape Armitage. [Fo114]. (c) SPRI LS2000-42-47
- E.A.Wilson. The toboggan race at the King's Birthday sports. *South Polar Times*, Apr 1903. (c) SPRI
- Programme of Concert for the King's Birthday. 8 Nov 1902. (c) SPRI BNAEms366/17/ER

- C.W.Royds. Royds, with Adelie Penguin. [R188]. (catalogued under Royds as his camera was used). (c) SPRI LS2000-42-78
- C.W.Royds. Blissett and Plumley with Adelie Penguin eggs. [R187]. (c) SPRI LS2000-42-213
- C.W.Royds. Emperor Penguins at Cape Crozier. [R237]. (c) SPRI LS2000-42-237
- Photographer Unknown. Adelie Penguin at empty nest. BNAE 1901-1904. Undated. (c) SPRI LS2000-42-240
- R.W.Skelton. Biological specimens: L-R: Emperor, King and Adelie Penguin eggs. The Emperor's egg was the first scientific specimen collected of this species, an earlier existing specimen being post-identified with certainty from this proven sample [Sk220]. (c) SPRI LS2000-42-272

- C.R.Ford. McCormick's or South Polar Skua. [Fo153?]. (c) SPRI LS2000-42-232
- C.W.Royds. Onlookers encourage Lt. Barne and the sledge party (Smythe, Plumley, Williamson, Crean & Weller) as he leads off to explore to the south-west; 12 Dec 1902. [R203]. (c) SPRI LS2000-42-26
- E.A.Wilson. Christmas fishing at the ship. *South Polar Times*, Apr 1903. (c) DHT

- C.R.Ford. The departure of the Western parties, 29 Nov 1902. [Fo145]. (c) SPRI LS2000-42-82

- C.R.Ford. One of the Western Party sledges, heading west. [Fo194]. (c) SPRI LS2000-42-201
- R.W.Skelton. Camping on morainic ice, near the Eskers 1 Dec 1902. [Sk233]. (c) SPRI LS2000-42-233
- R.W.Skelton. View of the Western Mountains from half way up the Blue Glacier. The highest peak is Mount Lister, to its left is Mount Hooker. 4 Dec 1902. [Sk238 CXV11/3]. (c) SPRI LS2000-42-263

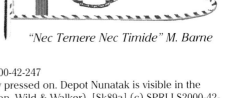

"Nec Temere Nec Timide" M. Barne

- R.W.Skelton. View up Glacier Valley, 12 Dec 1902. [Sk248]. (c) SPRI LS2000-42-156
- R.W.Skelton. Christmas Camp in the glacier moraine, spur of Terra Cotta Mountain. [Sk80a]. (c) SPRI LS2000-42-212
- R.W.Skelton. Looking down the glacier towards the Western Mountains. [Sk81a]. (c)SPRI LS2000-42-247
- R.W.Skelton. Allan's rest camp on the inland ice (near Polar Plateau) before the magnetic party pressed on. Depot Nunatak is visible in the distance (Armitage, Gilbert Scott, Evans, Quartley, Buckridge, Allan, Macfarlane, Handsley, Duncan, Wild & Walker). [Sk89a].(c) SPRI LS2000-42-225

- A.Quartley. Five men pulling Armitage out of a crevasse. *South Polar Times,* Apr 1903. (c) DHT
- R.W.Skelton. Depot Nunatak, taken on the return journey. [Sk94a]. (c) SPRI LS2000-42-243
- R.W.Skelton. The cliffs of Finger Mountain. Wild (left) and Armitage pose in the wind-scoop, 9 Jan 1902. [Sk98a]. (c) SPRI LS2000-42-252
- E.A.Wilson (prob). Six men sledging. *South Polar Times,* Apr 1903. (c) DHT

- C.R.Ford. Digging out the boats. [Fo162]. (c) SPRI LS2000-42-20
- R.W.Skelton. Watering ship, Evans, Cross and Heald. [Sk253?]. (c) SPRI LS2000-42-222

- J.J.Kinsey. Officers aboard *Morning* at Lyttelton, New Zealand. L-R: (back) Midshipmen Somerville, Pepper; (front) Lt. Doorly, Lt. Evans, Ch. Eng. Morrison, Lt. England, Capt. Colbeck, Lt. Mulock, Dr Davidson. (c) SPRI LS2000-42-14 -a photograph taken by Sir Joseph Kinsey.
- C.R.Ford. Armitage and the *Discovery* party greet Capt. Colbeck and the *Morning* upon arrival in McMurdo Bay. [Fo171]. (c) SPRI LS2000-42-32
- W.Colbeck (prob). Hauling fresh supplies from *Morning* to *Discovery*, Mount Erebus in the distance. From a lantern slide kindly donated to SPRI by the Colbeck family. (c) SPRI P62/71.5
- C.R.Ford. The departure of *Morning. South Polar Times,* Apr 1903. (c) DHT

Chapter Nine: The Second Winter
- R.W.Skelton. Hodgson on his round of the fish traps. [Sk176]. (c) SPRI LS2000-42-19
- E.A.Wilson. Polar Biology, title-piece. *South Polar Times,* Jun 1903. (c) DHT
- E.A.Wilson. Coloured drawing of a Jellyfish. McMurdo Strait. 1 Aug 1902. (c) NHM DF 217/1
- E.A.Wilson. "Collections Biological..." Cartoon of Hodgson. *South Polar Times,* Jun 1902. (c) DHT
- E.A.Wilson. Isopod and worm. *South Polar Times,* Jun 1902. (c) DHT
- E.A.Wilson. Notothenia. *South Polar Times,* Jun 1902. (c) DHT
- E.A.Wilson. Nymphon, a sea spider. *South Polar Times,* Jun 1903. (c) DHT
- E.A.Wilson. Sea-fir. *South Polar Times,* Jun 1903. (c) DHT
- E.A.Wilson. Cucumaria, a Sea Cucumber. *South Polar Times,* Jun 1903. (c) DHT

- E.A.Wilson. Mount Erebus. 26 Apr 1903. (c) SPRI 518
- E.A.Wilson. Crater Hill from Harbour Heights. Noon, looking south-east. 8 May 1903. (c) SPRI 1279
- C.R.Ford. Mid-day in May. *South Polar Times,* Jun 1903. (c) DHT

- E.A.Wilson. Auroral corona with two figures. (c) SPRI 1386
- E.A.Wilson. *Discovery* in Winter Quarters with Aurora. (c) SPRI 543
- E.A.Wilson. *Discovery* in Winter Quarters with Auroral streamers and curtains stretching from Crater Hill, past Crater Heights, the Gap and Observation Hill beyond Cape Armitage towards Black and White Islands *South Polar Times,* Frontispiece, Jun 1902. (c) DHT

- E.A.Wilson. "We wish all our readers a Merry Midwinter". *South Polar Times,* Jun 1903. (c) SPRI
- E.A.Wilson. Cartoon of Royds (prob) singing "Intrepid Souls" at the piano. *South Polar Times,* Apr 1903. (c) SPRI
- Menu for the Ward Room mid-winter dinner, 22 Jun 1903. (c) SPRI BNAEms366/17/ER
- E.A.Wilson. *Discovery* in Winter Quarters *South Polar Times,* Frontispiece, Jun 1903. (c) DHT
- E.A.Wilson. 'Poplar', the cat; "Stealing the night watchman's supper". *South Polar Times,* Apr 1903. (c) SPRI

- M. Barne. Caricature of 'The Pilot' (Armitage). *South Polar Times,* Apr 1903. (c) DHT
- E.A.Wilson. Polar Hieroglyphs. *South Polar Times,* Aug 1903. (c) SPRI
- Artist unknown. 'Ye Long Antarctic K/night'. (c) SPRI BNAEms366/17/ER
- E.A.Wilson. Taking observations in a blizzard. (c) CAGM 1930:634

- E.A.Wilson. Opalescent alto stratus and snow drift; looking north, 17 Aug 1903. (This picture has often been reproduced, most interestingly in Science Vol 292 Apr 2001, as the cloud formations it depicts play a key role in the development of the ozone hole over Antarctica). (c) SPRI 1245
- E.A.Wilson. Castle Rock below Mount Erebus, looking north-west 2 p.m. 3 Aug 1903. (c) SPRI 1271

Chapter Ten: The Second Sledging Season
D.M.Wilson & D.C.Lawie: Map showing the approximate routes of second season sledging 1903. (c) D.M.Wilson

- E.A.Wilson. Emperor Penguin Chick "painted in the position in which it was found frozen". Cape Crozier Sep 1903. (c) SPRI 461
- R.W.Skelton. Frozen Emperor Penguin eggs and chicks from Cape Crozier. Sep 1903. [Sk257](c) SPRI P83/6/1.2p32
- E.A.Wilson. Emperor Penguin "With a chick resting on its feet under the skin flap" Cape Crozier Sep 1903. (c) SPRI 439
- E.A.Wilson. Emperor Penguin " If hurried when carrying a chick, the adult overbalances and continues to thrust itself along on its stomach with its flippers never exposing the chick or using the feet for propulsion" Cape Crozier Sep 1903. (c) SPRI 445

- R.W.Skelton. Looking up the Great Western (Ferrar) Glacier from New Harbour entrance, 16 Sep 1903. [Sk283]. (c) SPRI LS2000-42-275
- R.W.Skelton. Looking up the Great Western (Ferrar) Glacier [Sk284]. (c) SPRI LS2000-42-203

- R.W.Skelton. Weller, waiting by a fish trap hole to harpoon a seal. [Sk278]. (c) SPRI LS2000-42-223
- R.W.Skelton. Weller's headless fish. [Sk271]. (c) SPRI LS2000-42-135
- R.W.Skelton. Barne's South-west party about to depart: L-R (front) Lt. Barne, Lt. Mulock; (back) Joyce, Smythe, Crean and Quartley. In the background (Dellbridge, Pilbeam, Wild, Allan, Croucher and Heald) [Sk275]. (c) SPRI P71/35p4

- Photographer unknown. L-R: Cross, Wilson and Whitfield, about to depart for Cape Crozier. (c) SPRI LS2000-42-75
- E.A.Wilson. Whitfield and Cross pulling the sledge for Cape Crozier [No cat #]. (c) SPRI P71/35/p19
- E.A.Wilson. Digging out the blubber stove at camp, after a blizzard, Cape Crozier. [W8]. (c) SPRI LS2000-42-p21
- E.A.Wilson. Emperor penguin rookery, Cape Crozier, looking east along the Ice Barrier. (c) SPRI 1461
- E.A.Wilson. Emperor penguin rookery, Cape Crozier, looking east along the Ice Barrier. (c) SPRI 1460

"Dread God" T.V. Hodgson

- R.W.Skelton. Seal and calf near Pram Point. [Sk267]. (c) SPRI LS2000-42-91
- E.A.Wilson. McCormick's (or South Polar) Skuas, nesting near Winter Quarters Bay. Undated. (c) SPRI 494
- E.A.Wilson. Fish taken from the stomach of a Weddell Seal, 27 Sep 1903. (c) NHM Z88fw
- E.A.Wilson. Four sketches of Weddell Seals. Various dates. (c) SPRI 1415 & 1416

- Jaeger. Advertisement for traveller's clothing from the Bruton Gallery Catalogue 1904. (c) DHT With special thanks to Jaegers

- A.B.Armitage. The commencement of pinnacle ice on part of the Saddle Mountain (Koettlitz) Glacier, showing the north face of Saddle Mountain (Mount Morning), 7 Dec 1903. [A14]. (c) SPRI LS2000-42-153
- E.A.Wilson. Sledging notes: "Inside your Jaeger blouse you can dry your spare mits, socks, saenegrass etc." (c) SPRI LS2000-42-69
- E.A.Wilson. Sledging notes: "Once in your Reinskin blouse all you have to do is jump into your sleeping bag." (c) SPRI LS2000-42-71
- E.A.Wilson. Sledging notes: "Waiting to be tucked in." (c) SPRI LS2000-42-72

- R.W.Skelton. About to head West: L-R: Skelton (sitting), Evans, Scott, Handsley (sitting), Feather, Lashly, 12 Oct 1903. [Sk281]. (c) SPRI LS2000-42-216
- R.W.Skelton. Just off: Lashly, Handsley, Scott; Feather, Evans, Skelton, 12 Oct 1903. [Sk282]. (c) SPRI LS2000-42-202
- R.W.Skelton. The side of the Western (Ferrar) Glacier, with Handsley, 9 Dec 1903 [Sk302] (c) SPRI LS2000-42-242
- R.W.Skelton. Western (Ferrar) Glacier, Cathedral Rock Ice fall, Windy Gully visible 10 Dec 1903. [Sk310] (c) SPRI LS2000-42-249

Chapter Eleven: The Return to Civilisation
- Period map showing the return route of *Discovery* through the Ross Sea, 1904, with additions by D.M.Wilson (c) SPRI LS2000-42-187/ D.M.Wilson

- C.R.Ford. (prob.) Sawing out Camp. [Fo200?]. (c) SPRI P71/35:p71
- R.W.Skelton. Weddell Seal head and shoulders. [S35]. (c) SPRI LS2000-42-233
- R.W.Skelton. Sawing out Camp. [Sk10?]. (c) SPRI LS2000-42-265
- R.W.Skelton. The dog team at full pace. [S26]. (c) CAGM 1969.169.2

- Photographer unknown. Adelie Penguins in ecstatic posture. BNAE 1901-04 location/date unknown. (c) SPRI LS2000-42-88
- E.A.Wilson. Adult Adelie Penguin, 23 Nov 1903. (c) SPRI 1490
- E.A.Wilson. Immature Adelie Penguin. Undated. (c) SPRI 417
- E.A.Wilson. Adelie Penguin in ecstatic posture. Undated. (c) SPRI
- Photographer unknown. Adelie Penguin. BNAE 1901-04 location/date unknown. (c) SPRI LS2000-42-87
- E.A.Wilson. 'The arrival of the relief ships'. (c) SPRI 69/10/2

- R.W.Skelton. View from Hut Point towards the Gap. The black bulb thermometer stand with the magnetic variation study hut behind. [S32]. (c) SPRI LS2000-42-62
- Photographer unknown. Dog team and Mount Erebus. [Fo?]. (c) SPRI LS2000-42-207
- G.A.Davidson. Wilson (left) with Ferrar, collecting the most southern Elephant Seal then recorded. (c) NHM Z88fw V30906

- R.W.Skelton. Using the Ice saw to break up the ice around *Discovery* - Observation Hill and the Gap in the background. [S1]. (c) SPRI LS2000-42-228
- R.W.Skelton. Dell and the dog-team, posing in front of *Discovery* - Ski slopes in the background. [S51]. (c) SPRI LS2000-42-193
- R.W.Skelton. Breaking the ice - a gun cotton explosion, Winterquarters Bay by Hut Point - looking towards Arrival Heights. [S48]. (c) SPRI LS2000-42-145

- C.R.Ford? *Terra Nova* (left) and *Morning* approaching Winter Quarters Bay as the ice breaks out of McMurdo Sound: 10p.m. [Fo203?]. (c) SPRI LS2000-42-190
- C.R.Ford. Cheering the approach of the relief ships from Hut Point. [Fo205]. (c) SPRI LS2000-42-220
- R.W.Skelton. *Morning* and *Terra Nova* (left) approaching Winter Quarters Bay as the ice breaks out of McMurdo Sound: 11p.m. [S65]. (c) SPRI LS2000-42-39

- R.W.Skelton. Winter Quarters Bay, looking south-west from Hut Point/ski slopes, the Relief ships arrived, about midnight 14-15 Feb 1904. L-R: *Morning, Discovery* and *Terra Nova.* [S73]. (c) SPRI LS2000-42167
- E.A.Wilson. Vince's Cross, 1904. (c) SPRI 1289
- R.W.Skelton. *Discovery* breaks free, the ice pack that surrounded her floating away. *Morning* is also visible. 16 Feb 1904, looking across Winter Quarters Bay from Hut Point to the Gap. [S83]. (c) SPRI LS2000-42-199

- R.W.Skelton. *Discovery* taking aboard coal and other supplies from Terra Nova, Erebus Glacier Tongue 19 Feb 1904 (Dellbridge Islands behind). [S94?]. (c) SPRI LS2000-42-36
- R.W.Skelton. Emperor Penguins on the Erebus Glacier Snout, 19 Feb 1904. [S87?]. (c) SPRI LS2000-42-134
- E.A.Wilson. Midnight, 19 Feb 1904, the last sight of Mount Discovery: SS *Morning* and *Terra Nova* following *Discovery* out of McMurdo Strait. (c) Private

- R.W.Skelton. Tabular iceberg - much worn. [S110]. (c) SPRI LS2000-42-175
- C.R.Ford. *Terra Nova* passing through bergs, from the deck of *Discovery.* [Fo209]. (c) SPRI LS2000-42-194
- R.W.Skelton (Prob). The Possession Islands, 24 Feb 1904. [S113?]. (c) SPRI LS2000-42-256
- E.A.Wilson. Sailing through the Possession Islands. (c) SPRI 538
- C.R.Ford. *Terra Nova* passing through bergs, from the deck of *Discovery.* [Fo209]. (c) SPRI LS2000-42-194

QUILT
AFRICA

JENNY WILLIAMSON
PAT PARKER

We would like to express our sincere and special thanks to the following people who, so willingly, gave their time and talents in order to help with the publication of our book.

Rob Williamson for the photography. Shelley Williamson and Jane Wheeldon for the design and layout. Brett Eloff for allowing us to print his wonderful photograph of Nelson Mandela.

Gaye Bertram, Suzanne Carr, Joy Cowen, Jenny Hearn, Helen Izikowitz, Linda Jones, Ronel Linde, Geraldine Lonsdale, Pat Perry, Susan Sittig, Carol Smith, Petro van Rooyen and Irene van Tonder for permitting us to feature their beautiful quilts.

Located in Paducah, Kentucky, the American Quilter's Society (AQS) is dedicated to promoting the accomplishments of today's quilters. Through its publications and events, AQS strives to honor today's quilt-makers and their work and to inspire future creativity and innovation in quiltmaking.

Library of Congress Cataloging-in-Publication Data

Williamson, Jenny.
    Quilt Africa / by Jenny Williamson & Pat Parker.
        p.   cm.
    ISBN 1-57432-852-2
    1. Patchwork-Patterns. 2. Appliqué-Patterns. 3. Quilting-Patterns.
    4. Africa in art. I. Parker, Pat. II. American Quilter's Society. III. Title.

    TT835.W537   2004
    746.46'041'096-dc22   2004001233

Additional copies of this book may be ordered from the American Quilter's Society,
PO Box 3290, Paducah, KY 42002-3290;
800-626-5420 (orders only please);
or online at www.AQSquilt.com.
For all other inquiries, call 270-898-7903.

contents

introduction

Jenny & Pat

For many years we have been inspired to make quilts utilizing the influences of Africa. This has proved to be easier than one would imagine!

We have a vast cultural and environmental diversity of sources from which to gain inspiration. Our scenery is spectacular and this opens up countless opportunities for creating landscape quilts or wallhangings. Our flora and fauna are unique and adaptations can be used with motifs chosen from these sources. Quilts can be made dealing with subjects that are specifically relevant to life in this country, celebrating the lives of our multi-cultural population, from whatever background, showing their lifestyles, either past or present.

Coming from our Eurocentric white backgrounds we owe an enormous debt design-wise to the many African cultures that have influenced us and have, in many instances, been our inspiration.

Over the years many quilters have said to us that they are either nervous, or do not know how, to use their African fabrics. Hopefully this book will encourage them to get out that stash of fabrics and 'Go for It'!

Our photographer, Rob Williamson

The photographic assistants

We have given instructions for the making of a number of quilts that, we believe, have an essence of Africa about them. Perhaps quilters will copy them exactly, or better still, use them as a starting point in creating quilts with an African flavor, using a combination of ethnic fabrics, shapes and colors and - what is more - have fun doing so!

shall we start?

We ask you to read the following notes before beginning a quilt from this book. They should help you to better understand our methods of instruction.

As so many wonderful books have already been written giving all the necessary details of the various techniques used in quilting, we see no purpose in repeating these details. We would, however, like to suggest the following guidelines that should help when making an African quilt or wallhanging.

Choice of fabrics
As far as the choice of fabrics is concerned, this is a golden opportunity to leave your "Comfort Zone".

Whether it be artwork or clothing, the people of Africa invariably choose an unpredictable variety of vibrant and seemingly clashing colors. Do not forget this when planning a quilt.

Audition the fabrics, choosing the ones which are most suitable for huts, trees, people, animals, birds, etc. Then move the fabrics around until the result is successful.

Do not be too inhibited. The greater the variety introduced, the more successful the end result.

Introduce some startling "Uglies".

Don't choose fabrics that look too realistic – naivete looks great!

Hand-dyed fabrics are good – particularly for backgrounds.

We recommend 100% cotton for HAND appliqué. When doing MACHINE appliqué, however, use whatever fabric gives the desired effect, whether it be cotton blends, satin, wool, silk, organza, netting, etc.

We are assuming that all fabric is 45" (115cm) wide. If this is not the case the given quantities will need to be adjusted. (More fabric needed if it is narrower and less if it is wider).

Hand appliqué
Due to the fact that it is often difficult to remove various marking pens and pencils, we prefer to use a method by which we do not have to mark the fabric at all.

Use a fine ball-point pen to trace the design onto iron-on vylene. We prefer to use a vylene that is thin and pliable, with bonding only on one side.

When tracing the design onto the vylene, always have the bonded side down. Cut vylene along the marked lines. (No seam allowance). Position the vylene onto the fabric as desired. The grain of the fabric is not important, rather iron the vylene onto the fabric to obtain the best effect.

Iron the vylene lightly onto the right side of the fabric, placing a plain white sheet of paper between the iron and the work. (Should you inadvertently iron onto the wrong side of the vylene, only the vylene and paper will have to be replaced, not the iron!)

Use a dry iron, no steam, but do not allow it to be too hot (e.g. wool setting or cooler, depending upon your iron), otherwise the bonding will melt and cause the vylene to adhere too firmly to the fabric. It is always advisable to test on a scrap before commencing.

After vylene has been ironed in place, cut a seam allowance of between $1/8$" (3mm) and $1/4$" (6mm).

Working on a flat surface, pin appliqué pieces to base. We find the tiny appliqué pins indispensable, as the long ones tend to get in the way.

We sew with either an Appliqué or Crewel (Embroidery) needle (Size 9 or 10), but we suggest that whatever needle is correct for you is acceptable. If you have young eyes and dainty fingers by all means use a 12!

Match the thread as closely as possible to the color of the piece being appliquéd. If the match is not perfect always go for a darker rather than a lighter thread.

Sew small blind hemming stitches about $1/8$" (3mm) apart. Pull thread firmly upwards towards you as you go.

Concave curves need to be clipped to release the tension.

Remove vylene as each piece is applied.

Machine appliqué
As in hand appliqué use a fine ball-point pen to trace the design onto the vylene. When tracing the design onto the vylene always have the bonded side up, and when ironing the vylene onto the fabric always have the bonded side down. Iron this onto the wrong side of the fabric.

Do not worry about the grain, rather iron the vylene onto the fabric to obtain the best effect. Use a dry iron, but do not allow it to be too hot. Place a sheet of clean white paper between the iron and the work.

Use a zigzag machine with a suitable foot (one which has no metal or plastic between the toes to block your view as you sew).

When doing machine appliqué fibre deposits build up very quickly around the bobbin area, so it is necessary to clean and oil your machine regularly. Make sure that the needle is sharp, as a blunt needle is the main cause of irregular stitching (We like to use a 70/10 or 80/12 size needle).

Always put a sheet of magazine paper underneath your work when machining i.e. between your work and the feed dog. This will act as a stabilizer and prevent the work from puckering. When stitching is complete remember to remove the paper from the back of the work!

Pull threads to back of work and cut off as you go. Birds' nests are for trees – not for the backs of quilts!

For satin stitch your stitches should be close enough to form a solid line, but not be so close that they bunch up and jam the machine. (If you let go of the fabric when

4

sewing, the feed dog should carry the fabric through without a problem).

For a more contemporary look alter your stitch lengths and widths until you get the desired effect. Alternatively you could turn in the raw edges and then finish off with a blind hemming stitch.

You may even wish to leave the raw edges and sew with a straight stitch.

Try using different threads. This is an area that can be such a lot of fun!

Remember that appliqué is a means of stitching one fabric to another. How it is done is not important as long as the end result is successful. This is where one can be really creative!

Anyone can do appliqué work. It is a medium that can be both rewarding and stimulating.

Piecing
Whether you are doing hand or machine piecing, it is imperative to work accurately. We use a $1/4$" (6mm) seam allowance throughout.

If your seams are not exactly $1/4$" (6mm) you will need to adjust our given measurements. We suggest that you sew 3 small squares together. Cut them $2^1/2$" x $2^1/2$" (64mm x 64mm). When they are stitched they should measure $6^1/2$" (165mm) from the left to the right hand edges. If they do not, adjust them accordingly.

Before cutting borders please measure your quilt top across the middle for both length and width. If your size is slightly different from the sizes given you will need to adjust your sizes accordingly. For example: the given width measurement is $40^1/2$" (1030mm) and your quilt top measures $41^1/2$"(1054mm) (difference 1"(25mm)) you will need to add 1" (25mm) to all the given sizes. The same applies to your length measurement.

When using the piecing templates, make templates as given, then add $1/4$" (6mm) seam allowance when cutting fabric. The arrow on the templates indicates the direction of the grain of the fabric.

Pressing
Pressing means literally what it says – press the iron gently onto the fabric. If you push too hard you will stretch the fabric.

Press the seams as you go.

Do not open the seams as it weakens them. Wherever possible press the seams towards the darkest fabric.

Press seams away from where you wish to quilt.

Signing your quilts
Make sure you personalize your quilts. Always sign and date your quilts – either on the front or back. Include any other information that you feel is relevant e.g. maybe the name of the person or the occasion for which the quilt has been made.

african dash

50" x 77¹/₂" (1.27m x 1.97m)
Helen Izikowitz

This quilt was inspired by the wonderful array of African fabrics which lend themselves so successfully to any traditional design.

43" x 52" (1.1m x 1.32m)
Jenny Williamson & Pat Parker
*Hand appliquéd, machine pieced
and hand quilted.*

This quilt depicts urban life as seen around
us at the present time. Small business is the
order of the day and budding entrepreneurs
are everywhere to be found.

every picture tells a story

chwe chwe magic

58" x 66" (1.48m x 1.68m)
Suzanne Carr
Hand pieced and hand quilted.

Interlaced rings of the fabric of African society.

30" x 45" (0.76m x 1.15m)
Jenny Williamson & Pat Parker
Machine pieced and appliquéd. Hand quilted. Background Indigo cotton named Chwe-Chwe by Xhosa people.

There is nothing quite like an African sky lit up by a full moon - hence our exaggerated use of vibrant colors.

moon madness

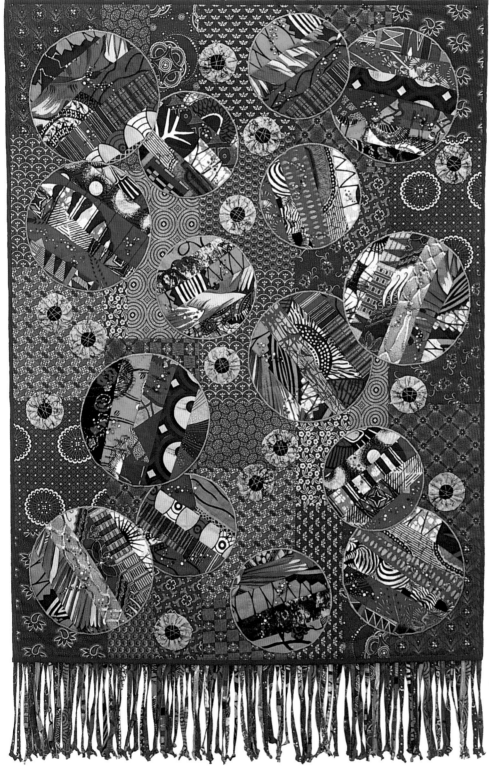

passages

25" x 30" (0.64m x 0.76m)
Helen Izikowitz

Design techniques using a variety of African
fabrics have assisted in my development
from traditional patterns to those of a more
abstract nature.

40" x 47" (1.02m x 1.2m)
Susan Sittig
Machine pieced, appliquéd, embroidered and quilted.

A few of my favourite wild flowers bring back wonderful memories of childhood holidays spent wandering in the mountains around Worcester in the Boland region of the Cape Province.

sentimental journey

fertility

43" x 43" (1.1m x 1.1m)
Jenny Williamson
*Machine pieced and appliquéd. Machine
and hand quilted.*

Will traditional fertility ceremonies die out?

27¹/₂" x 35" (0.7m x 0.89m)
Pat Parker
Hand appliquéd, machine pieced and hand quilted.

The Natal Midlands is a beautiful area of South Africa made up of rolling hills that extend to the peaks of the Drakensberg range in the far distance.

midlands meander

homeless

32" x 40" (0.81m x 1.02m)
Jenny Williamson
Machine pieced and hand quilted.

Every person needs a home, however humble.

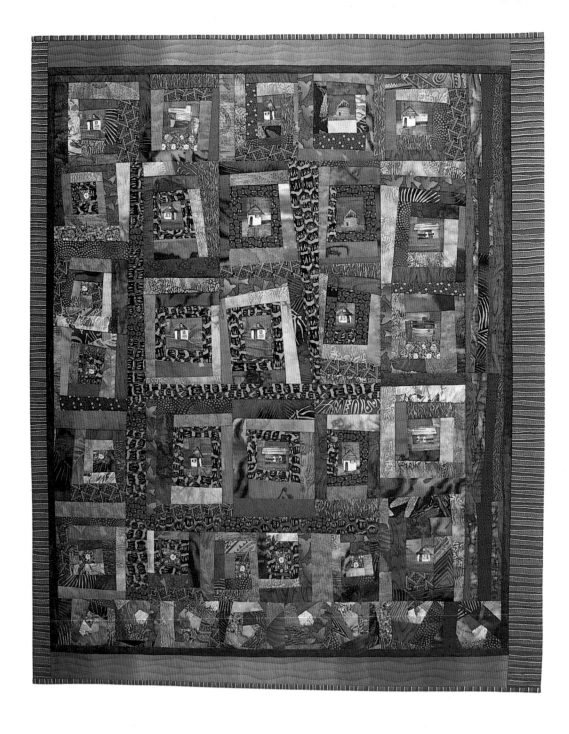

30" x 23" (0.76m x 0.58m)
Jenny Williamson
*Machine appliquéd, hand and
machine quilted.*

Wide open spaces refresh one's soul.

solitude

dreams do come true

40¹/₂" x 65¹/₂" (1.03m x 1.66m)
*Protea design - **Maretha Fourie***
*Machine pieced by **Geraldine Lonsdale***
*Machine quilted by **Petro van Rooyen***

Proteas are synonymous with the Cape of Good Hope. As it was not possible to buy fabric featuring this flower I decided to design and print my own. This decision sent me on a wonderful journey of discovery and at the end of a year, I had the protea fabric ready to use in my quilt - Geraldine.

37¹/₂ x 51" (0.95m x 1.3m)
Joy Cowen

The vibrance of Africa's colors and
traditions are most stimulating and the
simplicity and wonder of our natural
resources give me endless inspiration.

brave heart

Linda Jones

*Metallic thread used throughout to make it
look like chain mail.*

Haliaeetus Vocifer 20" x 35" (0.51m x 0.89m)
Ronel Linde

"The cry of the African Fish Eagle is
synonymous with wild Africa, and is perhaps
the best known of all African bird calls. It's
carrying ringing tones can be heard from a
great distance and stir excitement in most
of us at the splendour and challenge of the
sound. When one bird calls, it is often
answered by a second bird, sometimes in
a duet."

Quote from The Birds Around Us
Richard Liversidge.

african fish eagle

lycaon pictus - painted dog

22¹/₂" x 18¹/₂" (0.57m x 0.47m)
Ronel Linde
Machine appliquéd and quilted.

Wild dogs are classified Endangered by the IUCN Red list. There are only 250 free-ranging wild dogs in South Africa at the present time.

I have always been fascinated by these unfairly persecuted animals, as they have a very loving and caring pack set-up, where an entire pack helps look after the pups, and will feed any without mothers - a lesson for all of us, perhaps?

31" x 39" (0.79m x 0.99m)
Machine pieced and appliquéd by
Jenny Williamson *and* **Pat Parker.**
Machine quilted by **Ronel Linde.**

This is an endangered species which we have been fortunate enough to encounter on a few occasions when visiting game parks in South Africa.

Sometimes the wild dogs are referred to as "painted wolves" - not without reason - with their remarkable patchwork hides.

wild dogs

22

37" x 32" (0.94m x 0.82m)
Carol Smith
Machine pieced and quilted, hand embroidered and beaded.

Inspired by the little geckos that visit daily in my sewing room.

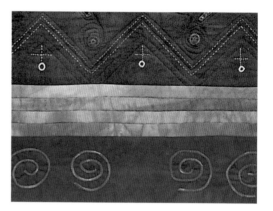

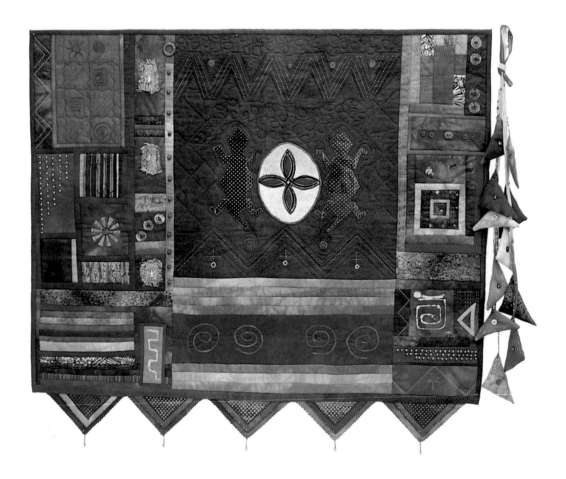

41" x 51" (1.04m x 1.3m)
Carol Smith
Machine pieced and quilted, hand embroidered and beaded.

In making this quilt I wished to convey the exceptional warmth of my country and its people.

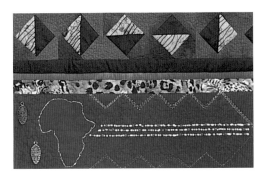

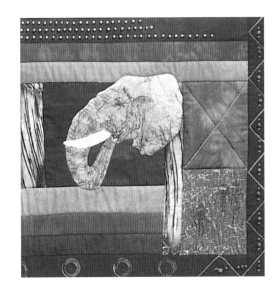

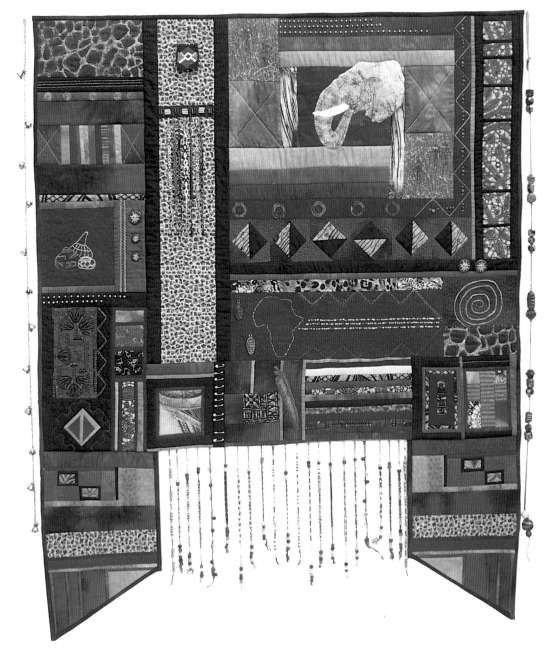

zambezi

17¹/₂ x 21" (0.45m x 0.54m)
Linda Jones
All machine work, with some hand embellishment.

My impressions of Africa while drifting down the Zambesi in a canoe in the early morning.

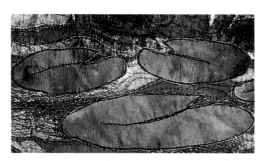

43" x 47" (1.1m x 1.2m)
Pat Parker
Machine appliquéd and pieced.
Hand quilted.

I continue to be fascinated by the many windmills that form an integral part of the Karoo landscape.

43" x 47" (1.1m x 1.2m)
Pat Parker

windmills on my mind

stars of an african night

49" x 56" (1.25m x 1.42m)
Suzanne Carr
Hand pieced and hand quilted.

Each star has a uniqueness portraying the individuality within our cosmopolitan country.

49" x 51" (1.25m x 1.3m)
Jenny Hearn

This quilt depicts the carvings on a granary door. The method of manufacture is derived from the African two-dimensional textile art, which includes techniques of embroidery and appliqué.

african idiom

coral and ivory

58" x 58" (1.48m x 1.48m)
Irene van Tonder
Machine pieced, hand appliquéd and hand quilted.

I wanted to convey the contrasting elements of the African bushveld.

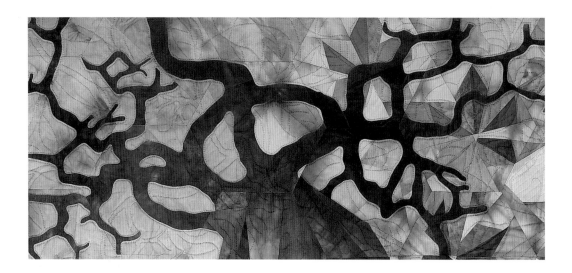

make an african quilt

african footprints

45" x 51" (1.14m x 1.3m)
Jenny Williamson & Pat Parker

Like people, animals can also be 'squares'. In fact we would even go as far as saying that our warthog is a prize 'nerd!' When making this quilt choose a selection of plain fabrics that look good together. Then add one patterned fabric to act as a "zinger."

Before starting this quilt please compare all shaded sections on drawing with similar sections on quilt photograph. You will see that these shaded sections have been strip

pieced. We will give you the cut size for each section and you should piece the sections as you wish.

Block size:
5" x 5" (127mm x 127mm). You will need 56 blocks, 7 across by 8 down.

Techniques:
We suggest this quilt be pieced by machine. The appliqué and quilting can be done by either hand or machine.

Materials:

Approximately 10 plain fabrics.	1/4 yard (0.25m) each	
Patterned fabric ("zinger").	1/2 yard (0,5m)	
1 Dark plain fabric to be used for a few background squares, the inner border, the central elephant and the binding.	1 yard (1m)	
Backing	49" x 55" (1.25m x 1.4m)	
Batting	49" x 55" (1.25m x 1.4m)	

Method:
Cut 56 blocks in plain fabrics 5 1/2" x 5 1/2" (140mm x140mm) (Each lengthwise strip is made up of 8 blocks).

Place all 56 blocks on audition board, moving them around until you are satisfied with the color distribution. Do not appliqué on the following blocks: C4, C5, D4, D5, E4, E5. This is where the central elephant will be appliquéd. (Make sure that your large central elephant will show up against the fabrics that you choose for these 6 squares).

Now trace your appliqué shapes onto paper and place these in position on your audition board. When you are happy with the distribution appliqué all shapes except central elephant onto background blocks. (Some blocks will be left with no appliqué).

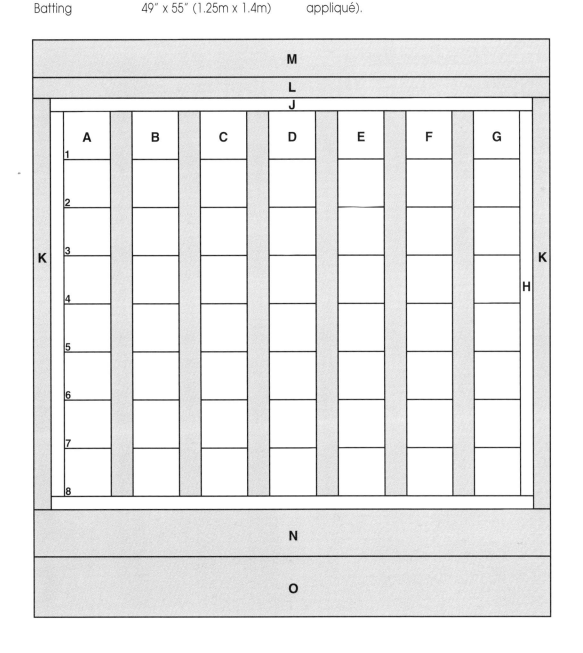

Sew blocks together so as to make up the 7 lengthwise strips (A) to (G). Set aside. Cut 6 lengthwise strips 40¹/₂" x 1¹/₂" (1030mm x 38mm).

Make 40 Prairie Points to insert at odd intervals between your lengthwise strips thus:

Cut 40 3" (76mm) squares. Fold across the diagonal once and then again to form small triangles. Tack along raw edge to keep in place. Overlap triangles to form groups of 3, 4 or 5.

Tack these groups of triangles in place as desired along edges of lengthwise strips. (A) to (G).

Join A, B, C, D, E, F and G alternating with narrow 1¹/₂" (38mm) strips to form quilt top.

Applique central elephant. (You should have the small elephant enlarged until it is your desired size.)

Cut narrow border in dark fabric as follows:
2 strips 40¹/₂" x 1¹/₂" (1030mm x 38mm) (H)
2 strips 43¹/₂" x 1¹/₂" (1105mm x 38mm) (J).

Sew strips (H) to left and right hand sides of quilt. Sew strips (J) to top and bottom of quilt.

Cut 2 strips 42¹/₂" x 1¹/₂" (1080mm x 38mm) (K). Sew to left and right hand sides of quilt.

Cut 4 strips as follows:
45¹/₂" x 1¹/₂" (1156 x 38mm) (L)
45¹/₂" x 2" (1156 x 51mm) (M)
45¹/₂" x 3" (1156 x 76mm) (N)
45¹/₂" x 4¹/₂" (1156mm x 114mm) (O)

Join (L) to (M). Sew to top of quilt.

Join (N) to (O). Sew to bottom of quilt.

Quilt as desired.

Bind quilt folding the binding to back of quilt so that it does not show on the front.

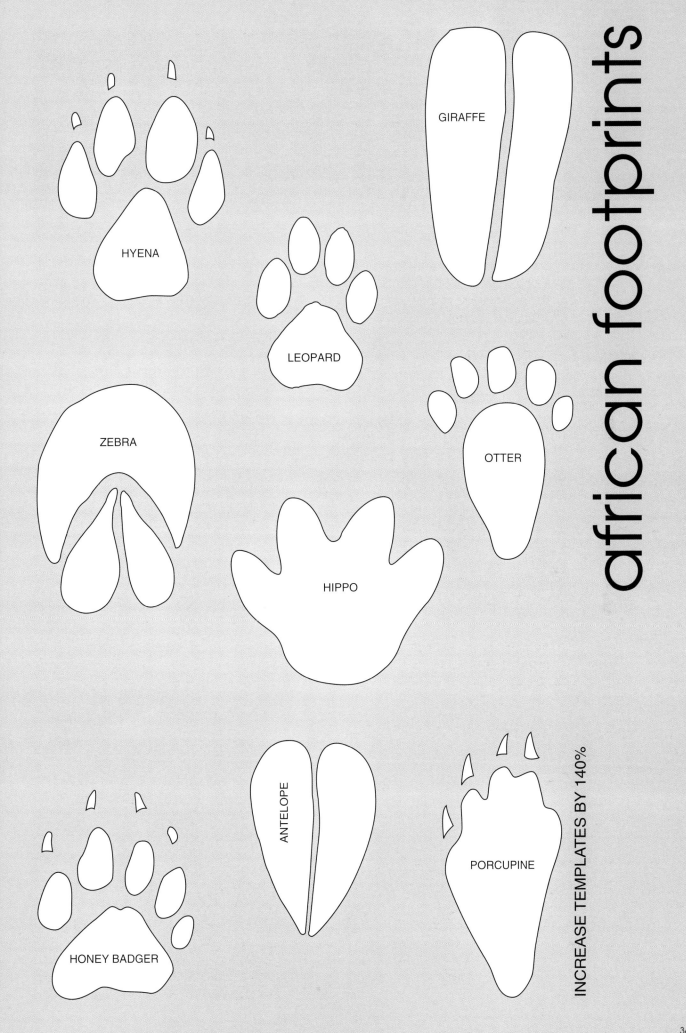

HYENA

GIRAFFE

LEOPARD

ZEBRA

OTTER

HIPPO

HONEY BADGER

ANTELOPE

PORCUPINE

INCREASE TEMPLATES BY 140%

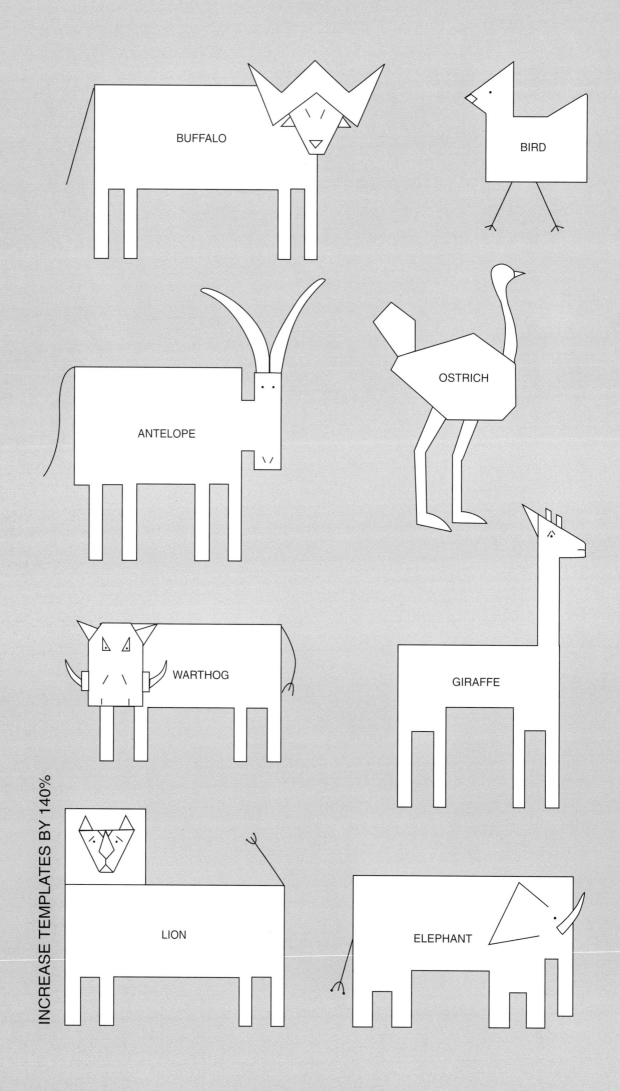

BUFFALO

BIRD

ANTELOPE

OSTRICH

WARTHOG

GIRAFFE

INCREASE TEMPLATES BY 140%

LION

ELEPHANT

RHINOCEROS

LIZARD

ZEBRA

FISH

GUINEA FOWL

HIPPO

LEOPARD

MONKEY

INCREASE TEMPLATES BY 140%

36

birds of a feather

40" x 50" (1.02m x 1.27m)
Pat Parker

This is a good beginners quilt as the design is so simple. The drawings for the guinea fowl have been reduced in order to save space.

You will need to enlarge them by at least 140% (more if desired). The beaks, eyes, crops and feet of the guinea fowl should be embroidered.

You will see that the templates are the same for all the guinea fowl. You can therefore design your own – move the templates around as you wish - the only limitation being that guinea fowl are not too good at doing 'headstands'!

Block size:
4" x 7" (100mm x 180mm). You will need 48 blocks made up of 4 different units 8 across by 6 down.

Techniques:
Can be pieced, appliquéd and quilted either by hand or machine.

Materials:
Dark fabric	2 yards	(2m)
Medium fabric	³/₄ yard	(0,75m)
Light fabric	³/₄ yard	(0.75m)
2 Contrasting fabrics	¹/₄ yard	(0.25m)
suitable for guinea fowls.		each
Fabric for heads of	³/₄ yard	(0.75m)
guinea fowl, innerpleat		
and binding.		
Backing	44" x 54"	(1.12m x1.38m)
Batting	44" x 54"	(1.12m x 1.38m)

Method:
Make template as given, then add ¹/₄" (6mm) seam allowance when cutting fabric.

Cut Triangles as follows:
(D) and (Dr) is Dark fabric,
(M) and (Mr) is Medium fabric and
(L) and (Lr) is Light fabric.

24 Triangles (D)
24 Triangles (Dr)
12 Triangles (M)
12 Triangles (Mr)
12 Triangles (L)
12 Triangles (Lr)

Each block is made up of 2 Triangles. Sew Blocks according to the 4 Units as illustrated.

Sew blocks together in rows as shown on diagram.

Make 3 of Row 1 and 3 of Row 2.

Alternating Rows 1 and 2 join 6 rows together to form quilt top.

Appliqué guinea fowl to quilt top as desired.

Measure your quilt top across the centre length and width.

Using the fabric bought for guinea fowl heads cut 2 strips 1¹/₄" (32mm) wide the

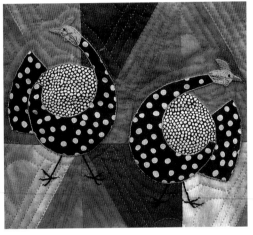

length of your quilt and 2 strips 1¹/₄" (32mm) wide the width of your quilt.

Fold in half lengthwise, (wrong sides together) then tack in position on all 4 sides to form pleat (pleat facing centre of quilt top).

Using dark fabric cut 4 strips 4¹/₂" (115mm) wide the same lengths that you used to cut your pleat.

Appliqué feathers to these strips as desired.

Using medium fabric cut 4 squares 4¹/₂" x 4¹/₂" (115mm x 115mm).

Join lengthwise strips to left and right hand sides of quilt.

Sew 2 4¹/₂" (115mm) squares to either end of widthwise strips.

Join these strips to top and bottom of quilt. Bind with same fabric used for pleat.

birds of a feather

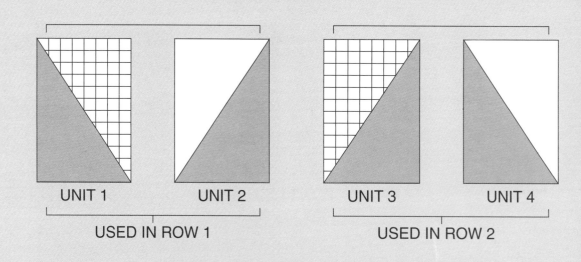

UNIT 1 UNIT 2 UNIT 3 UNIT 4

USED IN ROW 1 USED IN ROW 2

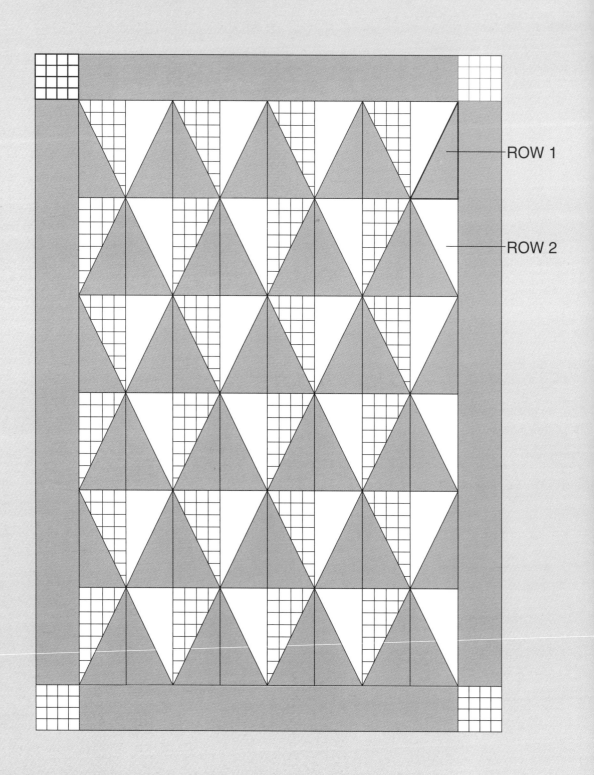

ROW 1

ROW 2

L   Lr
M   Mr
D   Dr

ADD ¼" (6mm) SEAM ALLOWANCE

desert sands

40" x 60" (1.02m x 1.53m)
Pat Perry

The earthy colors of this quilt contribute to the feel of the desert. However, the mood could change entirely with a different color scheme. The piecing may seem complicated, but if the step by step instructions are followed it will easily fall into place.

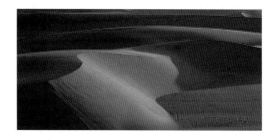

Techniques:
We suggest that this quilt be hand pieced. The quilting can be done either by hand or machine.

Materials:
Beige	1¹/₂ yards (1.5m)
Brown	1¹/₂ yards (1.5m)
Black	¹/₂ yard (0.5m)
Red	¹/₂ yard (0.5m)
Orange	¹/₂ yard (0.5m)
Batting	44" x 64" (1.12m x1.63m)
Backing	44" x 64" (1.12m x 1.63m)

Method:
Make templates as shown, adding ¹/₄" (6mm) seam allowance when cutting fabric. To save space templates (A), (B) and (D) have not been drawn to scale. Make these according to the measurements given on template diagrams.

Cut all fabric before you commence piecing.

Unit 1.
Make 10 according to piecing diagram.

Unit 2.
Make 3 according to piecing diagram. Piece quilt top one row at a time as follows, checking carefully on diagram as you work:

Row 1.
Join (A) to (A). Set aside.
Take 2 unit 1's and join 2 (C's) and 2 (Cr's) to each unit. Set aside.
Join another (A) to (A)
Sew these new units together.
Insert 6 (J's) to complete Row 1.
Set aside.

Row 2.
Add 4 (H's) to each of 3 Unit 1's.
Alternate these with 4 (D's).
Join Rows 1 and 2. Set aside.

Row 3.
Same as Row 1, except that only the top 3 (J's) should be inserted.
Join Row 3 to Row 2. Set aside.

Row 4.
Take up 3 Unit 2's.
Alternate these with 4 (D's).
Join Row 4 to Row 3.

Row 5.
Sew (A) + (B) + (B) + (A).
Insert 3 (J's).
Join Row 5 to Row 4.

Cut 2 strips (K) 40¹/₂" x 2¹/₂" (1030mm x 64mm). Join to top and bottom of quilt top.

Quilt as desired.

Bind quilt using brown fabric.

Having survived your walk through the desert how about a long (stiff!) drink?

K

ROW 1

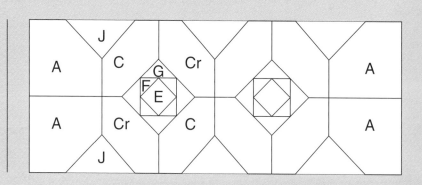

ROW 2

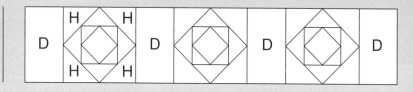

ROW 3

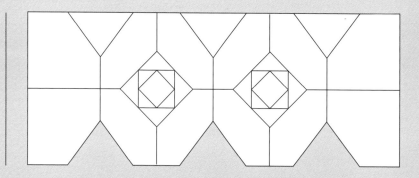

ROW 4

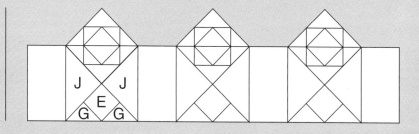

ROW 5

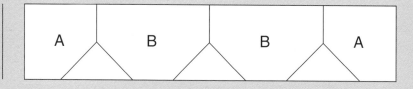

K

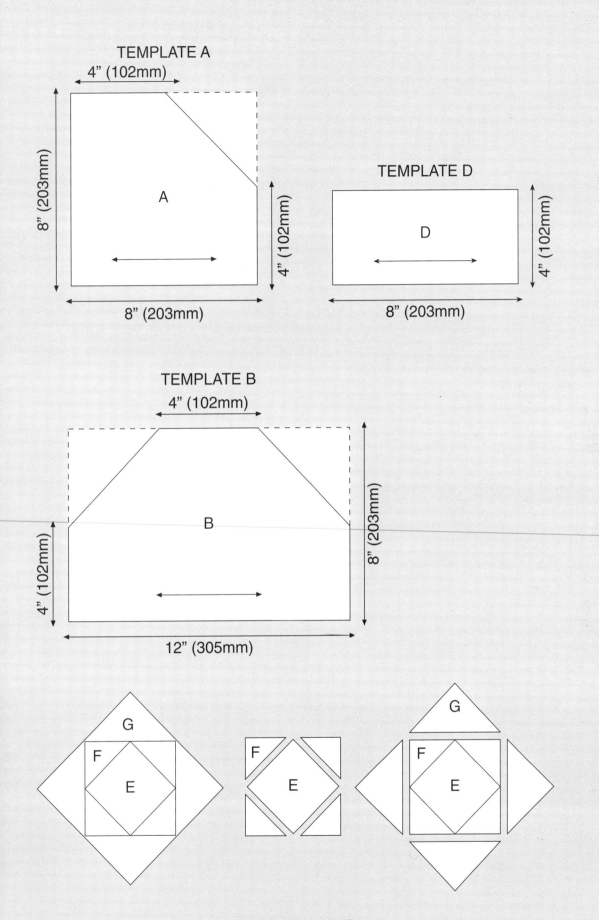

TEMPLATE A

4" (102mm)

8" (203mm)

A

4" (102mm)

8" (203mm)

TEMPLATE D

D

4" (102mm)

8" (203mm)

TEMPLATE B

4" (102mm)

B

8" (203mm)

4" (102mm)

12" (305mm)

G

F

E

F

E

G

F

E

UNIT 1 PIECING

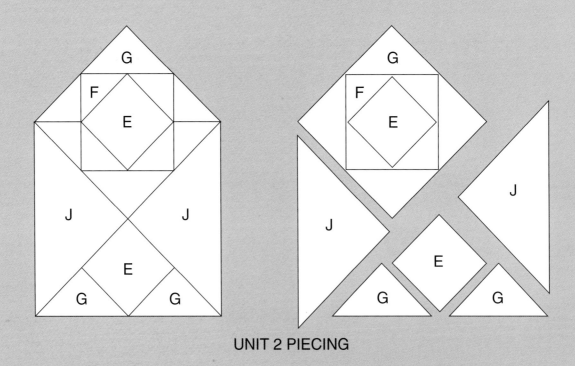

UNIT 2 PIECING

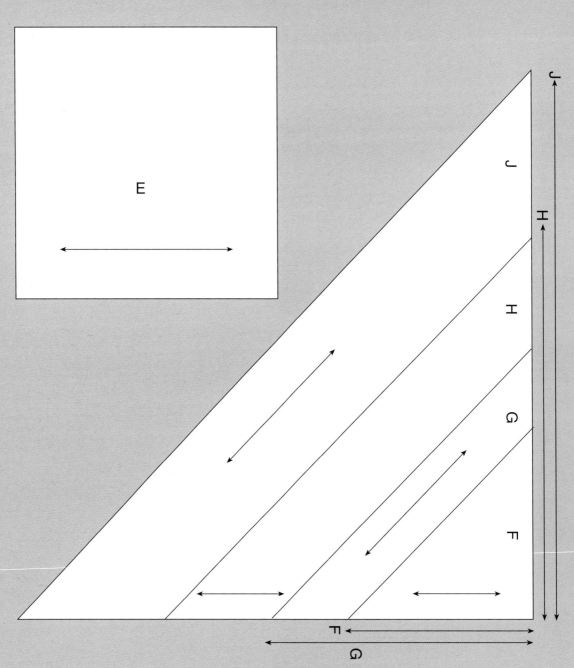

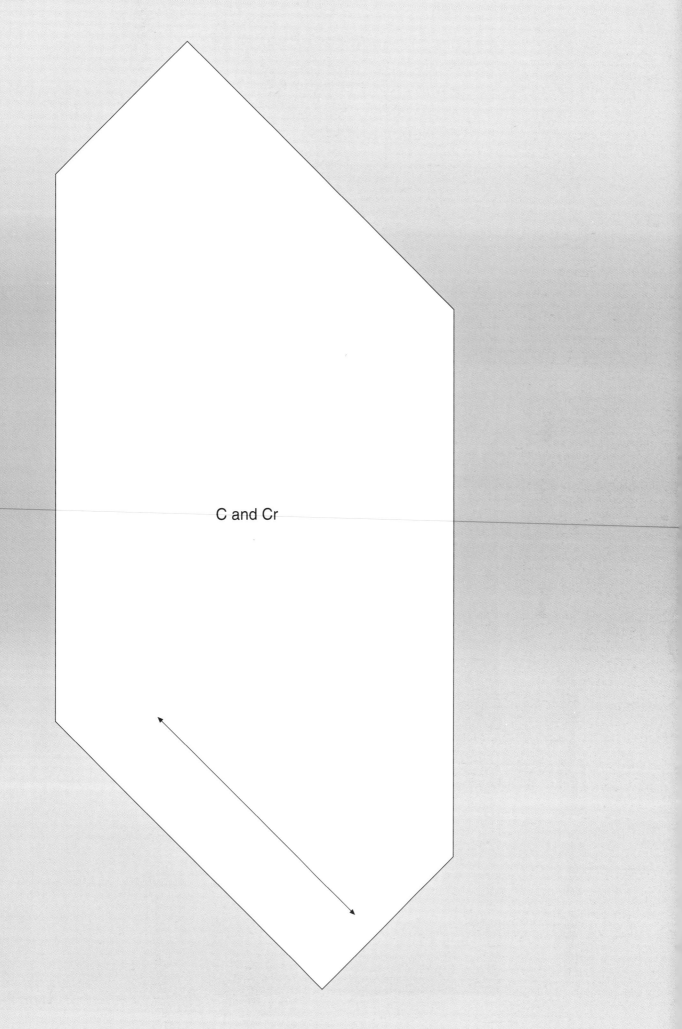

C and Cr

girls from egoli

48" x 64" (1.22m x 1.63m)
Pat Parker

I decided to have some fun on the fashion
front using the traditional African fabrics that
look so stunning on 'the right girl'.

Unfortunately, as I do not qualify, I dressed a
few models instead. Try this and enjoy!

Techniques:

This quilt can be pieced, appliquéd and quilted either by hand or machine. The instructions and templates given are for foundation piecing over paper. Should you decide to piece by hand make the templates by tracing the correct sizes given on our drawings then add your ¹/₄" (6mm) seam allowance when cutting fabrics.

Materials:

Green background fabric   2 yards (2m)
Black fabric   1 yard (1m)
Backing   52" x 68" (1.33m x 1.73m)
Batting   52" x 68" (1.33m x 1.73m)
As many African-type
fabrics as you can muster.

Method:

Using printed fabrics for (A) and green fabric for (B) and (C) make 25 Unit 1's.

Using printed fabrics for (A) and black fabric for (B) and (C) make 25 Unit 1's.

With printed fabrics only cut 50 triangles (D) exactly the same size as the outer edge of Unit 1. These triangles will be used with the Unit 1's to make up 25 squares, 5 across by 5 down.

Using color photograph as guide, place all Unit 1s and triangles (D) in position on a board, moving them around until you are satisfied with color distribution.

Piece 25 squares as shown on piecing diagram. Join squares in rows 5 across by 5 down.

Cut 4 strips in black 40¹/₂" x 1¹/₄".
(1030mm x 32mm). Fold in half, wrong

sides together and tack 1 strip to each side of joined squares ¹/₈" (4mm) from edge. Set aside.

You are now going to make 68 Unit 2's. Please check diagram **VERY CAREFULLY** as the green fabric will be in different positions on the squares depending upon where they are positioned on the quilt. Please note that on all 4 sides half the diagonals **WILL BE FACING ONE WAY AND HALF THE OTHER.**

Work first on the left side. Take 10 Unit 2s, join them together, then sew to left hand side of quilt top. Do the same for right side. Set aside.

Using printed fabrics make 4 Unit 3s for outer corners of quilt.

Cut 20 green squares 4¹/₂" x 4¹/₂" (115mm x115mm).

Now piece top and bottom sections of quilt as follows:
Checking carefully on quilt diagram, piece these sections together in 3 separate rows. Then join each set of 3 rows together, one for top and one for bottom of quilt.

Appliqué the Egoli girls onto these sections before joining them to quilt top as they will be easier to handle (the sections, not the girls). Check carefully that they face the right way up (you don't want half of them standing on their heads!)

Stitch these 2 sections to top and bottom of quilt.

Quilt as desired. Bind quilt with black fabric.

girls from egoli

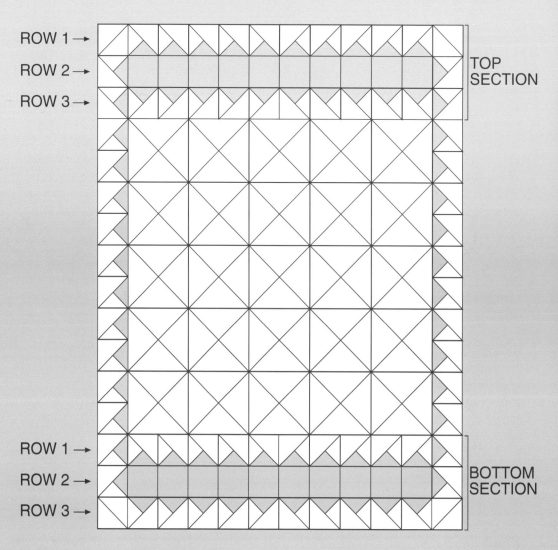

ROW 1 →
ROW 2 →
ROW 3 →

TOP
SECTION

ROW 1 →
ROW 2 →
ROW 3 →

BOTTOM
SECTION

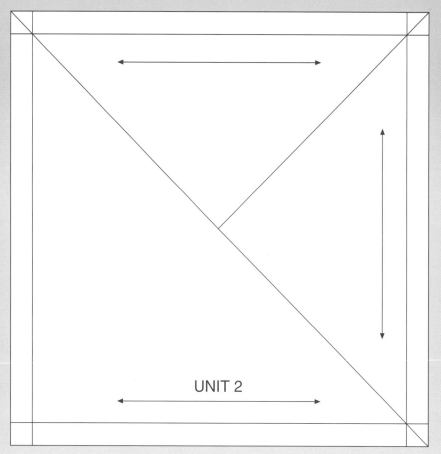

UNIT 2

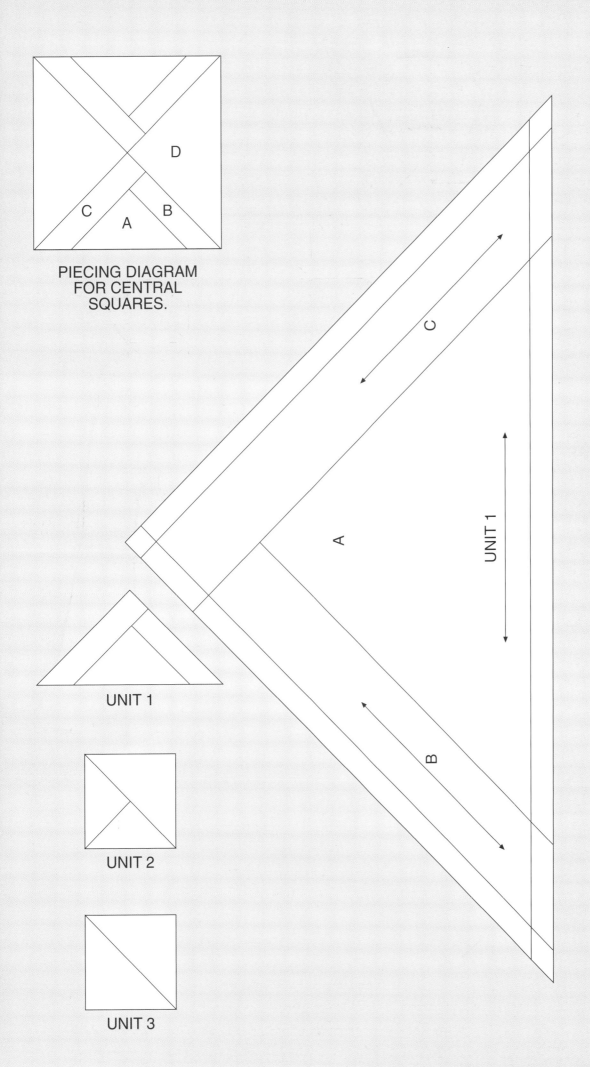

PIECING DIAGRAM
FOR CENTRAL
SQUARES.

D

C   B

A

C

A

UNIT 1

B

UNIT 1

UNIT 2

UNIT 3

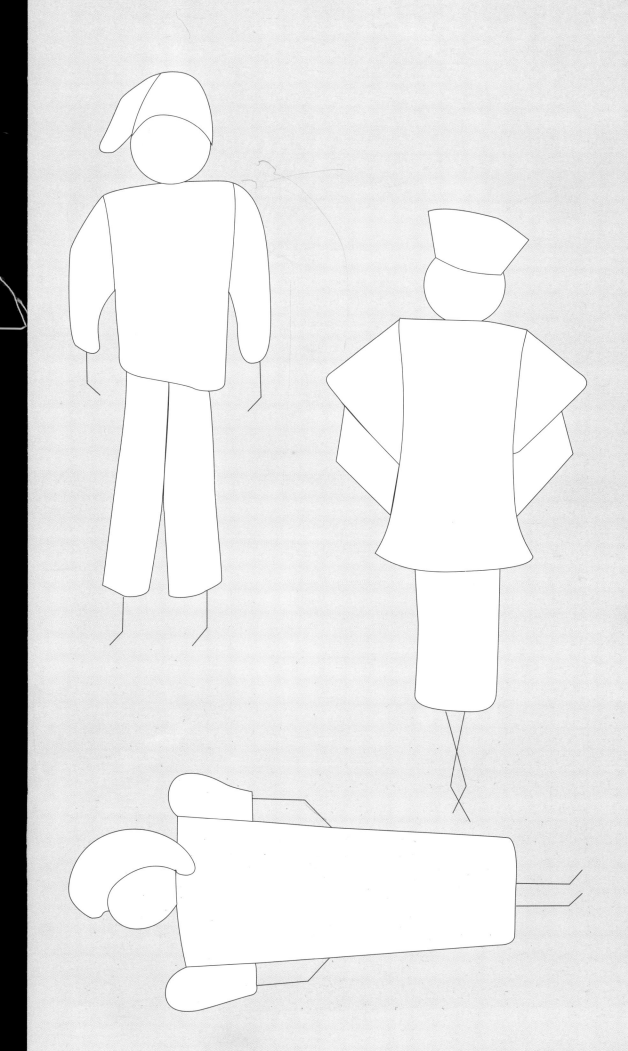

33" x 40¹/₂" (0.84m x 1.03m)
Jenny Williamson

This is a fun way to pass the time during endless boring waits for husbands, children, airplanes, etc.

These puffs are extremely easy and relaxing to make. They can be made from very small scraps of fabric.

Techniques.
The puffs are made by hand and then pieced together by machine.

Puff size:
Finished puff size 2¹/₂" x 2¹/₂" (64mm x 64mm) You will need 208 puffs, 13 across by 16 down.

Materials:
A selection of 3¹/₂" (90mm) squares of brightly colored prints.

Soft calico for back   2 yards (2m) of puffs.

Backing   36" x 44" (0.92m x 1.12m)

Binding   ¹/₂ yard (0.5m)

Polyester fibrefill for stuffing.

Method:
Using calico cut 208 squares 3" x 3" (76mm x 76mm). Using prints cut 208 squares 3¹/₂"x 3¹/₂" (90mm x 90mm).

Take 1 backing and 1 top square. With right sides together pin 2 corners of first side of square. Make a pleat in centre of top square so that the top and bottom squares fit exactly. Tack ¹/₈" (4mm) from edge of square.

Continue in this manner, keeping the centre pleats facing in the same direction, along the next 2 sides. Insert a small amount of filling (about the size of a walnut) into square and then tack the 4th side. Do not use too much stuffing as this will make the squares difficult to join.

We suggest that you pin the completed blocks to a board to check for a pleasing color distribution. Stitch puffs right sides together with a ¹/₄" (6mm) seam, completing a row at a time. (13 squares across).

Join rows (16 rows down), keeping seam allowance facing the opposite direction in each row to help with the matching of crosswise seams.

Measure the length and width of puff top across the 2 centres.

Cut the backing exactly to these 2 measurements.

Place puff top onto quilt backing and tack around all 4 sides.

Add binding.

Finally, tie top at corners of puffs at regular intervals to keep backing in position.

34" x 44" (0.86m x 1.12m)
Jenny Williamson & Pat Parker

To prevent becoming confused while making this quilt we suggest that you follow the instructions step by step and cross them out as you complete them.

Join as many small pieces of fabric together as you can to make up the required sizes for the borders. The more fabrics you introduce into this quilt the better it will look.

NB $1/4"$ (6mm) seam allowance used throughout. (This $1/4"$ (6mm) is already included in the given sizes.)

Techniques:
The appliqué, piecing and quilting can be done either by hand or machine. If you add embroidery, again either by hand or machine, this will add a further dimension to your quilt.

Materials:
Background fabric $\qquad$ $1^1/4$ yard (1.25m)
Batting $\qquad$ 38" x 48" (0.97m x 1.22m)
Backing $\qquad$ 38" x 48" (0.97m x 1.22m)
Binding fabric $\qquad$ $1/2$ yard (0.5m)
Small pieces of fabrics suitable for appliquéing your motifs.
Small pieces of brightly coloured fabrics suitable for the borders.

Instructions:
Using your background fabric cut out the following sizes:
1. $6^1/2"$ x $11^1/2"$ (165mm x 292mm)
2. $8^1/2"$ x $9^1/2"$ (216mm x 241mm)
3. $7^1/2"$ x $7^1/2"$ (191mm x 191mm)
4. $8^1/2"$ x $7^1/2"$ (216mm x 191mm)
5. $10^1/2"$ x $10^1/2"$ (267mm x 267mm)
6. $7^1/2"$ x $5^1/2"$ (191mm x 140mm)
7. $19^1/2"$ x $6^1/2"$ (495mm x 165mm)
8. $5^1/2"$ x $11^1/2"$ (140mm x 292mm)
9. $27^1/2"$ x $6^1/2"$ (699mm x 165mm)

Please have appliqué motifs enlarged by 210%. Now appliqué motifs onto backgrounds, adding embroidery if you wish to do so. Join your background pieces together as follows:-

Step 1.
Cut A $6^1/2"$ x $2^1/2"$ (165mm x 64mm). Add to base of 1. Cut B $2^1/2"$ x $13^1/2"$ (64mm x 343mm). Add to right hand side of 1. Join this unit to 4. Cut C $2^1/2"$ x $20^1/2"$ (64mm x 521mm). Add to right hand side of (1+4). Cut D $2^1/2"$ x $20^1/2"$ (64mm x 521mm). Add to left hand side of (1+4). Set aside.

Step 2.
Cut E $8^1/2"$ x $1^1/2"$ (216mm x 38mm). Add to base of 2.Cut F $2^1/2"$ x $10^1/2"$ (64mm x 267mm). Add to right hand side of 2. Join to 5. Set aside.

Step 3.
Cut G $2^1/2"$ x $7^1/2"$ (64mm x 191mm).

Add to left hand side of 3. Cut H $9^1/2"$ x $3^1/2"$ (241mm x 89mm). Add to base of 3. Set aside.

Step 4.
Cut J $7^1/2"$ x $5^1/2"$ (191mm x 140mm). Add to base of 6. Cut K $2^1/2"$ x $10^1/2"$ (64mm x 267mm).Add to left hand side of 6. Join unit 3 to unit 6.

Step 5.
Following the diagram join (1+4) to (2+5) to (3+6).

Step 6.
Cut L $3^1/2"$ x $20^1/2"$ (89mm x 521mm). Add to right hand side of joined piece. Set aside.

Step 7.
Cut M $19^1/2"$ x $3^1/2"$ (495mm x 89mm). Add to top of 7. Cut N $19^1/2"$ x $4^1/2"$ (495mm x 114mm). Add to base of 7. Cut O $3^1/2"$ x $13^1/2"$ (89mm x 343mm). Add to left hand side of 7. Cut P $3^1/2"$ x $13^1/2"$ (89mm x 343mm). Add to right hand side of 7. Set aside.

Step 8.
Cut Q $4^1/2"$ x $11^1/2$ (114mm x 292mm). Add to right hand side of 8. Cut R $9^1/2"$ x $2^1/2"$. (241mm x 64mm). Add to base of 8. Join 7 to 8.

Step 9.
Cut S $4^1/2"$ x $6^1/2"$ (114mm x 165mm). Add to left hand side of 9. Cut T $31^1/2"$ x $3^1/2"$ (800mm x 89mm). Add to base of 9. Cut U $3^1/2"$ x $9^1/2"$ (89mm x 241mm). Add to right hand side of 9. Set aside.

Step 10.
Cut V $34^1/2"$ x $2^1/2"$ (876mm X 64mm). Add to units (1+2+3).

Step 11.
Join units (7+8) to (4+5+6).

Step 12.
Add unit 9.

Your quilt is now in one piece and ready to be quilted and bound! We suggest that you shadow quilt around your motifs, adding just a few quilting lines to the borders to hold the quilt in place.

images of africa

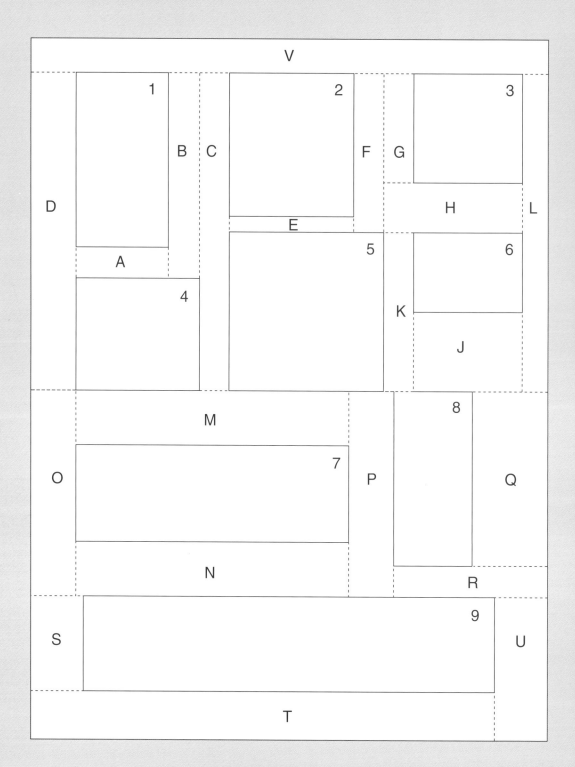

V

1   2   3

B   C   F   G

D   H   L

E

5   6

4   K   J

M

O   7   P   8   Q

N   R

S   9   U

T

INCREASE TEMPLATES BY 210%

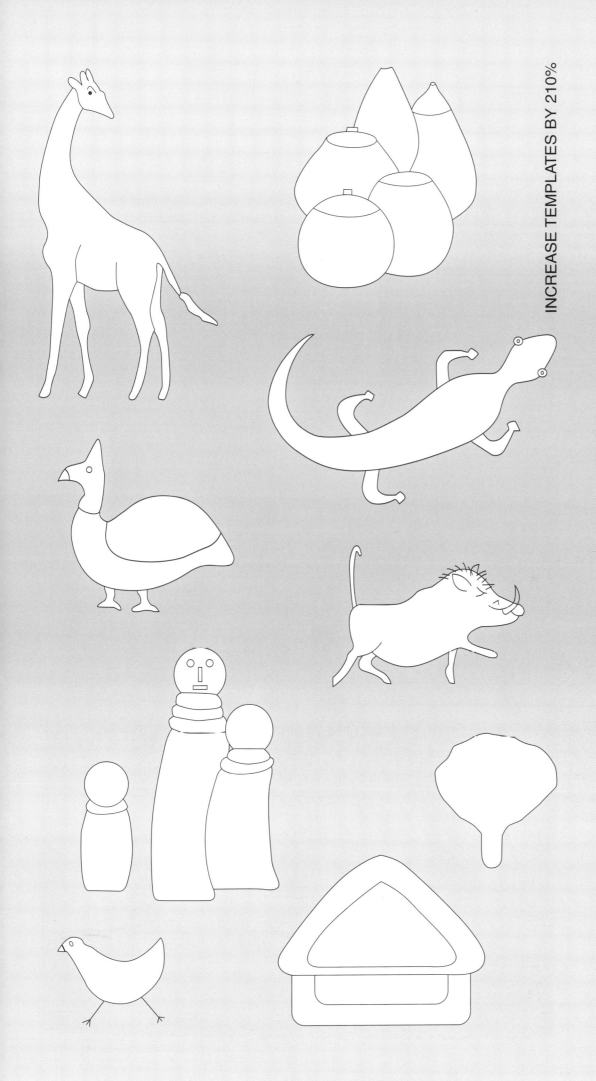

55" X 59" (1.40m x 1.50m)
Pat Parker

I was inspired to make this quilt by the vibrant ceramics of Ardmore made by the rural potters in the Champagne Valley of Kwazulu, Natal. Their pieces explode with color, frequently depicting the flora and fauna of our country. This is my tribute to Bonnie Ntshalintshali, award-winning artist from Ardmore whose tragic death occurred recently as a result of her contracting Aids.

Please note that the quilt diagram has been shaded in light, medium and dark. Kindly refer to this when cutting and piecing.

Teapot: Makheke Madondo, painted by Nelly Ntshalintshali

Milk Jug: Elizabeth Ngubeni, painted by Bonnie Ntshalintshali

Sugar Bowl: Pheneas Mweli, painted by Mirriam Ngubeni

Techniques:
Can be pieced, appliquéd, embroidered and quilted either by hand or machine.

Materials:
Light fabric	2 yards	(2m)
Medium fabric	1¹/₂ yards	(1.5m)
Dark fabric	1¹/₂ yards	(1.5m)
Narrow sashing on outside border.	¹/₂ yard	(0.5m)
Swags on border	³/₄ yard	(0.75)
Blue fabric surrounding windows.	1 yard	(1m)
Backing	59" x 64"	(1.50m x 1.63m)
Batting	59" x 64"	(1.50m x 1.63m)
Binding	¹/₂ yard	(0.5m)

Small pieces of printed fabrics suitable for all appliqué.

Method:
Using light fabric cut 4 rectangles 12¹/₂" x 16¹/₂" (318mm x 419mm) (H).

To save space the drawings for the 4 windows have been reduced. Please enlarge these by 210%.

Now appliqué the 4 windows.

The piecing of the central area is done in rows. Follow the rows downwards from left to right. The quilt diagram shows where to use medium and dark fabrics.

Row 1.
Using templates (A),(B), (C) and (D) make 5 half Saw-tooth Stars. Join together.

Row 2.
Cut 2 rectangles 12¹/₂" x 2¹/₂" (318mm x 64mm) (F) and 1 rectangle 10¹/₂" x 4¹/₂" (267mm x 114mm) (G). Using templates (A) and (D) add 2 points of central Star to (G). Join these 3 rectangles to 2 windows as shown.

Row 3.
Cut 2 rectangles 14¹/₂" x 4¹/₂" (368mm x 114mm) (P). Using templates (A), (D) and (E) piece as shown.

Row 4.
Same as Row 2.

Row 5.
Same as Row 1.

Now cut your borders as follows:
Using light fabric cut 2 pieces 36¹/₂" x 6¹/₂" (927mm x 165mm) (J).
Using light fabric cut 2 pieces 40¹/₂" x 6¹/₂" (1029mm x 165mm) (K) .
Using fabric bought for narrow sashings on border cut 4 pieces 36¹/₂" x 1¹/₂" 927mm x 38mm) (L). Cut 4 pieces 40¹/₂" x 1¹/₂" (1029mm x 38mm) (M).

Sew strips (L) to either side of (J).
Sew strips (M) to either side of (K).

Now appliqué borders.

Using templates (A), (C),(D) and (E) make 4 Saw-tooth Stars.

Join borders (K) to left and right hand sides of work. Sew 1 Star to either end of borders (J). Add to top and bottom of quilt.

Cut 2 strips 52¹/₂" x 2" (1334mm x 51mm) (N). Sew to top and bottom of quilt.
Cut 2 strips 59¹/₂" x 2" (1511mm x 51mm) (O). Sew to left and right hand sides of quilt.

Quilt as desired.

Add binding.

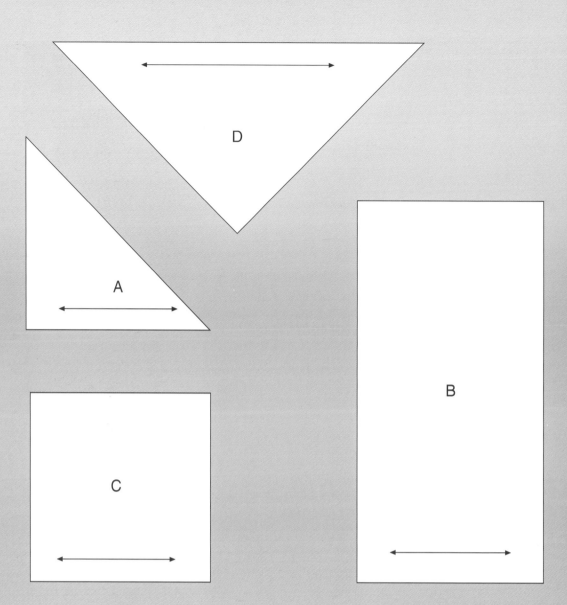
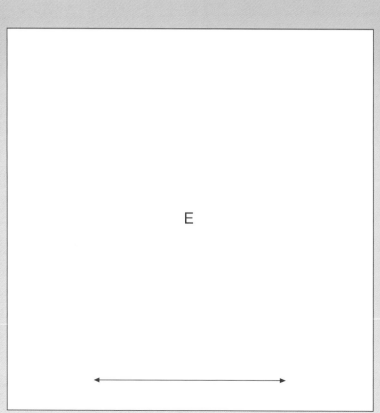

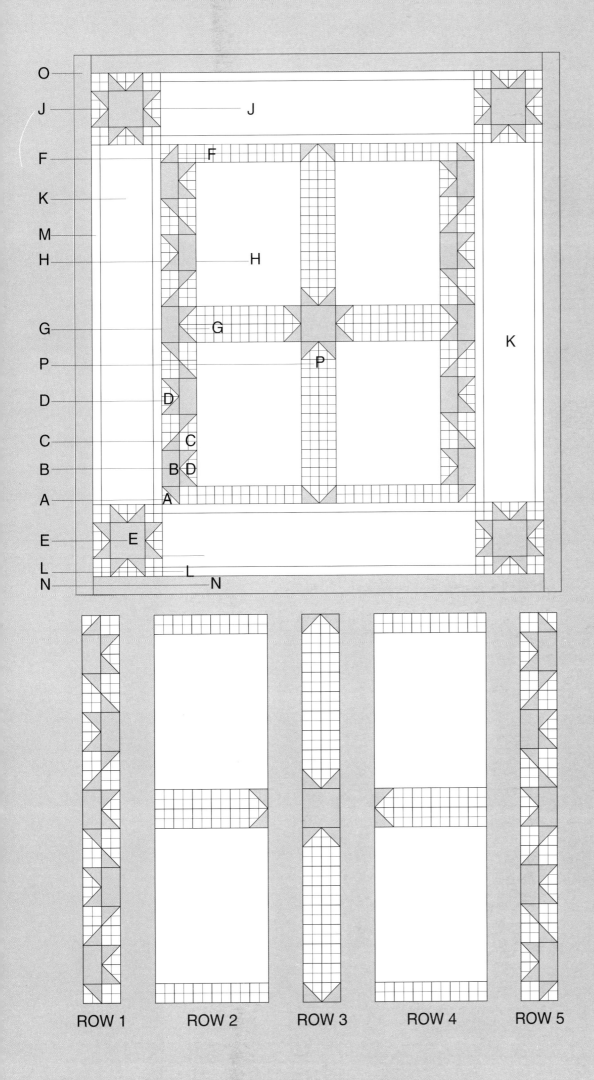

ROW 1   ROW 2   ROW 3   ROW 4   ROW 5

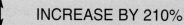

INCREASE BY 210%

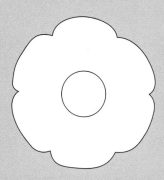

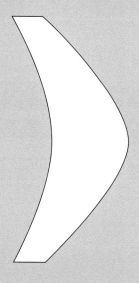

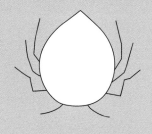

INCREASE BY 210%

INCREASE BY 210%

INCREASE BY 210%

miniature landscapes

9¹/₂" x 6¹/₂" (0.24m x 0.16m)
Jenny Williamson & Pat Parker

Two pictures were made using hand dyes and two with printed fabrics each giving a different atmosphere.

Techniques:

Hand appliquéd and embroidered. The hand appliqué technique used here is virtually the same as when using freezer paper. We find that iron-on vylene has so much more flexibility than paper and is therefore easier to use. Please make sure that you read our directions at the beginning of the book for using this technique.

Materials:

A piece of calico or seedcloth (14" x 11") (356mm x 279mm) (should be washed as fabric must be soft enough to work through by hand). Small pieces of cotton fabric suitable for a landscape scene, e.g.sky, mountains, water, etc. (hand dyes are good).

Method:

Trace landscape exactly as drawn onto vylene glue side down.

Number each piece on drawing and mark vylene with the corresponding number.

Cut vylene accurately along each line.

Choose fabrics starting with the sky and working your way forward to foreground.

Press vylene onto RIGHT side of chosen fabrics. Cut out each piece, adding seam allowances AS SHOWN ON DIAGRAMS. You will note that all the outside borders have 1" (25mm) seam allowances to give extra stability when framing.

Working from sky down carefully remove vylene and pin each piece in place to background calico. Check for visual impact. When you are happy with your choice re-iron vylene onto fabrics.

Starting with the sky, hand appliqué each piece onto background calico, working from background to foreground until picture is complete.

Add embroidery to enhance landscape.

miniature landscapes

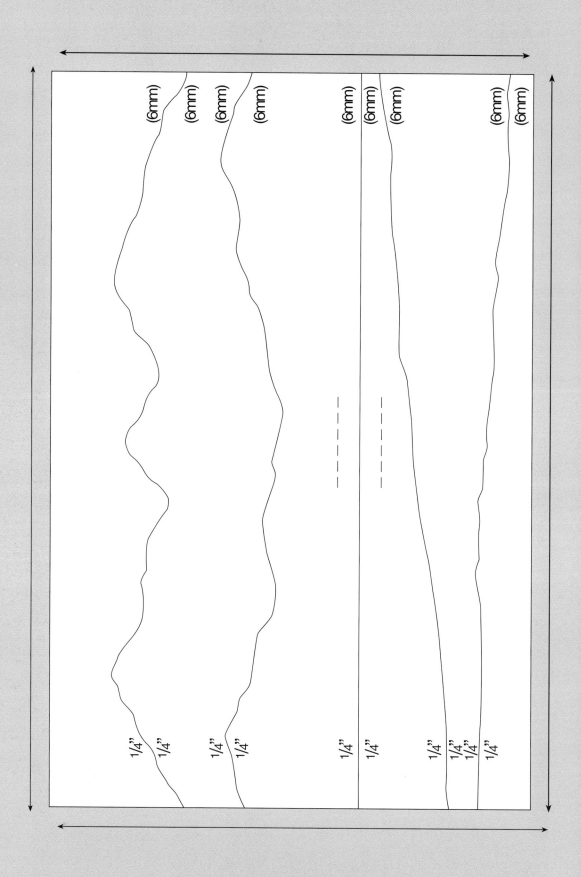

(6mm) (6mm) (6mm) (6mm) (6mm) (6mm) (6mm) (6mm) (6mm)

1/4" 1/4" 1/4" 1/4" 1/4" 1/4" 1/4" 1/4" 1/4" 1/4"

INCREASE DRAWING BY 125%

ADD 1" (25mm) ON ALL <u>OUTER</u> EDGES WHEN CUTTING FABRIC

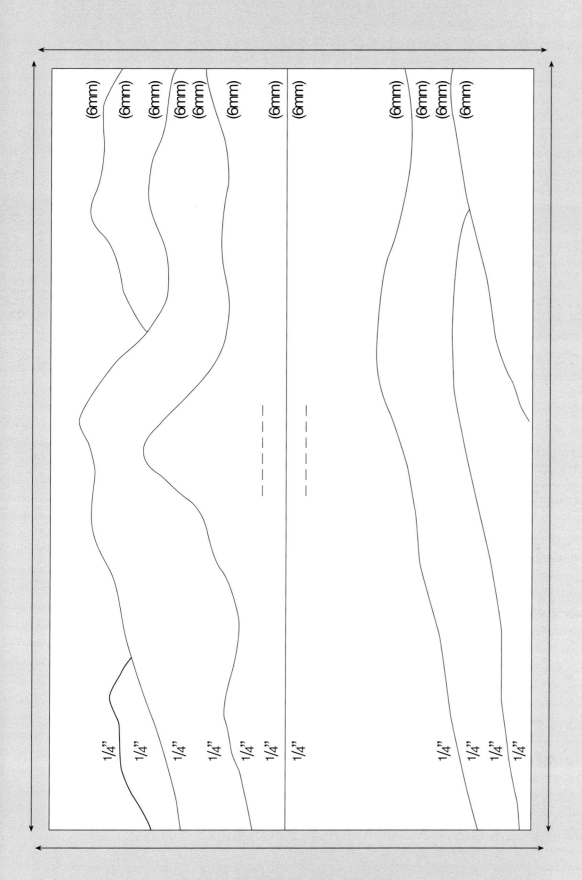

INCREASE DRAWING BY 125%

ADD 1" (25mm) ON ALL <u>OUTER</u> EDGES WHEN CUTTING FABRIC

mountain kingdom

48" x 48" (1.22m x 1.22m)
Pat Parker

Due to icy winds the people of Lesotho are reliant on their brightly coloured blankets for warmth and comfort. Hats are worn for protection against the burning rays of the sun.

Techniques

The appliqué, piecing and quilting can be done either by hand or by machine.

Block size

8" (203mm). You will need 20 blocks.

Materials:

Background	1¹/₂ yards	(1.5m)
Gold	¹/₂ yard	(0.5m)
Red	1 yard	(1m)
Hut roofs	¹/₄ yard	(0.25m)
Hut walls	¹/₄ yard	(0.25m)
Backing	52" x 52"	(1.32m x 1.32m)
Batting	52" x 52"	(1.32m x 1.32m)
Binding	¹/₂ yard	(0.5m)

Various scraps suitable for the appliqué on borders.

Method:

Make templates as given, then add ¹/₄" (6mm) seam allowance when cutting fabric.

Using color photograph as guide cut and piece 20 blocks. The numbers in piecing diagrams give the order in which the pieces should be joined. Join blocks 4 across x 4 down.

Draw border strips according to the size given in diagram, then add your ¹/₄" (6mm) seam allowance. Cut border strips and add corners made up of (C) + (D).

Appliqué herders, cattle and pots as desired.

Sew left and right hand borders to quilt top. Join a block to each end of remaining 2 borders, then sew to top and bottom of quilt.

Quilt as desired.

Add binding.

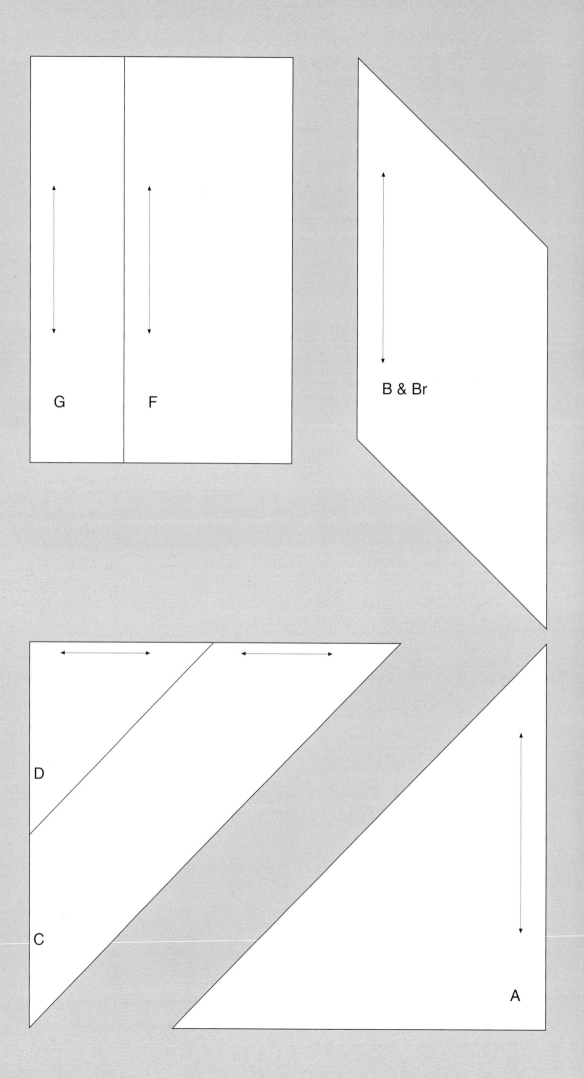

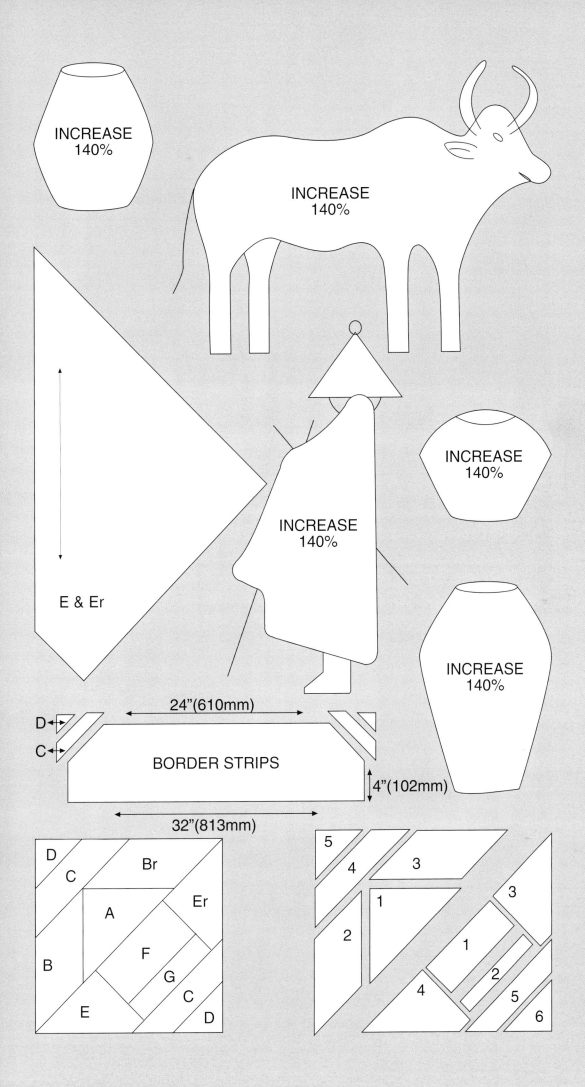

INCREASE
140%

INCREASE
140%

INCREASE
140%

INCREASE
140%

INCREASE
140%

E & Er

D

C

24"(610mm)

BORDER STRIPS

4"(102mm)

32"(813mm)

D
C
Br
Er
A
F
B
G
E
C
D

5
4
3
1
2
1
3
4
2
5
6

serendipity

51" x 54" (1.3m x 1.38m)
Jenny Williamson & Pat Parker

Here the Game Park fanatics could not resist mixing flora and fauna on their fabric fantasy!

Techniques
Can be pieced, appliquéd and quilted either by hand or machine.

Materials:
Background fabric on
which to appliqué. 2 yards (2m)
Inner border ³/₄ yard (0.75m)
Backing 55" x 58"(1.4m x 1.48m)
Batting 55" x 58"(1.4m x 1.48m)
Binding ¹/₂ yard (0.5m)
Small pieces of brightly colored fabrics suitable for animals and flowers. These small pieces will also be used for outside border.

Method:
Cut background fabric ACCURATELY as follows:
(A) 39¹/₂" x 16¹/₂" (1003mm x 419mm)
(B) x 2 39¹/₂" x 9" (1003mm x 229mm)
(C) x 2 42¹/₂" x 5" (1080mm x 127mm)
(D) x 2 39¹/₂ x 5" (1003mm x 127mm)
(E) x 4 5" x 5" (127mm x 127mm)

Using quilt photograph for reference appliqué shapes onto background.

Using inner border fabric cut:
(F) x 4 39¹/₂" x 2" (1003mm x 51mm)
(G) x 2 36¹/₂" x 2" (927mm x 51mm)
(H) x 4 2" x 2" (51mm x 51mm)

Join appliquéd background strips to inner border strips thus
(F) + (B) + (F) + (A) + (F) + (B) + (F)
Join 1 square (H) to either end of strips (G). Sew to top and bottom of quilt.

Sew appliquéd border (C) to left and right hand sides of quilt. Join 1 square (E) to either end of appliqué border (D).
Sew to top and bottom of quilt.

Using the same colored fabrics you have used for appliqué shapes cut 136 squares 2" x 2" (51mm x 51mm). Sew 2 strips of 32 squares to make (J). Sew to top and bottom of quilt.

Sew 2 strips of 36 squares to make (K). Sew to left and right hand sides of quilt.

Shadow quilt around appliqué shapes. Bind quilt.

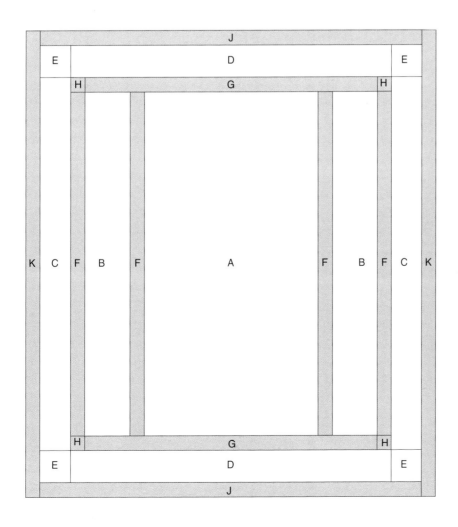

INCREASE TEMPLATES BY 140%

INCREASE TEMPLATES BY 140%

steps to freedom

43" x 54" (1.1m x 1.37m)
Jenny Williamson

"How can you possibly mix the fabrics of your crazy African stash in one quilt! Here's how. Let go with these steps to freedom!" This is an exciting quilt for beginners.

It is the traditional block "Patience Corner" and is most suitable for using your African fabrics.

Techniques:
Can be pieced and quilted either by hand or machine.

Block size:
12" (305mm) block, each block being made up of 4 units (see diagram). You will need 12 blocks, 3 across by 4 down.

Materials:

Black fabric   2 yards   (2m)
(This will be sufficient for
all Templates A, border
and binding).

Backing: 47" x 58" (1.2m x 1.48m)
Batting: 47" x 58" (1.2m x 1.48m)

As many scraps of African fabrics as you can find. The more you use the more successful your quilt will be.

Method:
Make templates as shown, then add ¹/₄" (6mm) seam allowance when cutting fabric.

For each 12" (305mm) block cut:
4 template A in black fabric
4 template B in scrap fabrics
4 template C in scrap fabrics

We suggest that you audition your fabrics to check the color distribution before sewing.

Join A to B pressing seams away from black fabric. Join C to (A + B) once again pressing seams away from black fabric.

Join 4 units as illustrated to form 12" (305mm) block. Make 12 of the 12" (305mm) blocks, then join 3 across by 4 down.

Borders:
Using black fabric:
Cut 2 strips 36¹/₂" x 1³/₄" (927mm x 45mm) (D)
Cut 2 strips 48¹/₂" x 1³/₄" (1232mm x 45mm) (E)

Using scrap fabrics:
Cut 4 squares 1³/₄" x 1³/₄" (45mm x 45mm) (F). Cut 2 strips 39" x 3¹/₂" (991mm x 89mm) (G). Cut 2 strips 57" x 3¹/₂" (1448mm x 89mm) (H).

Note:
Join as many scraps together as you need to make the required length.

Sew strips (D) to top and bottom of quilt. Join 1 square (F) to either end of strips E. Sew strips (E + F) to left and right hand sides of quilt. Sew strips (G) to top and bottom of quilt. Sew strips (H) to left and right hand sides of quilt.

Quilt as desired.

Add binding in black fabric.

steps to freedom

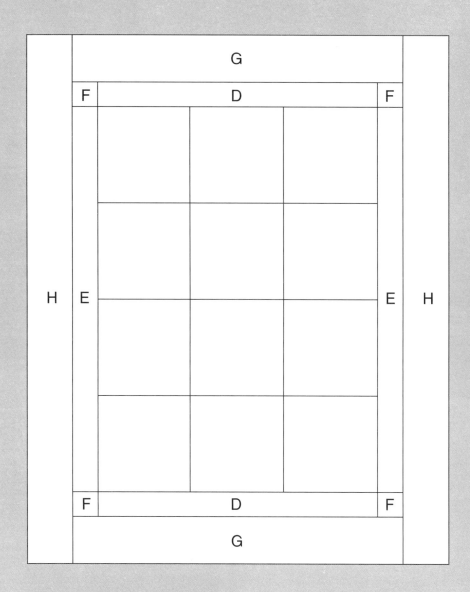

G

F   D   F

H   E   E   H

F   D   F

G

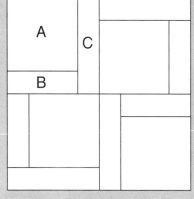

A

C

B

12" (305mm) BLOCK

A

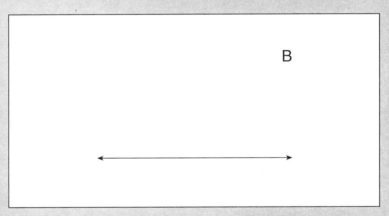

B

ADD ¼" (6mm) SEAM ALLOWANCE

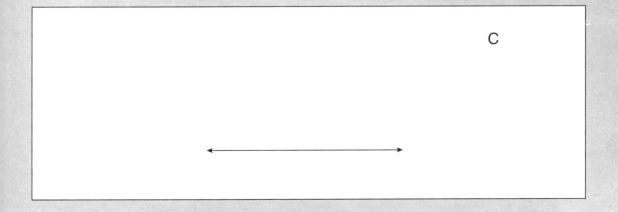

C

82¹/₂" x 94¹/₂" (2.1m 2.4m)
Pieced & appliquéd by Jenny Williamson
Quilted by Susan Sittig

This quilt is based on the traditional design 'Storm at Sea'. It is a very large quilt, but can easily be reduced in size. Simply make less units across and down.

Measure the borders in the same manner as we have given in the instructions below and then adjust your appliqué design accordingly.

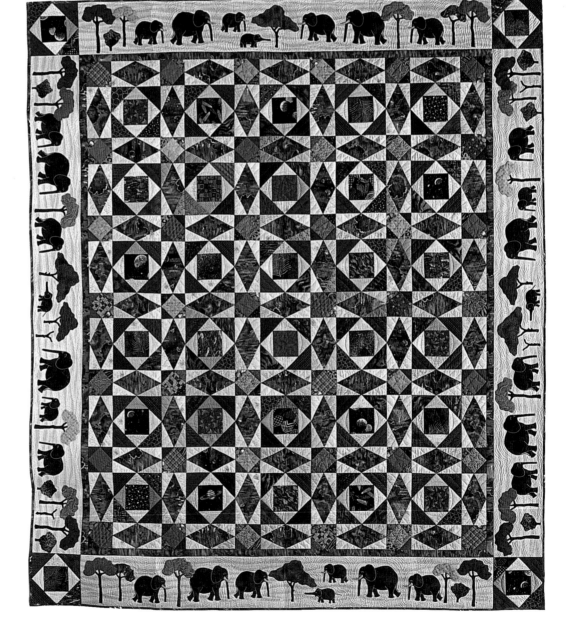

Techniques:
Can be pieced, appliquéd and quilted either by hand or machine.

Unit size:
The design is made up of 3 Units (see diagram).
Unit (1) is 8" x 8" (203mm x 203mm) – you will need 34. Unit (2) is 8" x 4" (203mm x 102mm) – you will need 71. Unit (3) is 4" x 4" (102mm x 102mm) – you will need 42

Materials:
This is a scrap quilt. Basically you need to divide your fabrics into 2 stacks, one with dark fabrics and one with light fabrics. Make sure you cut the darks and lights exactly as shown or you will lose the effectiveness of the design.

Dark fabric for inside border.   1 yard (1m)
Background fabric   2½ yards (2.5m)
for appliqué border.
Backing   86" x 98" (2.2m x 2.5m)
Batting   86" x 98" (2.2m x 2.5m)
Binding   1 yard (1m)

Method:
Make templates as shown, then add ¼" (6mm) seam allowance when cutting fabric.
Cut fabric thus:
(A) - dark
(B) - light
(C) - dark
(D) - dark
(E) - light
(F) - light
(G) - dark

Referring to Unit drawings make 34 Unit (1), 71 Unit (2), 42 Unit (3). Join Units in rows as shown on quilt drawing.

Note: Before cutting borders it may be an idea to measure your quilt top across the middle for both length and width. If your seam allowance is not 100% accurate your size will be slightly different from the sizes now given. If this is the case you will need to cut your border strips according to the length and width of YOUR quilt top. If your quilt measures 64½" x 76½" (1638 x 1943mm) proceed with sizes as given below.

Add inside border as follows:
Using dark inside border fabric - cut 2 strips 64½" x 1¾" (1638mm x 45mm) (H) - cut 2 strips 76½" x 1¾" (1943mm x 45mm) (J). Using a contrasting dark fabric cut 4 squares 1¾" x 1¾" (45mm x 45mm) (K)

Sew strips (H) to top and bottom of quilt. Join one square (K) to either end of strips (J). Sew strips (J + K) to left and right hand sides of quilt.

Using appliqué border fabric cut:
2 strips lengthwise 67" x 8½" (1702mm x 216mm) (L). 2 strips lengthwise 79" x 8½" (2007mm x 216mm) (M).

The drawings given for the elephants are too small as shown. Please enlarge these to a more suitable size.

Appliqué elephants and trees to borders. Sew appliqué borders (L) to top and bottom of quilt.

Join 2 Units (1) to either end of appliqué borders (M).

Sew (M + 1) to top and bottom of quilt.

Quilt as desired.
Sew on binding in dark fabric.

Having weathered the storm you quilters can now 'do it undercover'!

storm over africa

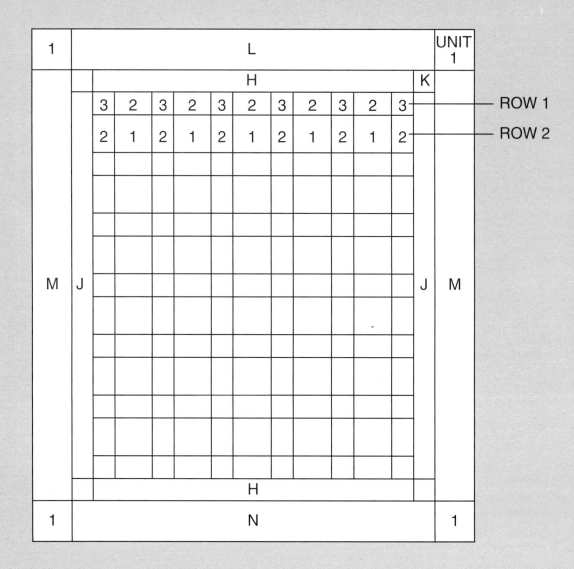

UNIT 1
1
L
UNIT 1
H
K
| 3 | 2 | 3 | 2 | 3 | 2 | 3 | 2 | 3 | 2 | 3 | ROW 1 |
| 2 | 1 | 2 | 1 | 2 | 1 | 2 | 1 | 2 | 1 | 2 | ROW 2 |

M J   J M

H
1
N
1

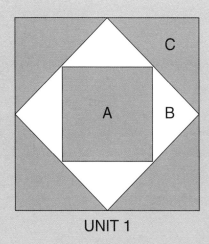

UNIT 1

C

A B

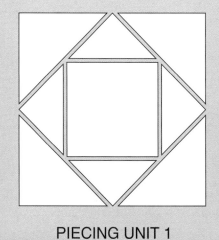

PIECING UNIT 1

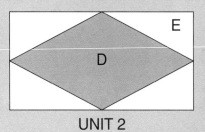

UNIT 2

E

D

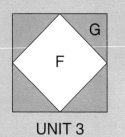

UNIT 3

G

F

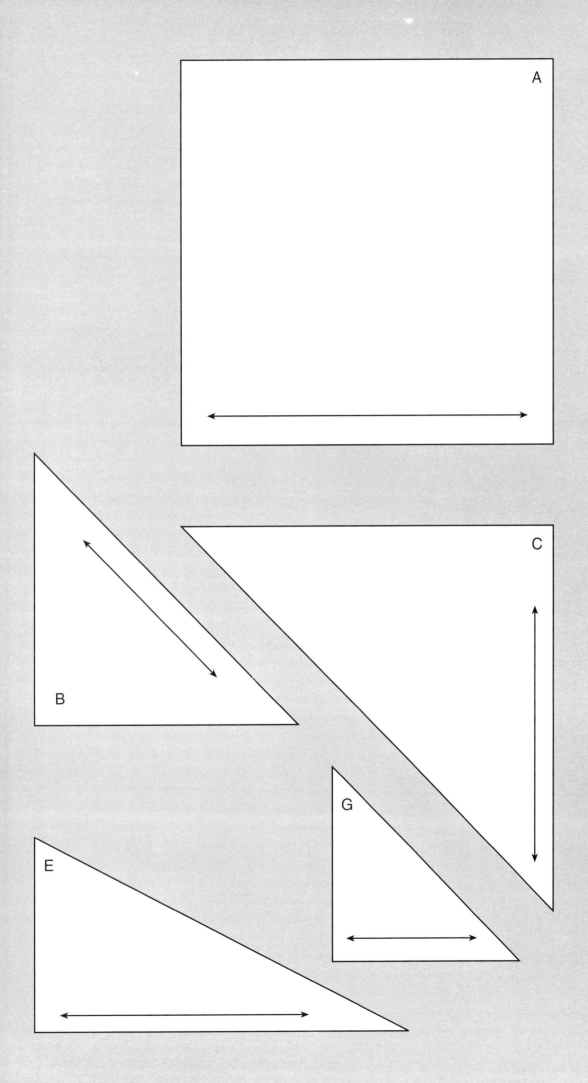

A

C

B

G

E

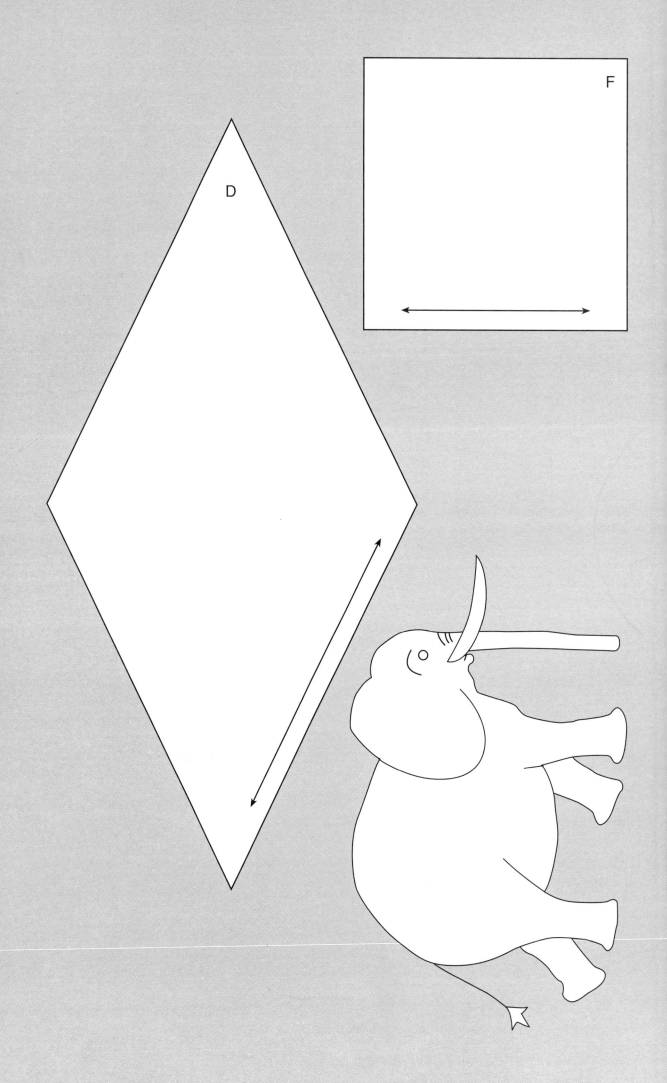

D

F

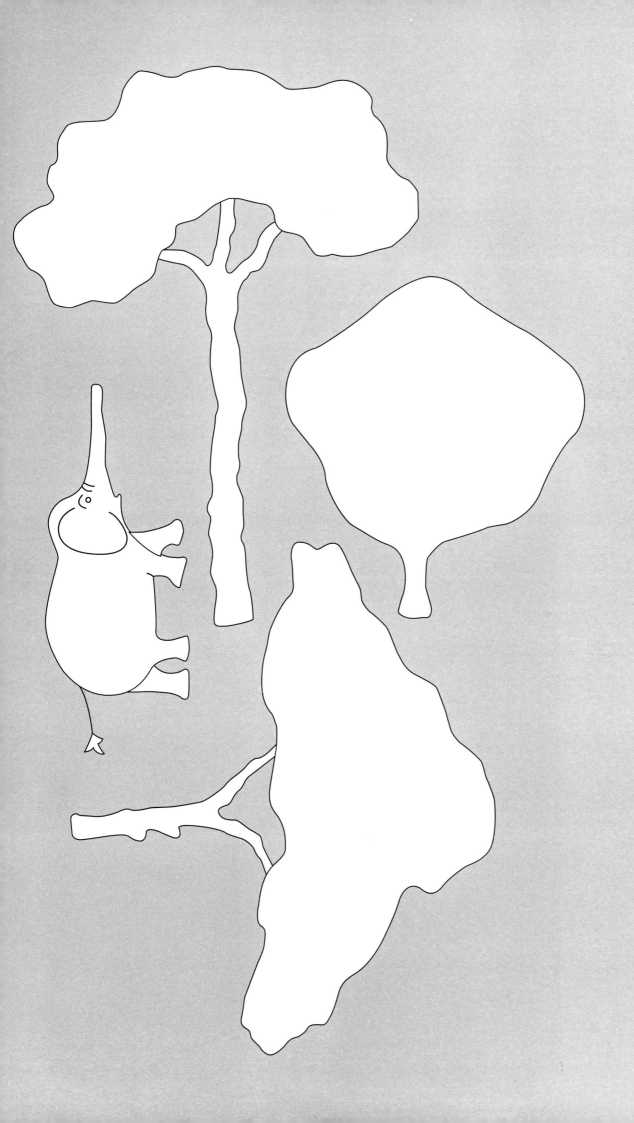

windmills for africa

41" x 41" (1.04m x 1.04m)
Machine Pieced by Gaye Bertram
Machine Quilted by Petro van Rooyen

This design was adapted from a mural painted on the wall of an African house.

The African artists have never seen a traditional quilt design book, yet it is interesting to note the similarity between their patterns and those of traditional patchwork.

Block size:
10" x 10" (254mm x254mm) You will need 9 blocks, 3 across by 3 down.

Techniques
Can be pieced and quilted either by hand or machine.

Materials
Black	1¹/₂ yards	(1.5m)
Off white	¹/₂ yard	(0.5m)
Red	¹/₂ yard	(0.5m)
Gold	1 yard	(1m)
Orange	1 yard	(1m)
Backing	45" x 45"	(1.15m x 1.15m)
Batting	45" x 45"	(1.15m x 1.15m)

Method:
Make templates as given adding ¹/₄" (6mm) seam allowance when cutting fabric.

Using color photograph as guide cut all fabric.

Following the Unit diagrams piece :

5 Unit (1)'s
4 Unit (2)'s
12 Unit (3)'s
4 Unit (4)'s

Referring to quilt diagram join all Units as follows:-
Join Units (1) and (2), 3 across by 3 down.

Join 3 Unit (3)'s together.

Repeat 3 times keeping each set of 3 separate.

Add 1 set of Unit (3)'s to left hand side and 1 set of Unit (3)'s to right hand side of quilt.

Join 1 Unit (4) to each end of remaining sets of Unit (3)'s.

Sew to top and bottom of quilt.

Quilt as desired.

Bind quilt using black fabric.

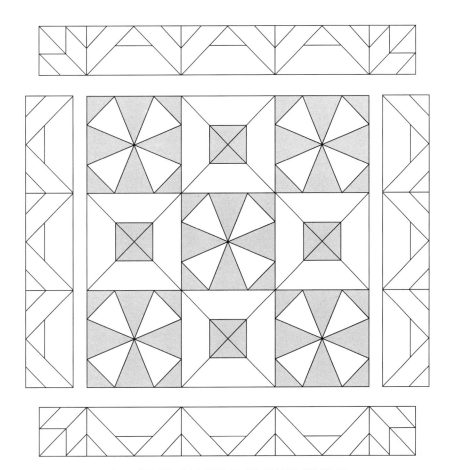

PIECING DIAGRAMS FOR QUILT

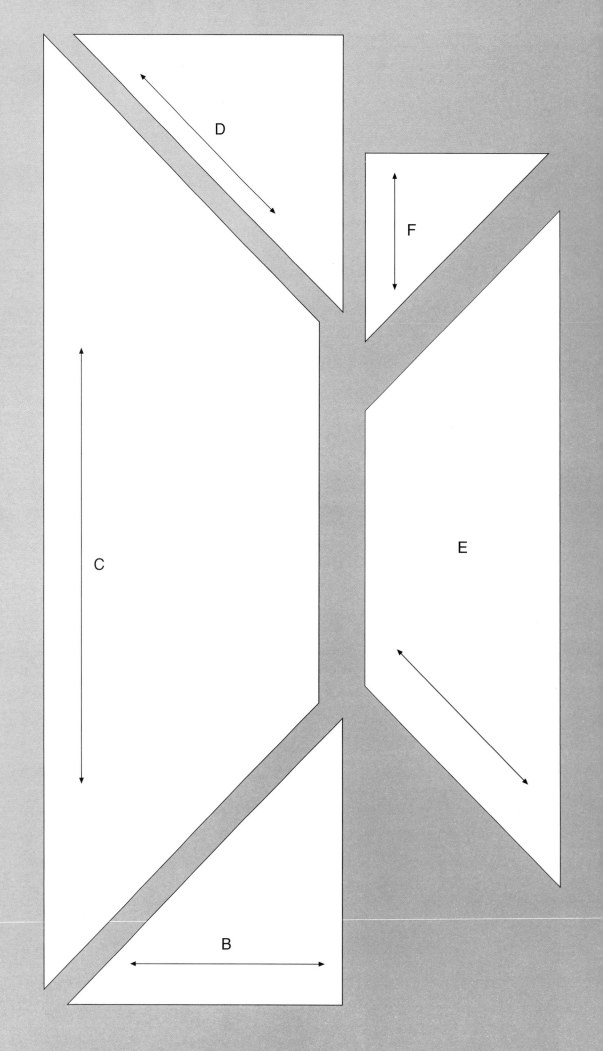

PIECING DIAGRAMS FOR UNITS

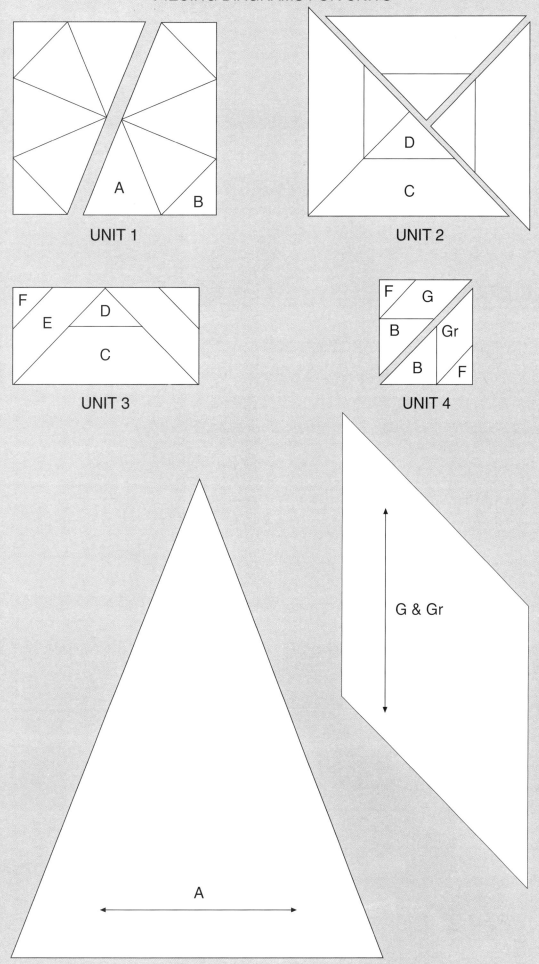

UNIT 1

UNIT 2

UNIT 3

UNIT 4

Other AQS Books

This is only a small selection of the books available from the American Quilter's Society. AQS books are known worldwide for timely topics, clear writing, beautiful color photos, and accurate illustrations and patterns. The following books are available from your local bookseller, quilt shop, or public library:

#6407   us$21.95

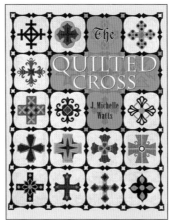

#6301   us$18.95

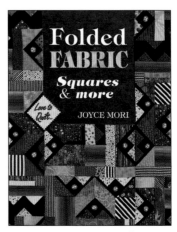

#6207   us$16.95

#6514   us$21.95

#6298   us$24.95

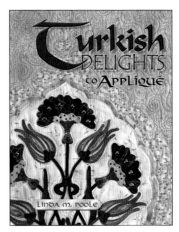

#6004   us$22.95

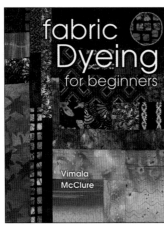

#6206   us$19.95

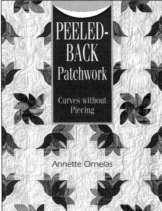

#6516   us$21.95

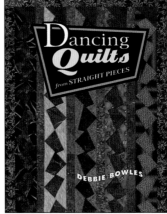

#6210   us$24.95